Who's The Boss of You?

Is Your Inner King Kong

Sabotaging Your Life?

KRIS WILLIAMS

ISBN

978-0-9933167-0-8

Cover design by Sophie Bennett

kittyinpink.co.uk

Acknowledgements

Many thanks go to Wendy and Del for giving me such constructive and professional feedback. Gratitude also goes to my daughters, Sarah (a copy editor in the making) and Alex, for their very detailed and encouraging feedback, notes and unwavering support. Love and appreciation goes to Paddy, for being with me at every stage of the long and challenging journey and for making so many useful and inspiring suggestions. I'd also like to thank my friends at South Lakeland Carers for their encouragement and suggestions – particularly Louise, whose genuine interest, insightful questions and discussions aided my motivation and helped me to come up with the title. And to John – thanks for sharing some of the madness of formatting with me.

Finally, deep appreciation and respect goes to those people who have agreed to let me use their stories – it's been a privilege to have joined you for part of your respective journeys to self-discovery. Thank you to all my clients - past and present - without you I wouldn't have experienced the true healing power of identifying and restructuring Core Beliefs.

May all your inner King Kong's be happy and cooperative!

For Paddy, whose loving support helped me to discover my own Core Beliefs and Inner King Kong.
To Sarah and Alex, who have taught and continue to teach me more than words can say.
And to Alan – my once arch nemesis, but now my unexpected and much loved and appreciated ally.

CONTENTS

Part 1

Ghosts in the Machine

Introduction	In the Land of Giants	i
Chapter 1	King Kong to the Rescue?	1
Chapter 2	A Baby is Born	9
Chapter 3	Core Beliefs Are Created	20
Chapter 4	There's No Place Like Home	33
Chapter 5	Friends, Lovers and…Workmates	54
Chapter 6	Money Makes the World Go Around	64
Chapter 7	Identifying Core Beliefs	75
Chapter 8	Out of the Shadows	91
Chapter 9	The Hidden Benefits	101

Part 2

Your Inner World

Chapter 10	What Dreams May Come	115
Chapter 11	The Child Within	126
Chapter 12	Deeper Travels Within	140
Chapter 13	Creative Approaches to Healing	151
Chapter 14	Finding Your Own King Kong	158
Chapter 15	Heal-thy Mind – Heal-thy Body	168

Part 3

Cellular to Celluloid

Chapter 16	All the World's a Stage	184
Chapter 17	Fear of Being Vulnerable - *The Aviator*	188
Chapter 18	Fear of Love and Adulthood - *A Taste of Honey*	198
Chapter 19	Fear of Being Weak - *The Iron Lady & Margaret*	209
Chapter 20	Sibling Rivalry - *In Her Shoes*	223
Chapter 21	The Southern Way – Denial, Repression, Humour – *Prince of Tides*	235
Chapter 22	Back to the Future – *The Kid*	253
Conclusion		266
Recommended Reading and Bibliography		270

INTRODUCTION

IN THE LAND OF GIANTS

Man is made by his belief. As he believes, so he is.

Johann Wolfgang von Goethe

We shall not cease from exploration, and the end of all our exploring will be to arrive where we started and know the place for the first time.

T. S. Eliot

By now, most people on the planet (at least the Western part of it, anyway) will have heard of The Law of Attraction (LoA). Basically, it concerns getting what you focus on, thoughts become things, and *'ask and you shall receive'*. This law of like attracts like recently became popularised by the book and film, 'The Secret'. However, if you look around, you can find books written on the subject anytime from the 19th century right through to now, only they didn't describe it as the Law of Attraction. In 1928, an artist and follower of the New Thought Movement, Florence Scovel-Shinn, wrote a book called *The Game of Life and How to Play It*. The New Thought Movement, which originated in the late 19th and early 20th century, contends that a higher power pervades all existence, and that individuals create their own reality via affirmations, meditation, intention and prayer.

Many New Thought writers, such as Scovel-Shinn, reference the Bible as their foundation text, although they approach its interpretation in a very unique way. For example, substituting 'Law', for 'Lord', as in '*Stand ye still and see the salvation of the Lord (or Law)*'. For someone like me, being given another way of interpreting the words and teachings in the Bible is useful and intriguing. It's also amazing to consider that these Universal Principles were all there in the Bible – it just needs to be read in a certain way to unlock its deeper, metaphysical meaning. Such as this from Isiah: '*My word shall not return unto me void, but shall accomplish that where unto it is sent.*' In LoA terms, this means that your words (and especially your thoughts) attract experiences that resonate on the same vibration: like attracts like. Whatever energy you send out has to come back to you in a like manner – so be careful what you send out.

In 1964, a renowned English magician/mentalist, Al Koran wrote a book called, *Bring Out the Magic in Your Mind*, in which he describes how the latent powers of your mind, 'can be harnessed to bring you prosperity, success, health and vitality'. The 'secret' then, if there ever was one, is in the fact that it's your beliefs (which generate our thoughts) that are at the core of your ability to manifest the things you desire. The most powerful beliefs we have are held within the subconscious and have been there for a very long time.

The Law of Attraction operates on the premise that we co-create the world we live in, that thoughts are energy and that they shape everything you see and experience in your life. If you are aware of this and accept it as true, then you may have been encouraged by what it promises, and so endeavoured to put it into practice; but, despite your erstwhile efforts, you may regularly have encountered obstacles with your hopes and dreams not always turning out the way you visualised them. Even though you may have read the books, attended the seminars, watched the films, and repeated the affirmations until you were hoarse, you still might not be consistently manifesting all those wonderful things that would make your life that much better. Understandably, repeated failure can easily lead to disillusionment - especially when all your efforts seem to have been in vain.

One important thing to bear in mind here is that the LoA is working *all* the time – even when things happen that aren't so pleasant. The key is that it's what you *believe* that determines what you get – every time. But it's not always easy to know exactly which beliefs may be sabotaging all our efforts and so producing such things as lack, ill-health, difficult relationships, and jobs we hate. This then, is the crucial factor in the equation. If we were to break down the Universal Principle of the Law of Attraction into a simple formula, it might look like this:

Desiring + Asking + Imagining + Believing = Seeing

You would probably agree that the first two components of the equation are the ones we find easiest and spend a lot of time doing. When we consider Imagining, and how detailed, well-defined and filled with emotion those visualisations need to be in order to be effective, we often begin to struggle. These are the areas that the books, etc., spend most time explaining. What often isn't given much clarification, however, is the Believing element. Most people working with Universal Principles don't realise that Believing goes much deeper than the surface belief that you can have whatever you ask for. It is here that - without realising it - you come up against those hidden, underlying beliefs about whether you deserve and have a right to those things. It's these, often unrecognized, beliefs which can be responsible for the ultimate success or failure of your manifesting endeavours.

Ostensibly, this isn't a book about the Law of Attraction: although once you've got a better understanding of the subjects it covers, you might find out why the LoA doesn't always work for you in the way you would like (remember, it is working all the time!). Within the pages of this book you will find possible explanations for why you struggle to create that life of abundance – and by *abundance* I mean plenty of everything, not just money. It might seem that you have no control over how things pan out, that you have behaviours that have a mind of their own, and that unwelcome experiences seem to come out of nowhere - often at the most inopportune moments. These 'ghosts in the machine' trip you up and cause all manner of problems whenever you try to get on in life. At crucial moments something happens that pulls the rug out from under you – you get ill, or you lose interest or confidence just before you're about to make a success of something, maybe you just never seem able to complete training courses or gain an educational qualification, or you find it hard to sustain relationships beyond a certain point. It seems that these events are out of your control: surely getting laryngitis just before an important job interview is a cruel twist of fate or just stress, and nothing to do with your internal belief system? Who would deliberately *create* an illness when they're about to achieve something that has been their goal for such a long time, something that they spent years and lots of money to train for and get qualified in?

Well, the answer is, yes, you are ultimately responsible for these seemingly external attacks on your happiness and wellbeing. The thing to remember is, you may have created what's behind all of this 'bad luck', but you didn't do it consciously. Deep within you is an army of protectors that were created in your childhood to keep you safe. This book is about these 'ninja' forces which have no concept of time moving on, of you growing and developing into an adult, or of the fact that their behaviour is damaging to you or your life in any way. They act out of a permanent present, obeying instructions (by now completely outdated), and carrying out their mission to the best of their ability. (This could also apply to behaviours carried over from 'past' lives: I go into more detail about this in Chapter 12.)

It may seem odd to refer to these psychological aspects as if they had a personality and a life of their own; but in a way, they do. Imagine that at any given moment in time a part of you becomes split off and gets stuck in that moment. What you're dealing with is an aspect of you that still exists within you. In every adult there is any number of scared, confused, gleeful, fearless children that all want attention at once, or cling, terrified to a teddy bear. Unfortunately, they want attention according to the rules that were set up at the time of their creation. They have no awareness that as they continue to function in every facet of your life, blindly obeying out-of-date rules, they are damaging you as a whole.

The most pervasive of these hidden beliefs were created at crucial developmental periods throughout your life when you may have encountered difficulty, danger, trauma, or just repeated negative behaviours or attitudes. The hidden beliefs were created as a defence mechanism, a way of protecting you from harm - perceived or real. This isn't necessarily the kind of danger where you can potentially be physically harmed: it can be, and often is, the result of the fear of being rejected or abandoned – usually by your parents and family. At the time of their creation (most commonly during the first 3 - 4 years of childhood) the methods of protection, however extreme, were necessary and advantageous. Other, less obvious beliefs were created as a result of you being part of a family and even wider community. These are the beliefs that are handed down from generation to generation and are the backbone of family attitudes, values and unspoken rules. These beliefs govern how we feel about money, health, status, success, relationships - every aspect of life and of living in the world.

Regardless of when or how they were created, beliefs go on to take on a life of their own. Unfortunately, once they are activated, they continue to do their work behind the scenes. The belief system that was created by the repetition of family attitudes to life will constantly be in operation in the background, directing the decisions we make every step along the way of adulthood. If the beliefs were created from a place of fear, such as with trauma, and you find yourself faced with a situation that could be considered a threat, the beliefs will do what they were created to do - protect you: and they will use whichever means necessary to fulfil that objective, even if that means making you ill.

The emotional injuries and irritations with family or friends; the fearfully anticipated reactions of colleagues; the inability to manage your money; the disregard for your health or general welfare; habitual worry; repetitive fantasies or obsessions - are all examples of these beliefs leaching from the unconscious and being played out in the current events of your everyday life. *'Yesterday's best choice made by the child in a land of giants may now be very limiting to the grown adult.'[1]*

This book, then, is a guide to identifying those beliefs - your 'hidden selves' - and to getting to know them better and finding ways of negotiating with them so they don't continue to sabotage your aspirations, relationships, health or career. The name I prefer to use to describe these hidden selves is, 'Core Beliefs': 'Core' because they are at the very centre of our being, which implies they can be difficult to uncover or identify, and even more difficult to change or remove. This internal belief system can go by different names depending on which self-help approach and/or psychological theory you're working with. You might encounter them as: Drivers and Injunctions (Transactional Analysis); Sub-personalities (Psychology); Parts (Internal Family Systems model); or Cognitive Behaviours and Schemas (Behavioural Psychology). In his book, *Imagine Yourself Well*, metaphysical author Frank DeMarco, describes these beliefs as 'robots' that function automatically. 'It's a matter of programming, for they always function exactly as designed...until we consciously contact them and update their files'. Regardless of the label they go by, they are all pretty much the same thing - renegade aspects of the psyche.

In my fifties, I am an amalgamation of all my life's experiences. Some are visible and therefore easy to see - scars from falls and accidents; physical imperfections from various conditions; facial expressions that reflect how I feel about certain experiences; the clothes I wear and how I have my hair - being the most obvious examples. And then there are those experiences I hold deep within me: the marks and imprints of a life of love, loss, pain, joy, fear, hope... All the things that make me who I am - or at least, who I *think* I am. Some of these life impressions are so well hidden

[1] **Dave Spenceley** – *Introduction to TA* www.ta-psychotherapy.co.uk

that even as a therapist with many years' experience, I have had to work hard to uncover them. To a trained or interested observer, my behaviour in any given moment will give clues as to which aspect of my personality is uppermost - in that moment. The manifestation of a particular belief or set of beliefs will manifest in many different ways and my behaviour will change so subtly and seamlessly from moment to moment, that it is almost impossible to know who is at the fore, and therefore influencing my decisions, etc.

As I've said, these are the parts of us that unconsciously affect our behaviour, attitudes and expectations. Every single person on the planet will have a cast of parts or Core Beliefs operating in the background. It doesn't matter if they are rich or poor, powerful or weak, famous or unknown, or even if they have had relatively secure and loving childhoods, the Core Beliefs will be there – it's just that some are more obvious than others. You might have a complex range of beliefs and parts in operation[1], perhaps not all the time, but certainly at times of stress, anxiety, pressure or even when you are in a situation that in some way mirrors or triggers an emotional memory of the situation that caused them to be set up in the first place.

Before we go any further, it is important to note that what I am describing is not the manifestation of Dissociative Identity Disorder (formerly Multiple Personality disorder), whereby the personality of someone who, as a child, suffered repeated and severe physical, mental and/or sexual abuse would become fragmented or split into several identities, each having their own age, gender, gestures, and distinctive way of talking. In this instance, DID is literally a survival device. What I'm referring to is a lot more subtle, and not anywhere near as damaging as what someone with DID experiences. However, having said that, there is a commonality in that the identities - or in our case, parts - have been created in order to protect the person. In the case of DID, it's a protection from the psychological trauma of remembering and reliving their abuse, as opposed to merely trying to avoid what is perceived by that part to be a *potentially* dangerous situation.

I also want to make clear that what I'm describing isn't necessarily the psychological results of acute neglect, abuse or the cumulative failures experienced within crucial relationships. Those are extreme, but unfortunately, not uncommon examples of experiences that set up Core Beliefs. If, as a child, you were exposed to constant abuse or neglect, what I describe in this book will no doubt only form the tip of the iceberg. By having a greater understanding of Core Beliefs, you will begin to appreciate the whys and wherefores of your behaviour - most likely exhibited in your relationships and/or health. These problem areas will be obvious to you, but you may not be aware of the underlying causes - the Core Beliefs - that were created by that early life experience or experiences.

If you have experienced severe abuse, then as valuable as this book may be in shining light on otherwise concealed causes of problems, nothing would be as important or healing to you as seeing an experienced therapist who can help you to make greater sense of how your experiences created your Core Beliefs and how they might be affecting you as an adult, and so provide you with the means to restructure those Core Beliefs once and for all.

In reading this book, you will discover what kind of life events can trigger the creation of Core Beliefs, from the seemingly mundane to the more traumatic. In an attempt to make this clear, in Part 1, I will explain the rudiments of why healthy attachment is so important to babies and small children, and why this basic human need is fundamental to the development of emotionally healthy young people and therefore, psychologically secure adults - adults who will have little problem in manifesting all they could ever want. I will tell the story of why and how some of my own Core Beliefs were created, and I will use case studies from my therapy practice to highlight other aspects of dealing with Core Beliefs.

In Part 2, I will provide you with a personal model of working with Core Beliefs, with various methods and exercises designed to help you identify and understand your own Core Beliefs. The exercises can be done alone, but it would be much more beneficial either to do them with a friend you can trust or, better still, with a therapist. Of course, you don't have to do any of the exercises in order to benefit from them. Merely reading this book and thinking about those aspects that might apply to you will be of benefit in some way.

I will also be looking at the role dreams play in helping us to gain insight into our deep-seated fears, drives and behaviours. They have played a crucial role in my own Core Belief work and the work I do with my clients. I will give examples of dreams and their interpretation that show just how much your inner self is working on your behalf to help you gain awareness of ways to deal with personal issues and Core Beliefs. Dreams hold the key to the treasure chest that is our inner being. They are the form of communication most often utilised by our subconscious or higher self as a means of getting us to pay attention to how we perceive the world and our place in it. Exploring your dreams can be like excavating a deep mine and discovering a rich source of precious gems. By paying attention to the messages sent by your inner guide, you in effect convey to it that you take your inner life as seriously as your outer one. What you get in return is an abundant flow of significant information that can lead you to even greater treasure.

From time to time I use terms such as higher or greater self, or inner guide. However, it isn't necessary to believe that we are spiritual beings in a physical body in order to gain understanding, healing or insight from the words and ideas in this book. If it helps, exchange phrases such as 'your greater being' for 'your subconscious mind'. As far as I'm concerned, these phrases are interchangeable and will make no difference to the overall meaning of the book.

In Part 3, I have used films - both fictional and biographical - to illustrate the creation and lasting effects of Core Beliefs. As a therapist, I believe in the healing power of metaphors, myths and stories, and use them extensively in my work both as a counsellor and hypnotherapist. For this reason, I chose movies as a method of exploration mainly because they can be such a powerful story-telling medium, but also because those I have chosen demonstrate how damaging Core Beliefs can be, how they operate behind the scenes just waiting for their cue to step up on stage, and how they can be managed and possibly even overcome.

As well as my experience as a therapist and personal development facilitator, this book largely came out of my own personal experiences. As someone who is committed to self-development and growing self-awareness, I have been (and continue to be) on what has often been a painful, sometimes scary, but ultimately exciting and rewarding journey to uncover, identify and challenge my own Core Beliefs. I am still in the process of figuring out how they operate and on finding ways to get them to take on new, healthier, less limiting roles. It's a slow process, but one that's well worth the effort. Through the exploration of my dreams, the learning and awareness I gained by doing my own extensive Core Belief restructuring, and the inspiration and guidance I have received along the way, I am now at a place where I am learning to embrace those aspects of myself that formed my Core Beliefs, and have begun to make friends with their over-enthusiastic creations.

Having begun this personal journey to my core self, I feel that combining certain aspects of my own personal story, case studies from my therapy practice, and the stories within the films I have used as examples, will provide you with a comprehensive overview that will help you to understand what may be at the heart of your own personal issues, be they in relationships - work or personal – financial, health, or career difficulties.

Although the main thrust of this book is to help you to gain insight and understanding of your inner mechanisms, there will be times when consider the broader context of you beyond the physical. To this end, therefore, I also include spiritual considerations that I believe may be of assistance to you. It is my hope that, should you be expecting a psychological style self-help book, these occasional forays into the realm of metaphysics do not get in the way of your overall enjoyment of the book or the potential applications for your life that it has to offer.

I begin this journey into Core Beliefs with the film that formed the basis of my workshops and this book: King Kong. What better way to open a book that has a section devoted to films and how they can help us to explore the creation of Core Beliefs, than with this perfect example? It doesn't matter if you've never seen the film (either the original - which I discuss here - or the latest version), you will still be able to enjoy using the story to help you better understand how Core Beliefs are created in our younger years and how they can continue to operate out of awareness for many of our adult years.

[1] What I am describing is not Dissociative Identity Disorder (formerly Multiple Personality Disorder), whereby the personality of someone - who as a child suffered repeated and severe physical, mental and/or sexual abuse - would become fragmented or split into several identities, each having their own age, gender, gestures, and distinctive way of talking. In this instance, DID is literally a survival device. I also want to make clear that what I'm describing isn't necessarily the psychological results of acute neglect, abuse or the cumulative failures experienced within crucial relationships. Those are extreme, but unfortunately, not uncommon examples of experiences that set up Core Beliefs. If, as a child, you were exposed to constant abuse or neglect, what I describe in this book will no doubt only form the tip of the iceberg. By having a greater understanding of Core Beliefs, you will begin to appreciate the whys and wherefores of your behaviour - most likely exhibited in your relationships and/or health. These problem areas will be obvious to you, but you may not be aware of the underlying causes - the Core Beliefs - that were created by that early life experience or experiences.

PART ONE

GHOSTS IN THE MACHINE

Chapter 1

KING KONG TO THE RESCUE?

Though this be madness, yet there is method in't.

Hamlet – (Act II, Scene II)

Every man has inside himself a parasitic being who is acting not at all to his advantage.

William S. Burroughs

You will now be aware that many of the blocks, fears, indecision, behaviours, and inner conflicts we hold as adults are a result of our Core Beliefs. As we grow and evolve, we will adopt different sets of values and beliefs: some of which will be embodied as yet more Core Beliefs. As adults, it's unlikely that we will ever again create a set of beliefs as intractable as those we created as children. This is partly due to the fact that our brain and the way we view the world is pretty much established by early adulthood. However, the brain continues to change and develop throughout life, but at a much slower rate. There are many factors that go into the creation of a belief - repetition of an experience being just one of them; and so, for this reason, beliefs formed as adults are not as robust, and so are unlikely to take hold as easily as those we created as children, when our brains had more 'plasticity' and were in the process of becoming.

Inner conflict arises when parts of us are still holding on to the old beliefs. Symptoms may vary from an inability to speak up for yourself; becoming immobilized when someone confronts or shouts at you; remaining unsuccessful; or sabotaging any success you achieve so as not to attract attention to yourself. The *raison d'etre* of a Core Belief is to keep you safe, and one of the best ways of doing this it to make you invisible. Of course, this isn't a literal invisibility.

If you look back over the instructions you were given as a child by your care-giver, eg, 'be careful', 'watch yourself', 'be quiet', 'try harder', etc., you will have some idea about how innocuous they may appear; however, if they are repeated often enough and with enough emotion - even if delivered with a caring intention that may appear to be quite useful - they can actually be insidious and damaging in the long term. For example: An office worker was unable to ask his boss for a promotion or higher salary. When he was a little boy he asked his mum not to hug him in front of his friends. Unfortunately, his mother never hugged him again. His innocent request and his mother's reaction had instilled in him the deeply held belief that 'if I ask for what I want I will be rejected'.

Enter King Kong

The story of King Kong fits perfectly with the setting up and continuing influence of our Core Beliefs. An innocent abroad, Fay Wray finds herself in hostile surroundings, totally out of her comfort zone and natural environment - the big city. She is on a desert island making a film and has been kidnapped by the natives and offered as a sacrifice to Kong, who dutifully comes and takes her off into the jungle. On the way to his lair at the top of a sky-scraping mountain, Kong is attacked by several big, bad creatures: one of which - significantly for Kong and our analogy - is a Pterodactyl (a massive, bird-like dinosaur). Now, Kong believes that these creatures don't just want to pick a fight with him, he believes that they also want to get their claws on Fay Wray; and, as he's taken quite a shine to our heroine, he doesn't want to give her up. Each time they are attacked, Kong bravely comes to the rescue to save Fay Wray from being torn to pieces. Although Kong is a threat, Fay Wray recognises that he is protecting his precious cargo in a way that is absolutely necessary and crucial for her survival in that dangerous situation *at that time*. Unfortunately, Kong perceives all-comers as potential predators, even the hero who is trying to save Fay Wray from a horrible death.

Eventually, the handsome hero outwits Kong and successfully saves the heroine, returning her to the ship that will carry her back to the relative safety of her homeland. However, the director of the film, recognising Kong as a sure-fired money-maker, ensures that this giant of a creature also accompanies them on their return journey to civilisation - the concrete jungle that can be every bit as cut-throat and dangerous as any wild, untamed wilderness.

Back in the metropolis, Fay Wray is now in her natural setting. This is familiar territory: she knows how to operate in this environment and can make informed, mature decisions about her life there. Fay Wray is about to prosper from the capture of King Kong: she will go from being a poverty-stricken unknown, to a successful celebrity. On stage in a large theatre, she nervously parades in front of a manacled Kong. His captors (and Fay Wray), think they have him under control and that he is now powerless to do anything unless they let him. The packed auditorium is filled with an awe-inspired audience, and cameras flash as photographers try to capture the definitive image of Beauty and the Beast. King Kong, angry at his imprisonment and interpreting the noise and blinding flashes of light as a threat, believes Fay Wray is in danger and literally goes ape. He escapes his bonds and does his utmost to protect her. He is following his instincts and doesn't realise that in this setting, his behaviour is inappropriate and only serves to put her in a more damaging situation.

Later, he plucks her from the safety of her hotel room and takes her - as he did in the jungle - to the highest place he can find, the Empire State building. Once there, he comes under attack from several fighter planes (pterodactyls!). With Fay Wray once again in jeopardy, he gently puts her down so that he can attend to the unremitting threat that surrounds them. Again, what Kong has no way of knowing is that his primeval, instinctive behaviour is putting his precious Fay Wray in danger. His role in all of this is to protect and save her from harm at any cost. Of course, this results in Kong being killed, and he falls to his death onto the busy street below. Fay Wray is shaken, possibly traumatised once again, but lives to face another day of life in the big city.

King Kong and Core Beliefs

Now let's look at this story from the perspective of the creation of Core Beliefs. As with any analogy, we may have to tweak it a little to make it fit, but most of what occurs in the setting-up of beliefs is neatly held within the story of Kong.

Imagine Fay Wray in the jungle represents the child encountering a new situation. The child is out of its safe, familiar, natural, and (mostly) predictable environment. In this frightening (and/or repeated) situation, they experience something that is so scary and so beyond their ability to comprehend, that a 'part' (King Kong), with a belief that the world is a dangerous place, is created to protect them should they encounter a similar situation again. Unfortunately, the trigger for the re-emergence of the part isn't necessarily an exact (or most times, even similar) replica of the original experience. All that needs to happen is for the child, teenager, or adult to encounter a situation that creates a similar *emotional* response, i.e. fear. Out of awareness, and without being prompted, the part - or Core Belief - will kick in to do its job, to carry out orders and to do so in any way it can.

Fay Wray in the city is now the adult version of that child. She is more than capable of navigating her way around this world. She can make informed decisions based on skill, knowledge, and previous experience. She will undoubtedly make mistakes - everyone does - but she will learn from those mistakes and will hopefully use the learning gained from them to help her grow and mature accordingly. She will have aspirations and dreams about what she wants out of life, where she wants to go and how she might get there. She will have amassed a great many resources and skills that she can call upon whenever necessary in various situations.

Unfortunately, she still has operating within her the part that has never let go of the belief that it needs to protect her. King Kong attached himself to her in the jungle and went back with her to civilisation. As far as he - the part of her that believes she is not safe in certain situations - is concerned, she is still a vulnerable child who needs protecting. He persistently goes to any length to fulfil his role of defender and protector, going so far as to cause her more pain and to put her wellbeing in even greater peril.

The fact that our Core Beliefs operate retroactively is of great significance when we come to fix them in the present. To them, we are still helpless, vulnerable innocents. As children, we don't have the capacity to make judgements based on past experience or understanding, and have a very limited perception of how life and the world functions. At that time, this part or belief is deemed essential to our survival. We felt so threatened by the frightening situation or repeated experience that in our limited understanding we truly did believe we might die (and for some that may have been true). We know on a visceral level that if we ever encounter that situation (or feeling of impending danger) again, something must be done to protect the defenceless child.

Consequently, whenever we feel threatened, anxious, nervous, exposed or vulnerable, King Kong will never fail to come to the rescue. What we have to do is figure out just what our own personal King Kong looks like (and by that I don't mean giving it a physical description), and what experience (or experiences) created him in the first place. When we know that, we can get some idea as to what his mission is: for example: you will be safe if you keep quiet; you will be safe if you stay hidden/invisible; you will be safe if you are good; you will be safe if you always please others before yourself, etc. We then have to explore ways to undo the beliefs that were created back in the childhood jungle, and bring them into the present day metropolis of adulthood. But remember, despite evidence to the contrary, the part of us that holds these beliefs is our friend:

it never acts out of spite or malice, but from instinct and the deep seated desire to keep us safe.

For this reason, it - or they, for there can be many versions of our Core Beliefs - will not go without a fight. They must be convinced that times have changed, that you have grown into a mature, rational, perceptive, competent adult (even if we don't always feel that way!). They have to be persuaded that their services - as they are - are no longer required. That you are more than capable of making decisions and judgements for yourself based on your years of experience: that you are able and willing to make mistakes - in fact, it's important for your growth and development that you do - and that you will learn from them and (hopefully) not repeat them. That not every situation is a dangerous one that can harm you - some feelings of anxiety or apprehension are perfectly natural (such as when giving speeches, asking for a raise, saying no to a bossy relative, going on a first date, etc.), and are not the response to a life-threatening situation.

In dealing with your inner King Kong, you must learn to recognise and examine carefully the hurtful attitudes you encountered as a child. This shouldn't be too difficult as they will still hurt now. The reason behind identifying them isn't so you can apportion blame - which never solves anything - but so you can be sure you don't inflict these hurtful attitudes on yourself.

When your parents, primary care-giver, siblings, or even teachers, repeatedly spoke to you in such a way, belittling you and your efforts, making fun of your fears and worries, invalidating your attempts at the challenges you faced, or worse, calling you hurtful names, you will likely continue this self-degradation into adulthood. These verbal put-downs and personal attacks are powerful suggestions if repeated often enough, but if they are reinforced with facial expressions such as disgust, disappointment, irritation, or even met with stony silence, then they can cause lasting damage that goes to make up our sense of who we are and how approved of we feel in the world.

The following chapter explores in more detail how Core Beliefs are created. It includes aspects of my own voyage to my true self - the self that I began with as a baby; a baby that, as far as familial issues, behaviours and attitudes were concerned, began its physical life as a blank slate.

Chapter 2

A BABY IS BORN

*At the heart of personality is the need to feel a sense of being
lovable without having to qualify for that acceptance.*

Paul Tournier

*Our birth is but a sleep and a forgetting. Not in entire
forgetfulness, and not in utter nakedness, but trailing clouds
of glory do we come.*

William Wordsworth

We come into this world a being of pure potential. Despite our background, we can be, do, and have anything we want. The world of possibility and probability stretches out before us, ready to be chosen, discovered, and created. Adventures beckon, to be filled with challenges surmounted, loves won and lost, success achieved, riches gained, reputations made... The possibilities are as endless as atoms in the universe.

Unfortunately, as physical beings, we are susceptible to the social influences, vagaries and issues not only of our parents, care-givers and other family members, but also from previous generations. From the moment of birth (and even *in utero*), a baby absorbs data from its immediate environment in the form of shadows, sounds, sensations and even intuitive, or psychic impressions. It will be sensitive to the emotions; not only of its mother, but also of those she has contact with, and her environment. We could also add that this new human being will also bring with it its own spiritual intentions, a blueprint of what it would like to achieve and how best to do it; nonetheless, free-will allows for many deviations from the 'path' at any time and in any way.

Back in the seventeenth century, a philosopher called John Locke proclaimed that, at birth, the mind was a *tabula rasa*, a blank slate. This burgeoning science of psychology and rationalism eventually developed into the doctrine that there is no such thing as inherited psychic awareness or inborn traits or memories. For the purpose of this book, I will focus mainly on the brain as a 'receiver' filtering experiences that then go on to create impressions which are then superimposed over the psychic awareness we possessed when we entered the physical body. It is these 'physical' impressions that influence the creation of Core Beliefs. However, there will be certain traits, physical conditions and mannerisms that we brought through with us from our greater self and have little to do with how we were raised.

The second it emerges from the womb, a baby is bombarded by an immense amount of both subtle and profound detailed information about the world and how to operate - and thus survive - as a physical being within it. These messages come at it from all directions, and are taken in and filtered via the five senses and its still powerfully present intuition (this usually diminishes in intensity as we mature). In its first months of life, a baby's survival is at the heart of every movement, cry, grasp and gurgle. By roughly eighteen months, when it is able to communicate with the seemingly omniscient creatures around it (on whom it is dependent for its survival), a baby will begin to use verbal language instead of just body language and unintelligible noises. A baby has no way of knowing when or if its hunger will be satiated, its thirst quenched, its pain eased; or, equally as important for its survival, its need for physical contact met. It has to trust that its primal form of communicating its bodily needs, loneliness, fear and discomfort will not be ignored, because the alternative could literally result in its death. We are all born with a strong will to live, to survive at any cost, regardless of how seemingly intolerable the conditions we were born into might be.

For the first three to four years of life, a baby's brain is developing at a rate faster than at any other time of its life (puberty, being a very close second). Brain development, or learning, consists of the process of creating, strengthening, and discarding connections - or *synapses* - between neurons (a cell that transmits nerve impulses). Synapses organise the brain by forming neural pathways that connect the parts of the brain governing everything we do - from breathing and sleeping to thinking and feeling. At birth, very few synapses have been formed. Those that are present are primarily those that govern unconscious bodily functions such as heart rate, breathing, eating, and sleeping.

Throughout a small child's early years, and in response to its experiences, the formation and development of synapses occurs at an incredible rate. By the time children are 3 years old their brains have approximately 1,000 trillion synapses, many more than they will ever need. The synapses that get used the most are strengthened and remain intact, but many are gradually discarded: a process known as 'pruning'.

At these times of vigorous, crucial development, the brain is at its most malleable. This 'plasticity', also known as 'neuroplasticity', refers to the changes in the neural pathways and synapses that take place in response to changes in behaviour, environment and, more crucially, stress. This understanding of the flexibility of the brain to change and adapt to environmental and emotional stimuli, replaces the formerly held belief that the brain is a physiologically static organ. It is now recognised that the brain changes throughout our lives and not just in childhood. However, the developmental years of a child and young person's life, when the brain is more flexible, are those that most affect their behaviours and attitudes as and when they become adults.

During this time of plasticity, a child's brain could be likened to a blank canvas. As a baby or toddler interacts with the world and its primary caregiver(s), marks are being made on the canvas, with every experience leaving an impression. Some of these experiences, if repeated often enough or with enough emotion, will create an almost indelible mark while those experiences that are fleeting will not have a lasting effect and will eventually fade away. This is how we grow a brain and how we learn - by repetition. The more often we do something, the more likely it is to become habit, and thus, a way of life or of being.

The result of various hues and shades of paint being applied to the canvas determines the final work of art that emerges. For most of us, our paintings are somewhere between the idyllic nirvana of fantasy and the hell-like torment of a nightmarish world. The thing is, depending on our first experiences of being human, as adults we each of us carry around our very own work of art that depicts our version of the world and what we can expect to find in it: whether it's a safe place and we can anticipate a life filled with little or no nasty surprises, or a dangerous place with the potential for harm, pain and suffering always on the horizon, or anything in between.

Am I safe? Checking the signs.

Research now shows that interaction with other people and our environment is as vital to the growing and developing brain as are the elements of the food we eat - such as proteins, fats and vitamins - and that these experiences can cause the brain to develop in different ways. But we are more than our body. We - and therefore our thoughts - are made up of energy and so naturally, and often unknowingly, respond to the energy/thoughts of others. This is what it is to be intuitive or psychic; and so, as we are all energy forms, we are all psychic. Thus, negative experiences - from undisputable abuse to subtle and 'psychic' messages from caregivers about how they feel about you, themselves, the nature of life, living and the world - can have a profound effect on the development of the brain. This in turn affects how a baby perceives its immediate environment and those that inhabit it: Can they be trusted? Will my needs be met sufficiently and in a timely manner, or will I be left hungry, cold, wet? Will I be abandoned and left to fend for myself? Will they hurt me? Are they angry? Did I do the right thing?

A baby - or any physical being for that matter - is aware on a psychic level of the moods and intentions of those it comes into contact with. How many times have you sat next to someone and just felt your energy drop, or felt uncomfortable? In some instances it will be so subtle that it will slip under the radar, but at other times you will just get a feeling about someone. You won't know why, but you just don't like them, or trust them. This is why we have intuition, as a survival device (one that we'd be wise to trust and develop as we would any other useful skill), and it's this that serves us most in those early years of family life.

On the whole, your family will behave in ways that - although common to families all over the world - are unique to that particular grouping. They may have possibly lost touch with their inner being, or Greater Self - the part of us that is often referred to as the 'soul', or 'higher self' - which then gets buried under years of forgetting, causing people to move further and further off course. No matter how many nudges they receive in the direction of their 'true north', their sensitivity to their Greater Self and awareness of its existence within them is so deeply hidden that they have no conscious knowledge of it, and so are unable to recognise the 'signs' for what they are. They become closed off to themselves and their natural ability to connect with their Greater Self, and the greater selves of others.

It's difficult for a baby to over-ride these influences. They are still in the process of adapting to being physical, making adjustments and trying to stay on track, as memory of who and what they are recedes further and further into the background with each day and with each new physical experience. They become entranced by the 'reality' of their world. They are now in such a dense environment that it's difficult for the subtle messages from their Greater Self to get through. As adults, they will continue to be bombarded with data and instructions from other physical beings around them: physical beings that have also spent many years accruing layer upon layer of physical, impenetrable fog. This has the effect of buffering the child from its true north and Greater Self.

As this baby grows, it collects more and more evidence that the world (i.e. its inhabitants) is potentially dangerous and cannot be trusted or relied upon. They need greater and greater protection from those things that could harm or damage them, and so they create their Core Beliefs, their King Kongs, to help them stay safe and navigate their way through life. It is for the child's benefit that they exist and operate. As you will see later in the book, this belief system is designed to enable us to fit in with our family and so provide us with a safe haven and - the ultimate goal of us all - approval.

The child may mature and become a fully functioning adult; but the scared and fearful child still exists within, believing that it still lives in a dangerous world and that it still needs to be protected. They have absorbed the fears and attitudes of the children that still exist within their parents, who similarly carry the fears and attitudes of their parents and their parents before them. They are part of a chain linking us back through the generations, but it's a chain that can be broken. It is necessary to re-educate the Core Beliefs about the real world, the 'now' world you live in. As you do this, they will finally let go of outdated, limiting beliefs and fears and so gradually relinquish control of you and your life. It may even be possible to re-programme them so that they move forward towards becoming integrated within you: operating in harmony, providing you with the memory of innocence and trust and openness to new possibilities that you were born with. They have a lot to offer the adult version of themselves, just as you have a lot to offer them. It's a two way connection that needs to be established between each and every version of your physical being. Movement and adaptation is imperative for a healthy and happy life.

Thankfully, not all childhood or teenage experiences are harsh or negative ones. This in turn means that not all Core Beliefs are rampant saboteurs out to scupper our chances of lasting happiness. If you have had care-givers that actively encouraged you in all your endeavours, dreams and aspirations, if they picked you up when you made mistakes, dusted you down and told you that your attempt was a courageous one; if, when you were scared, they smiled and hugged you as they reassured you that you were safe; if they did all the things that loving, caring guardians can do to provide you with a safe haven of comfort and security, then you will have a plethora of Core Beliefs that tell you it's ok to not get it right the first time (or second, or third) because at least you had a go and that you can learn positive lessons from what we think of as mistakes. You will feel safe to voice your opinions and desires - you will even know clearly what those desires are.

Perhaps your family's attitude to money was positive, and instilled in you a sense of abundance and plenty. They may have had good health and seemed not unduly concerned with illness, germs and disease. Your parents may have demonstrated the enduring comfort of a stable, lovingly committed relationship. With all this love, support and positive experience behind you, you will probably go on to achieve, if not huge success and the happiest of relationships, then at least a solid, secure family and/or career base, and a relatively healthy body.

Sadly, there are some families that experience an inordinate amount of hardship and repeated cyclical patterns of dysfunctional behaviour. We are all aware that systematic abuse will increase a child's risk of becoming a damaged teenager who may go on to exhibit or develop self-destructive behaviours such as, eating disorders, sexual promiscuity, self-harming, and general delinquency. (It's important to note that not all children who exhibit these behaviours will automatically have had an abusive childhood.) This mistreated or troubled teen then grows up to be a desperate adult with drug and alcohol problems, depression and anxiety, and even suicidal tendencies. Again, these are often the more obvious wounds of a life of abuse and neglect, and this book isn't about the lasting damage caused by acute attachment disorders: there are plenty of books and studies that more than adequately cover those issues and areas of development. The aim of this book is to show how even the subtlest of messages from our caregivers, those we may have regular contact with, and even from the environment of our family home, can have a profound effect on how we function as adults.

It isn't just the messages we pick up from family and friends or the community at large that can have a profound effect on how we view the world. Below is an example of how a seemingly innocuous television programme contributed to the establishment within a young girl of a deep fear of life and death, her world and the people in it.

Marie's Story

At 15 years old, Marie's life was plagued by her belief that the world is intrinsically dangerous. It's hard to know exactly when in her young life she began to fear her environment in such a profound way: there is no evidence of abuse or serious neglect during her early years. However, when Marie was eight or nine, she loved to curl up with her mum on the sofa to watch Casualty (a family drama set in a hospital A&E department). She remembers being frightened by the realisation that people die - often in horrific ways - and that she was powerless to prevent it. Her belief that the world (and life) is unpredictable and dangerous, had created such a strong fear within her, that she was unable to sleep without first checking that her bedroom windows were locked. She also had to ensure that her arms were safely tucked under the duvet, and she would cross the road rather than risk passing a parked car that had someone sitting inside.

In therapy, Marie finally began connecting her seemingly irrational fears to experiences from her past, and was thus able to begin the slow journey back to empowerment and self-confidence. She was able to discover and communicate with a part of herself that was still a frightened little girl needing to snuggle up to her mum on the sofa: a little girl who believed she was in danger and needed to be protected. She learned how to comfort this Inner Child, to reassure it that all is well and that she is safe. The TV programme wasn't the only thing responsible for creating her world view (more of this later), but it certainly added to the fear she had of living in a world she felt she had little or no control over.

In his seminal book, *Your Inner Child of the Past*, leading psychiatrist, W. Hugh Missildine, states that:

> *'As a child, you naturally reacted to your parents' attitudes. During the developmental years, a young person internalises these attitudes - and you still do, using these attitudes on yourself. Long before adolescence, you began a process of 'internalising' these attitudes, absorbing and integrating them into your way of considering, treating and guiding yourself.'*

Regardless of how our own personal Core Beliefs are created, what's important is that we identify where our habits, behaviours and attitudes originate (are they ours or our parents?) and so reclaim our power by exploring and examining closely those ways of viewing the world that get in the way of us living the life we want.

Art restorers and conservationists now use a new x-ray technology that can see through many layers of paint and thus reveal the under-painting and drawing that made up the first attempts of the artist to create their masterpiece. Similarly, if you were to look closely enough at the marks and impressions on your own personal work of art, you would no doubt see the hint of something hidden in the background, something that had been laid down in your early years and may no longer even be a memory in the conscious mind. Or it could be the remains of an experience that produced fear within us as children: something so subtle and seemingly inconsequential, that we fail to accord it any significance in adulthood. Unfortunately, these 'ghosts in the machine' are very much alive and kicking in the subconscious where they have a very active - and to them, meaningful - life. It is these ghosts, their discovery, identification and subsequent removal or re-structuring, that we explore in more depth in the following chapters.

Chapter 3

CORE BELIEFS ARE CREATED

If you want to change the fruits, you will first have to change the roots. If you want to change the visible, you must first change the invisible.

T. Harv Eker

Our parents can show us a lot of things: they can show us how we are to be and what things we ought to strive for, or they can show us how not to be and what things we ought to stray from. Then you may have the kind of parents that show you all the things about you that you want to get rid of and you realize those traits aren't yours at all but are merely your parents' marks that have rubbed off onto you.

C. JoyBell C.

In 1961, my mother had already given birth to three children. Now she was pregnant again with what she hoped would be her last child. During the pregnancy, she dreamed that she had given birth to a blue-eyed, blond haired boy whom she named Alan. This dream made her very happy because, if it came true, it would mean she would have the last child to complete her ideal family of 2 boys and 2 girls. The order would also be perfect - girl, boy, girl, boy.

In August of that year she went into labour. Things didn't go too smoothly and the baby struggled to be born. The umbilical cord was wrapped around its neck and so no matter how much my mother pushed, the baby's journey into the world did not progress, and the cord would tighten even more - something that put the baby's life in danger. Holding the baby's head, the doctor turned its body in order to unwind the cord from around its tiny neck. And then I was born. Not my mother's dreamed of blue-eyed boy with curly blond hair, but a blue-eyed girl with wavy fair hair.

There is no doubt in my mind that my mother loved and bonded with me from the moment she laid eyes on me - I later had the privilege of seeing her almost smother my two baby girls with love and kisses, so I know she had a thing for babies! And I'm equally sure that I was doted on and was the centre of her universe for the first 22 months of my life - which is when she gave birth to a lovely baby boy, who just happened to have blue eyes, and blond, curly hair, and whom she named, Alan.

None of the above information was ever kept secret from me as I grew up: why would it be, it's fairly innocuous in the scheme of things. Like any curious child, I would ask my mother about our family and about what happened when I was born. She would smile as she told me about her dream baby and how I came along instead, and she would laugh when telling the story of how I had the cord so tightly wound round my neck that every time she tried to push me out, I would literally 'boing' back in again. I have no recollection of how I felt or reacted to these stories of my place in my family or of my indecision as to whether to be born or not; and, as I grew up, I never gave it much thought. It was a family story to go with all the other family stories and didn't especially warrant special, or even much, deliberation.

As an adult many years later, I attended a course in Bach Flower Remedies. We were asked by the facilitator to choose a flower card that we felt attracted or drawn to. Some people knew instantly and, not wanting to lose their chosen card, dived on it before anybody else could grab it. I sat staring at the scattered cards as I mused, and considered, and dithered, and deliberated... Soon I was the only one who hadn't chosen. The facilitator leaned forward, picked up a card and handed it to me. The flower on the card was a Scleranthus. On reading a description of this plant to include in this book, I was struck by something that fits uncannily with what I now know about my Core Beliefs. '*Scleranthus annuus* is a tiny plant with green flowers, and can be very difficult to find because it *blends in with the background*.' Now, those people reading this book who know me well will be wondering how that last bit has anything to do with me and my personality. As a child, I always wanted to be centre stage - a desire so strong I went on to spend several years as a professional actor. I will soon explain the seeming contradiction of me hiding in plain sight.

However, the facilitator chose that card for me because Scleranthus is a remedy given to those who find it difficult to make decisions. She then went on to explain that the card we were drawn to (or, in my case, given!), is our life card: it describes our personality and/or how we approach life. Suddenly, my difficulty at being born made sense: I simply hadn't been able to make up my mind! However, a few years later, the joke of me as a baby being reluctant to be born became more serious when seen in the light of the potential spiritual implications of my decision to become physical.

Today, as an adult who has practiced for many years as a therapist, I can understand so much more about my place in my family and my relationship with my younger brother. Most of the time we got along as most siblings do - fighting over toys, calling each other names, playing games together - the usual stuff. However, as soon as I went to school, I realised that my little brother was going to have what I wanted, what I craved - my mother's undivided attention. This is where attachment issues come in.

I wasn't yet two when my brother and rival was born. I still needed a lot of attention and nurturing, especially as I was still too young to clearly communicate my needs verbally. Like with any baby, I would have had a reasonable awareness that I would be fed, watered, changed or eventually comforted whenever I was upset, but being left alone would still have felt like abandonment and rejection, and so would have been interpreted on a subconscious level as a threat to my survival. Understandably, my baby brother needed my mother's attention more than I did - he was a helpless baby, after all. But at not yet two years old, none of that would have registered with me. What I experienced was my mother leaving me to cry in order to tend to his needs (and I'm sure, in desperation to get attention, I cried a lot!), and my brother being cuddled and crooned over - something that I realised had somehow changed for me. I am sure I upped the ante as far as attention seeking was concerned, hence the need to be the centre of attention. At first I used tears and tantrums, but as I grew older I found other ways of gaining that much-needed attention.

Don't get me wrong, I'm not claiming that all my ills stemmed from the fact that I had a baby brother: there are plenty of people in the world who share that experience. The point I am trying to make is that attachment issues and the creation of Core Beliefs can be triggered by the least abusive or neglectful of environments, and that everyone who has experienced being part of a family will, by default, have their own set of issues and beliefs. Some will be so subtle and harmless that they make little or no real impression on that person as they mature. Even so, they will be present, just very deeply hidden and disguised, and so seemingly non-existent.

However, in my situation, I not only had competition for survival to contend with (a primal need as opposed to a conscious one), I also had the story (when I was old enough to ask about it) that my brother had been joyfully anticipated and expected instead of me. Consequently, every time I saw my mother give my brother attention (especially when it superseded my need or desire for attention), I would interpret it in the light of him being more deserving of that love and affection than me. Even as a young child (and woe betide anyone who doubts the ability of any child to pick up subtle messages from those they interact with), I will have made a kind of 'felt' sense of that story. I was never able to articulate the feelings it created within me: the knowledge that I had been responsible for usurping the much wanted, dreamt of, blue-eyed boy's place in the family, and subsequently, the world (not to mention the possible pain and distress my emergence into the world would have caused my mother). I would have known on a profound level that I needed to work extra hard, be that much nicer, likeable, even more lovable than my brother if I was to stand any chance of getting a look-in on the attention front. But I didn't know how to do that. The only weapon I had at my disposal was to demand more and more of my mother's attention by crying louder, more often, and over the tiniest of infringements and slights. This was a battle of survival that I could not afford to lose.

Trauma and Core Beliefs

Wind forward two years. I am now a cute four year old with long, light-flaxen tresses. Despite my daily battles for mum's attention with my arch nemesis, life is pretty good. We live on a newly built housing estate filled with young families, so I have lots of playmates. We are some of the lucky ones as our council maisonette looks out onto a fairly large patch of grass.

One of my special friends at that time was a young man who lived across from the grassy area outside of our block. He was about thirteen when I was born, and apparently took a shine to me straight away. In my mother's words, he was 'slow'. Of course, none of us kids knew what that really meant and even if we did, it didn't make any difference to us, we just knew he liked to play with us - me especially. How lovely it must have been for me to be singled out by someone so popular: someone who wasn't interested in my kid brother.

And so, one summers evening, this boy who was now a young man of seventeen, took each of us in turn for a ride around the green on the crossbar of his bike. My dad would do that too, sometimes, when we went to visit family on another part of the estate. It was great to feel the sensation of speed, to have my dad pay attention to me and for me to have him all to myself. So when this young man, my special friend, came to give me my turn on the bike, I was really excited. I was even more thrilled when, instead of doing the one lap of the green as he had done with all the other kids, he carried on and headed towards a back road that skirted a golf course. I felt so lucky and very special: I was getting a real treat.

Some of you, I'm sure, will have read between the lines and have a fairly good idea what happened next. (There's no way of putting what follows in a gentle way, so I apologise if it seems blunt.) My friend took

25

me somewhere secluded and raped me. I don't remember much of what happened - just bits and pieces which, thankfully, didn't include much about the actual rape. As I sat on the crossbar of the bike on the ride home, he asked if he could kiss me. I said an emphatic 'no' - I didn't like my friend anymore. I now know that what he had actually said was, 'Do you mind if I kiss you?' At just going on four years old, I couldn't quite figure out the syntax of that question: all I knew was, he had asked a question and it involved him kissing me, which I absolutely did not want. So I was really confused (and even more distressed), when he went right ahead and kissed me, even though I had so clearly said no. (I want to reassure those readers who may be upset or disturbed by this disclosure, that I did tell someone about what happened and the man was arrested and prosecuted for his crime.)

We now have the makings of a very complex set of Core Beliefs (such as 'I am not safe if I am visible', 'It is dangerous to be thought of as special', 'You can't trust people'), to add to those that had already been set in place by the birth of my brother and the unspoken complaint my mother might well have inferred when describing (however non-accusatorily) the pain and anxiety during labour that my birth had caused her. It would be many years later before I began to put the pieces together and come to realise just how these events contributed to the creation of my Core Beliefs and continued to operate in the background - that is, out of my awareness - sabotaging most of my adult endeavours in one way or another.

As I've said, not all Core Beliefs are created as the result of traumatic experiences. Because of the shock to the system - which would imprint the experience not only on the brain, but also within the body as cellular or tissue memory - Core Beliefs set up by trauma will undoubtedly be more difficult to re-structure once they've been identified. Below is an example of the beliefs set up by repeated (and in this case, conflicting), messages from a care-giver. In this particular instance, the instructions are verbal, but they could just as easily be non-verbal. We will also see how much they can affect how we behave in later years.

Michael's Story

As a small child and young teen, Michael had been given the conflicting instructions, 'Think / Don't think', by his mother. On being sent to the local shops with a list, Michael might find that he needed to improvise - usually because they were out of X, or they only had a larger or smaller version of Y. He would come home with the groceries and his mum would ask him why he had bought X instead of Y. Michael would say he thought it was best to get that than nothing at all. His mum's response was often to shout at him, telling him, 'Well, don't think, you think too much!' It could just as easily have gone the other way if Michael thought it was best not to improvise. For that he would get, 'That's just your problem - you don't think.' It's not that Michael's mother was a woman intent on creating confusion in her young son's mind: she was just a woman struggling to raise a family almost single-handedly.

Like all of us, as an adult, Michael often finds himself in situations where a decision has to be made; but, instead of calmly weighing his options and going for what he feels is best, he will be paralysed into non-action because of his underlying fear of making the wrong decision. He literally can't think straight, and so can spend a long time thinking too much about his options. He feels a physical discomfort whenever he needs to make a decision; and, depending on how important the outcome of that decision is, he may even defer to others and coerce them into making the decision for him in order to relieve this discomfort or stress about getting it wrong. He doubts himself and doesn't trust his ability to choose wisely. If he had never discovered the origin of this doubt or mistrust, he would easily continue to believe it when family or friends accuse him of being indecisive, slow, or a ditherer. As a result, people may grow impatient when he can't make a decision quickly enough or contemplates the consequences of his decisions for too long and in too much detail: something that adds even more stress to an already stressful situation.

What is actually happening in these moments of indecision is that the adult Michael has been momentarily supplanted by the child Michael. Unconsciously, he will be replaying any one of the scenarios where his mother told him that he thinks too much, he shouldn't think, or he just doesn't think. His brain will freeze, much like a computer when it's trying to carry out too many instructions at once. The child Michael, will be desperate to get it right in order to please his mother, as the opposite - her displeasure - is painful, and feels like being banished from the safe haven of love and security.

The Core Belief, 'It's not safe to think and/or not to think', was set up to remind Michael of this fear of abandonment and rejection so that he could recognise it whenever a similar situation next occurred. That way he would be able to avoid getting it wrong and stay safe. Consequently, there is a part of Michael that will come to the fore whenever he has to make a decision. How activated it becomes will depend on the importance of that decision being 'right' and acceptable, and what he perceives will be the consequences of getting it 'wrong'.

For most (possibly all) of us as adults, we will have deep-rooted commands operating within us that act like an instruction manual. Do X and Y happens; if you don't want A to happen, then do or don't do B; F will happen whenever G is activated, etc. Imagine a child surrounded by giants who control its every move, experience and emotional response. If we don't get it right (whatever 'it' might be), we run the risk of losing the approval of our parents, which equates with danger.

In his book, *In Defence of Children*, psychiatrist, B. I. Beverly, recognised that a child is:

> *'expected to understand, appraise, and adjust himself*
> *to those adult standards as an adult would. By great effort*
> *and well-meaning, he may act rightly hundreds of times; yet*
> *any such desired behaviour is usually ignored, while one*
> *wrong act on his part brings down upon him the wrath of the*
> *gods - his parents, older relatives, teachers and other adults'.*

When finding themselves in a situation that in the past may have resulted in being on the receiving end of the displeasure of an adult, it will be the child, still functioning within the adult, that comes into operation. It is the child within that is going to respond: and no child wants to incur the ire of giants, nor does it want to challenge their wisdom - they are, after all, not only perceived as a giant by the child, but also as an omnipotent God!

As adults, the instruction manual still exists; but it's so deeply hidden we've mostly forgotten about it and wouldn't know where to begin looking for it even if we did remember. However, whenever we receive a message from 'out there', our inner parts or child, studiously look for a match in their survival manual in order to find the right way to respond.

What follows is an example of how a powerful, enduring set of Core Beliefs can be created and how they can go on to engender debilitating and enduring mental health issues. Again, for obvious reasons, I've changed the name of the person involved. This person has struggled with OCD (Obsessive Compulsive Disorder) for the whole of her adult life - she is now in her mid-forties.

Jean's Story

Jean was seven years old. Her father had been decorating and there were lots of DIY products around, including White Spirit. It was a hot day and, feeling thirsty, Jean went to the fridge to get herself a drink of lemonade. She had poured herself a glass and was happily drinking the contents when her father told her to stop and questioned what she was drinking. Had she mistaken White Spirit for lemonade? He hadn't seen her get the lemonade - he'd only seen her drink from the glass. Was she sure it was lemonade? Knowing he'd been using white spirit, he was afraid she had inadvertently poured that into the glass by mistake.

Jean knew it was lemonade she'd been drinking, but her father was, in effect, telling her she couldn't trust her own actions or senses (there is, after all, a marked difference in smell and taste between lemonade and white spirit). This inability to trust her own judgement went on to become complex OCD. This seemingly innocent incident left the young Jean with a fear of imminent death; and, from that day on, she became an anxious child. The OCD itself lay somewhat dormant for the next several years and no-one - not even Jean - would have noticed there was a major problem waiting in the wings to be triggered.

When she was 19, Jean's father died. At first she managed her grief reasonably well. However, one day 'out of the blue', Jean became aware of what seemed to be her first OCD symptom. Talking about it later, Jean would describe this moment as the 'the turning on of a light switch'. From then on, she was unable to function rationally. She questioned everything she did and became overwhelmed with intrusive thoughts - the 'what-if's' - self-doubt, and compulsions.

For Jean, it has been very difficult to understand and come to terms with the possibility that as an adult she is still responding to, and obeying the instructions from, her deceased father. It's the very fact that he was no longer around to protect her from herself that caused Jean's OCD to emerge from the recesses of her mind and take hold so strongly. Seven year old Jean (and the Core Belief) had been relying on her father for all those years to help keep her safe. While he was there, the part of her that had established the Core Belief that she can't trust herself, was in abeyance. It will, however, have been keeping things running in the background ready to come to the fore as and when needed. In order for Jean's Core Belief to relinquish control, she first had to find a way to make it all right that she challenge her father's wisdom, that she will be safe in doing so and won't come to any harm if she installed her own wisdom in its place. But, in doing this, there will be a sense that she is not only disrespecting her father but that, on a visceral level, she is putting her life in danger.

This is just one example of how pervasive Core Beliefs can be and how difficult it can be to alter them; it isn't just a matter of being able to identify the cause. These beliefs are entrenched in our psyche and it will take a lot of persuading, negotiating and hard work uncovering the various layers before a Core Belief, or set of Core Beliefs, can be successfully eradicated or transformed into something that works for you in a way that is positive and productive.

I will describe the methods that helped Jean begin the journey towards positive mental health in Part 2. I wish I could say that Jean is now enjoying a life free from symptoms; but, unfortunately, at the time of writing, she is still struggling to vanquish the fearfulness and anxiety that keeps her trapped in a world that she feels she needs to manage and control very carefully. It's not that uncovering and working with Core Beliefs is not helpful, it's that the deeper entrenched they are in the psyche, the longer and more intense the process.

For a more in-depth view of OCD and how pervasive its hold can be if not treated early enough, see Chapter 17, '*Fear of Being Vulnerable*: *The Aviator*, which describes Howard Hughes' struggle with OCD, its creation in early childhood, and how it went on to dominate and ultimately destroy his life.

In the following chapter, we will look more closely at the role families play in the setting up of Core Beliefs. We all of us will have experienced life within a family of sorts, and so there isn't anyone on the planet who will have reached adulthood completely untouched by the etchings on the brain of life at home.

Chapter 4

THERE'S NO PLACE LIKE HOME

Deep inside us, we know what every family therapist knows:
the problems between the parents become the problems within
the children.

Roger Gould

How one handles success or failure is determined by their
early childhood.

Harold Ramis

In Chapter two, I touched on how the brain develops and how family environments can affect that development. In chapter three, I gave a more personal description of childhood experiences and how they contribute to our understanding of the world around us and our place in it. In this chapter, I intend to go into more detail regarding being part of a family and how our home life impacts in such a way as to affect us way beyond our young years and well into adulthood. Some of what you're about to read may be similar to what we've already covered, but I don't think it does any harm to re-visit those concepts and theories and go into them in more detail.

We already know that the reactions of parents (or primary care givers) to their child greatly determines how that child will feel about him/herself. Of course, parents are innocently perpetuating the parental attitudes that they experienced growing up. It's a cycle that cannot be broken unless we stop to examine our attitudes and discover where they originated. Very rarely does an adult create an attitude from scratch. We may think we are operating within our own set of rules and values, but we may never have actively chosen those behaviours, or to hold particular standards, morals or principles. If they seem different to those of our parents, it's possibly because you have adapted them somewhat over the years - especially if you have lived apart from your parents for many of your adult years. The way your beliefs appear on the surface may seem far removed from those of your parents', but dig a little deeper and you'll no doubt find they are the wellspring of your most deeply ingrained behaviours and attitudes: as it was for their parents for them, and so on back through the generations.

Home is where the heart is. It's also the location of the main blueprint for the adults we were to become. In order to figure out what contributed to making you who you are today, you need to go back and examine the original plans. Of course, you might not be in a position to question grand, let alone great-grandparents about their childhood and how they were parented, but being able to examine your own in as much detail as you can should afford you a good enough idea of what you're dealing with. With those plans brought out of the darkness of ignorance, you will be able to make appropriate alterations according to your own design and choosing.

I'm reminded of old, black and white haunted house films where someone standing outside sees a window to a room they didn't know existed. They check the original plans of the house and, sure enough, the room is marked on the blueprints but has been sealed up. Often in these films, the characters discover that some terrible deed took place in the room, or perhaps it harbours something malevolent that needed to be imprisoned. For us, that hidden, boarded up room, is likely to hold information about our past that can lead us to awareness of our present circumstances. As frightening as the story behind the secret room may be, once it is uncovered, true healing can begin. In our film analogy, it may require something as drastic and dangerous as an exorcism in a desperate attempt to expel the demons. Again, for our purposes, an exorcism of our childhood ghosts, as scary as it may feel, can lead the way to relief and liberation from past pain and distress.

Of course, the demons and ghosts of the past will be different for everyone. I'm not suggesting that the monsters of childhood are always shocking or harrowing in any way. Hopefully, not all of us will have had traumatic experiences growing up, but none of us will have been able to avoid the inevitability of parents as purveyors of familial and cultural attitudes. In fact, it is more likely the all-encompassing atmosphere and mind-set of our families as opposed to a single trauma that determines our sense of self-value and worth. Add to this the societal (and, in these high-tech days, even global) attitudes and moral codes our parents live(d) by, and you can see how the emerging personality of a small child can be so profoundly and unwittingly influenced and manipulated.

What this means ultimately, is that we go through life trying to recreate or in some way simulate the emotional atmosphere of childhood and the home we knew as children. I don't think I've ever met an adult who, when recalling staying away from home as a child - even if with grandparents or friends - did not feel the misery of homesickness. Even for those whose childhood was blighted by neglect, poverty, intolerance or even outright abuse, staying overnight in another home, with all the unspoken rules and expectations, would result in feelings of strangeness and of being lost.

Obviously, some of this can be ascribed to the fact that every family has its own set of rules around eating, sleeping, and sharing time together. A small child experiencing a family environment that is alien to its own, is naturally going to feel a fair amount of discomfort and unease. As an adult then, it's easy to see why we might strive to simulate that familiar 'at home' feeling wherever we live. This may provide us with a comforting sense of security, but it's also likely to bring with it the constraints and disquiet of our childhood home. Given a choice, we would not willingly choose to recreate all aspects of our early years; however, even the more negative aspects of family life can give us that much sought after sense of familiarity - sought after by our Inner Child, in any case.

What this also implies is that in seeking to reproduce our childhood home, we are also then led to seek out relationships that closely mirror those we had in childhood. We might joke about men who want to marry a woman just like their mother. What we mean is that they are looking for someone who will care for and treat them in the same way. A man who unfavourably compares his wife's or partner's way of doing things - such as cooking - with that of his mother, is a good example of the little boy within wanting to be 'safe' at home with his mum. The same can equally apply to his relationship with his father. If this man ever feels stressed or not in control, he will most likely be even more demanding: expecting everything to be exactly like it was in his childhood home.

He may not necessarily be very close to, or loving of his mother or father, but then it's not the person he wants to replicate but the experience of familiarity that they represent. If his mother doted on him, then childhood for him may have been a time when he could do no wrong, when he was allowed to make mistakes and still feel like he was loved and cherished. Even if his mother was indifferent to him as a boy, as an adult he would be trying to win her love and approval. This might result in him wanting every opportunity to show her how good he is by staying loyal to her way of doing things - even when she's not there to see it. The little boy within would not be able to understand this nuance, all he would know is that something vital is missing from his life and he must do all he can to reinstate it in order to continue to survive. By siding with another, he risks alienating himself even further from his mother (or father): and so his significant other can never be allowed to reach the status he has ascribed to his omniscient parent.

Message Received - Loud and Clear!

As a child, we absorb and imitate every gesture and facial expression of our parents in a bid to ensure their continued love, warmth, affection and approval. Their attitudes toward us - gleaned from these, often subtle, signals - determine how we feel about ourselves and the world. For a baby and toddler, there is often no other means of judging these things except through the mirror of our parents. It is from these early interactions that we ascertain how lovable (or not) we are.

I recall a time when my daughter was about 3 years-old. She had done something 'naughty' and checked out just how much trouble she was in by leaning in close to examine my face. I knew instantly that she was reading my expression in order to judge if her behaviour had incurred my displeasure. As I saw the expression of quizzical dismay on her face, my heart went out to her and I knew that it was something she must do almost minute by minute in my company – checking my face for signs of possible disapproval. This was the only way she had available to her of gauging whether or not she was still loved and valued.

In that moment, I realised how easy it is for us as adults to underestimate the power we have to bestow our approval or rejection on our children (regardless of whether they are our own or someone else's) with something as casual as a look, so providing them with a strong or weak sense of self-worth. If this was something that was repeated on a regular, day to day basis, imagine how damaging that would be to the fragile ego of a child. Imagine how much more potentially damaging a dismissive, disappointed or critical tone of voice can be – especially if heard over and over. Combine such facial expressions or gestures of disgust and intolerance with a verbal attack on the self-value of a child, as in, 'you're so stupid', 'you clumsy idiot', the child will turn this in on itself and those comments then become, 'I am stupid', 'I am clumsy and an idiot'

Very often, these messages received as children from those entrusted with our care, if repeated often enough and strongly enough, can result in a young person who only ever feels 'at home' when being spoken to in similar ways. Think of the teenager who seems to deliberately provoke adults into speaking harshly to them. I've worked with young people in the care system that would repeatedly goad any adults who got close to them emotionally until they responded in a similar manner, that of an adult shouting and threatening them with harsh consequences for their behaviour.

At this point, it would not be unusual to see a glimmer of a smile on the teen's face. On the surface, this could be construed as a sign of pleasure at having 'broken' the adult responsible for their care, proving that they're just like all the other adults in their life; however, more often than not, it's a sign of relief and reassurance. Such a young person can only take so much kindness, warmth and patience in an adult they are close to before they feel compelled to literally crank up the tension between them to the point of eruption. It's the discharge of this built up energy that can cause the flicker of a smile: now the young person is on familiar territory in which they are on the receiving end of anger and threats. This is the world they are used to and know how to operate within. However strange it may seem, this is their comfort zone of familiarity, and it's one they will seek out in all relationships until and unless they have repeated experience of warmth and genuine affection from people they can trust. If this doesn't happen often enough, then as adults, they will continue to twist and manipulate relationships and circumstances so that they resemble those from the past.

Of course, most of us will have grown up sharing our home with more than our parents: we may have also shared that hallowed space with other siblings (some may have even spent many childhood years with a grandparent also resident in the family home). The number of siblings you have and where you are placed within that hierarchy will have naturally contributed to your self-concept as an adult. It makes a huge difference to your experience of growing up if you were the eldest, youngest, middle or only child.

Another aspect to this web of relationships is the place your parents occupied within *their* family. For instance, if you are the eldest, then their attitude toward you may be a reflection of their own experience of being the eldest, or even of being the youngest in their own family. Gender will also play an important part in this complex mix of relationships and interactions. A father who only had brothers may find himself over-indulging his daughters. An adult who was an only child may have very little tolerance for childishness within their children as they wouldn't have witnessed or experienced this kind of immature behaviour as children themselves, particularly if their parents found it difficult to indulge their own childlike selves by playing games, acting silly or making things up. An only child of these parents might often be chided for their foolish, puerile antics and told to 'grow up' or 'act your age'.

Jenny's Story

Jenny was twenty five when she came to see me for hypnotherapy to help her with sleep problems, lack of energy due to Chronic Fatigue Syndrome (Myalgic Encephalomyelitis – M.E.), and a less than healthy diet. She would often lie in bed awake until all hours, unable to sleep for the constant thoughts that ran through her mind whenever she lay down to rest. On top of this, the M.E. meant she was often too exhausted to go to work. Weekends and evenings were spent either sleeping (something she could do easily at any time other than at bedtime), or playing computer games. She also ate too much unhealthy food – particularly at night.

During the course of our work together it transpired that Jenny was the eldest of two. Her brother no longer lived at home and had spent some time in the army. Jenny felt that whenever her brother came for a meal (which was often), he, her mother and step-father would criticise her and accuse her of malingering. It seemed to her that they didn't believe she had ME and thought it was just laziness. This particularly affected Jenny as she had always been an active young woman who enjoyed walking and swimming - neither of which she could manage since being diagnosed with

M.E. several years earlier. Jenny's relationship with her brother was always fraught, as they competed for their mother's attention and affection.

Jenny had always felt as though her brother had been on the receiving end of all that was withheld from her - positive attention, being valued, and having her opinions and ideas listened to with respect. As she entered adulthood, this became more and more apparent, and her status and voice within her family seemed less important than that of her younger brother's. As the first born (and a girl), she was expected to do more around the house and was a valued provider of support to her mother when she and Jenny's father separated; and yet, even this emotional support didn't result in her gaining the attention and appreciation from her mother that she craved.

I gently pointed out to Jenny that M.E., although physically real, is often the result of emotional and/or psychological issues. I explained that M.E. could be thought of as 'me'. The characteristics of M.E. in the field of Meta Medicine[2] include thinking we're not good enough, always striving to do or be better, not taking care of ourselves, abandoning hope, and feeling a lack of purpose. The body literally gives up the effort to exist or be human. When you scratch beneath the surface of aching muscles, headaches, fever and exhaustion, there is a deep desire to hide, to exclude ourselves from social activity or intimacy.

Jenny's situation fitted this description perfectly. Once she realised and accepted that her M.E. was the result of her Inner Child desperately trying to win the affection and attention of her mum, and that it was a

---

[2] Meta Medicine holds that disease always correlates with unresolved conflict such as might follow a significant emotional event. The intensity and length of the conflict determines how severe the disease is. The nature of the conflict determines *where* the disease affects the body-mind. Our body reveals what is happening at a subconscious level. When the conflict is resolved, the body heals.

genuine physical expression of her feelings of worthlessness and her belief that she could never be as good as her brother, she was able to restore herself to health. Within weeks of beginning therapy, she had lost some weight; was feeling more positive about the future; held a family meeting where she explained assertively that she would no longer tolerate being picked on and not taken seriously; was going for walks and swimming at the weekend instead of lying in bed, watching TV or playing on her computer; and had gained enough confidence at work to let her supervisor know that she wasn't willing to discuss work issues during her breaks or lunch (something that had happened almost on a daily basis). Needless to say, Jenny no longer considers herself to be someone with M.E.

Family Roles and Family Rules

Whenever someone comes to me for counselling, I always warn them that they aren't the only ones in therapy - whoever they share their lives with is also going to experience changes in their life. Naturally, it won't be at the same level as the person doing the therapy, but they would definitely feel the ripples of change on some level - particularly if they are part of the reason for the person seeking therapy in the first place. Anyone embarking on a therapeutic journey would do well to bear this in mind, and make sure that their loved ones or family members are aware of the possible repercussions of their treatment.

For Jenny, there were a few occasions when the changes she was making to her life and way of being were challenged - particularly by her brother - but she was prepared for this and was therefore able to stick to her guns. It's important to take things slowly so as not to throw others into such a state of anxiety and confusion about the changes taking place within the person they knew so well, that they consciously or unconsciously do all they can to sabotage anything that upsets the status quo.

Virginia Satir, considered the 'Mother of Family Therapy', made popular, in part, the idea that we have roles within the family system. She believed that these ways of being were learned in childhood as we tried to navigate our way through family interactions and hidden agendas. In her book, *Peoplemaking*, she describes four roles within a family as:

*1. **The Placator** - this is the people-pleaser in the family. They have low self-worth which they try to hide by doing all they can to please others and keep the peace within the family. They never disagree, and apologize for everything - even when they haven't done anything wrong. Their emotional survival depends on their winning the acceptance of other family members, and so they will always be the mediator in family disputes as this lessens their feelings of low self-esteem and vulnerability. This person is on everybody's side and effectively prevents people from working through their issues together in a productive way.*

*2. **The Blamer** - this person is always right and will find fault in everything. They bolster their low self-worth by putting themselves one up at all times. They will disagree, criticise, point the finger and dictate how everything should be done within the family. Their way is the best and only way.*

*3. **The Computer** - or the seemingly cool, calm and collected one.* They hide their true feelings from themselves and others by distancing themselves (emotionally) through the use of long words and intelligent sounding, complex sentences. They do this by seeming to be in total control, reflected by the lack of emotion in their voice and/or their body language. If they do demonstrate emotion, it is usually contempt or boredom with what they are hearing or witnessing within the family.

4. The Distractor - this person will do everything in their power to keep family discussions or disputes from getting too close to inner feelings. They will speak in irrelevancies, move about all the time, never directly answer questions, and will often use humour and/or sarcasm to divert attention away from what's really going on.

These roles within the family aren't always rigid and so clearly defined. Depending on the situation, each family member can move between these roles taking on one or other of the stances, as and when necessary, in order for them to feel safe and emotionally secure. This means we are unable to determine whether a response is coming from our true self, or from these habitual, adaptive roles.

As well as these stances within the family, there are other roles that we may take on in order to fit in with what's expected and accepted. Remember, this isn't a definitive or strict list of roles, and we may find that we recognise ourselves in more than one. Quite often, these roles are covertly assigned to members of the family.

Have you ever encountered a situation, perhaps in work, where there are two (or more) people who seem to behave in the same way? They might be the attention seekers, always ill and always speaking about how stressed they are and how many problems they have. If you listen to two of these people conversing, you will often be able to detect an element of competition between them for who is the worse off / most ill / more stressed. This interaction demonstrates that it's difficult, in an on-going relationship, to accommodate the same, or very similar, roles. It's as though there's only room for one of each and so a play-off will take place every time they meet in order to establish who has the right to that role.

Of course, that's a very simplistic way of looking at a very complex set of behaviours and attitudes. It would be impossible (and not very helpful, in my opinion) to label individuals, or even families, as being completely one type or another: especially as we move and shift in our ways of being almost on a daily basis. However, by recognising these traits within relationships, you will be able to more easily understand your own way of being, your own personhood, when interacting with others – particularly within your family. Added to the four stances outlined by Virginia Satir (five if you count the role of *The Leveller*[3]), there are other roles that come into play within family interactions.

When working with clients, I describe the family and the roles they've taken on, or have been allocated, as being like a group of actors performing in a staged production (more on this later), with the theme of this drama becoming the organising principle[4] of the family. (The theme might be addiction, abuse, criminal behaviour, subversion, ambition, illness, over or under achievement, pretence, fantasy – anything that binds the family together in a common framework of being.) What differentiates these roles from those of Virginia Satir's - which include parents - is that they are mostly determined by your birth order within the family.

For simplicities sake, I have listed these roles in a way that corresponds with birth order; however, this isn't an exact science and it is possible to embody more than one of the roles, which can also be influenced by gender and culture. Depending on who is describing them,

---

[3] The *Leveller* uses words that match their body language, tone of voice and facial expression. If they take on any of the other four stances, it is because they choose too, and not out of a need to bolster their fragile and vulnerable self-esteem or self-worth.

[4] Defined in Wikipedia as: *A core assumption from which everything else by proximity can derive a classification or a value.*

some of these roles go by different names, but nonetheless share common traits. What follows then, is a generally accepted description of the most commonly identified roles and their various names. You may also recognise similarities between some of these roles and those defined by Virginia Satir.

Family hero / Caretaker / Good girl/boy / Model child

Most often the oldest child: however, this can also be determined by gender. For instance, the eldest daughter in a family with illness / addiction as its organising principle will often take care of the other children, assuming the role of parent even to an older brother. They may even assume the role of a surrogate spouse or confidante. These are the dutiful sons and daughters who strive, and are expected to be good, at all times. They take on responsibility for the emotional wellbeing of the family. They grow up quickly, rarely play or act the fool, and believe they have to earn their worth. Parents (and teachers) have high expectations of them and so can easily invalidate their efforts if they are not deemed good enough.

The family Hero is not allowed to make mistakes, often being told that they should know better if they do something childish. They are placed on a pedestal, admired and held as a good example by one and all. An only child will exhibit many of the traits of maturity and the need to please parents and people in authority as the eldest child, only to a greater degree as they don't have younger siblings to play and share fantasy worlds and games with, or to practice negotiating and sticking up for themselves.

Problem child / Rebel / Scapegoat

Usually the second child in the family: they exhibit almost opposite traits to those of their older sibling. They will not do so well at school and will be more inclined to truant. They are the naughty one who distracts the parents from any marital problems as they join forces to sort out their problem child. This also works for other siblings who can use the Rebel child as a Scapegoat. They carry the responsibility of being the one who isn't expected to do or behave well. No one is surprised when they get into trouble or mix with other problem children, but they will always be keenly aware of their parents' (and teachers') disappointment in their misdemeanours, lack of motivation or achievement.

As the Scapegoat, other siblings will often get them to be the voice of dissent within the ranks as everyone expects them to cause trouble, challenge authority and provoke disagreement. They are less prone to denial, showing a greater tendency toward honesty, however painful or unpleasant for those on the receiving end. I've always felt that for these children in particular it can be extremely difficult to free themselves of this role, as the other members of the family are unwilling to take on this provocative responsibility. It's as if other siblings can hide their own transgressions behind those of the Rebel. Therefore, siblings will sabotage any attempt made by the Scapegoat to shake off this challenging and isolating role within the family.

Lost child / Adjuster

When I was learning first aid, something that stuck with me and seems to fit so many of life's situations was that, at the scene of an accident, you don't go straight to the person who is making the most noise, but instead go to the quietest one. If someone is kicking up a fuss and vocally expressing their pain, then you can rest assured that they are intrinsically ok. However, if someone is quiet and lying motionless, then the chances are they are in shock and may be suffering from more serious injuries.

This scenario can be equated to the family system and roles. The Rebel, and to a lesser extent, the Mascot (who we meet next), is the noisy, kick up a fuss, get in everyone's face, child. They let you know if they are angry or disgruntled - and how! They are truly hurting, of that you can be sure, but they have the ability to express their hurt in the moment by letting you know about it. The Lost child is like the quiet accident victim. They will sit quietly in the background watching the chaos erupt around them, waiting patiently for their turn for attention. They escape the pain of being ignored or forgotten by spending hours alone engrossed in a book, absorbed in the TV, or listening to music. It's not so much that they have their needs ignored: it's more that no-one recognises that they have any needs to be ignored in the first place. Because of this, it's easy to overlook the lost child and assume that they're getting on just fine.

The Mascot / Clown / Protected one / Eternal child

Usually the youngest child, they can never be allowed to grow up and must be protected at all times from the harsh realities of life. It's the job of the family Clown to divert attention away from difficult situations, and their comedic antics are a means of diffusing tension and pressure within the family. They aren't allowed to be serious or express sadness. Part of their job is to help keep their parents (and other adults they come into regular contact with) young.

Because they are considered the baby of the family (even well into adulthood), and therefore fragile and in need of protection, they are often excluded from family dramas that might cause them distress. As long as they are able to cavort, act daft and make people laugh, all is safe within the family. It's a huge responsibility and one that they are never likely to be allowed to grow out of. Other members of the family may exhibit similar traits – sense of humour, ability to clown around, etc. – but there can only be one youngest member of the family, and so the role is theirs for life (if they so choose, that is).

These are by no means the only roles that can exist within a family. Other roles might be, 'the talented one', 'the pretty / plain one', 'the stupid / clever one', 'the sickly, weak one', etc. Whatever your role (or roles), you will find it difficult to move away from the perceptions others have of you, even as an independent adult.

The Theatre of Life

Now we return to the analogy of the family as a troupe of actors forever playing the same roles within the same production. Each of them have had the same script and have learned it off by heart. When they reach certain scenes, they all know how they are supposed to act, what they are to say and to whom, and what the end of that scene will look like. With that scene successfully concluded, they can move on to the next scene and then the next, and then the next... Everyone knows their part, and everything in the garden is rosy as long as everyone does what's expected without deviation from the script or adaptations to their character.

Now, imagine one of the cast of characters decides that they no longer want to play that role. After all, they didn't ask for it, it was given to them at the start of their contract with the troupe. It was possibly the only one available at the time they joined the cast and they didn't have any say in the matter. Only now, they've had enough of being that character: they'd like to try something different. Perhaps they feel stuck in a rut, unfulfilled and disappointed and frustrated with how things always turn out the same for their character. They've heard it's possible to change roles mid-performance, or to maybe even leave the production all together. Whatever it takes, they are going to try for a new role, a new outcome for the production and for them.

They may have decided this without consulting the other members of the cast. In the wings, they may have tested the waters by mentioning their dissatisfaction with the way things are and their desire to change roles. Without a doubt, if they mentioned their intention to another member of the cast, that 'actor' will have told them it's not possible, or that there aren't any other roles available for them, or that it will cause too much trouble within the troupe and so it's best to just leave things as they are. They may even have been warned that they will never be allowed back in the troupe if they leave their particular production, or try to change it in any significant way. And so they have a choice: they can give up all thoughts of changing their role and continue to go along with the play as it is, or they can make a stand and take their chances.

Let's imagine they decide to risk everything by trying out a new character with different lines and a different idea of how certain scenes could end. They wait in the wings for their cue, take a deep breath and join the other actors on stage, ready with their new lines. The moment arrives when they get their cue from one of the other actors. Instead of just reeling off their usual line, they pause and then respond differently. For a moment there is confusion on the faces of the other actors. One of them repeats the line and waits for the correct response. All eyes are on the errant actor as the others wait for their correct cue; only, once again, they are given the 'wrong' line. They look at each other in bewilderment, they've no idea what's going on and even less of an idea how to respond. This isn't the kind of play where you can improvise and make things up as you go along. How will they know how or when the scene ends if people just go off script like that?

Now all the other members of the cast are affected. If one line takes one of them off track, that means that they, too, will be off track. They begin to panic, wondering where this is going. They all do everything in their power to bring the wayward character back in line. They will go through various approaches to get things back the way they were, when everyone knew their part and stuck to it. They will coerce, ignore, dismiss, and undermine the changes the nonconformist player attempts to introduce. If none of that works, they will resort to threats, subtle at first, but slowly escalating to outright intimidation and accusations of their being responsible for ruining the play and for the potential break-up of the troupe.

Bringing this analogy back to the family, there is real fear here for everyone. As one person begins to change, it has a ripple effect that causes changes in everyone else. The one with the most to lose - usually the most dominant member of the family - will do all they can to ensure that the rest conform to what they believe to be the right way of being. Of course, in order to accommodate this family system, all members need to relinquish power and control, which ultimately means the sublimation of their true self. As with Core Beliefs, the family's attitude, behaviours, structure, hierarchy and place of power was established in previous generations, and is handed down from one generation to another.

This is an example of co-dependence within the family. There are unwritten rules that stipulate what each member of the family must do in order to achieve approval from everyone else. Individual wants, desires and feelings must be ignored and supressed in order for the family's organising principle to be upheld. It's these inherent rules that ultimately determine your success or failure with the Law of Attraction. As long as they are in operation, it won't matter how many affirmations you repeat, how clearly you visualise your goal or even how excited you get about achieving it – it is those beliefs created as a child that will define your life experiences.

Family Rules Ok

From a very early age we learn the rules of the family into which we've been born. Some are flexible, others more rigid. Authoritarian families have too many rules, chaotic families have too few. There are overt rules - rules that are obvious and clear - such as, 'Male family members get bigger portions of food', 'Female members cook the meals and clean the house', 'Dad decides what gets watched on the TV', 'Younger children go to bed before the older ones', 'Everyone goes to church on a Sunday', 'Homework has to be done before you can go on the computer'. Not all of these rules will be stated verbally, but by the actions of family members, we get to know which rules apply to us.

Then there are the covert, unspoken and hidden rules. 'Women shouldn't enjoy sex as much as men (if at all)', 'The rich get richer, the poor get poorer', 'Men don't show or talk about their feelings, unless it's when they're angry', 'Girls are fragile', 'Money is hard to come by', 'having children is a sacrifice'. Some of these rules infer social, gender, religious or cultural based attitudes; others are concerned with family secrets and shame.

Whatever your family rules, your life as a young person – and adult – will be governed by them, and there is every chance that you will perpetuate them when you have your own family. As an adult, you may have a level-headed, intelligent and mature view of life and the world. However, your Inner Child might see the same situation through the emotionally tinted glasses of past family relationships and rules. Even when this concept of the child actively existing within the adult is understood and accepted intellectually, there is a strong tendency to minimize the significance of feelings that stem from childhood.

In the following chapter we will look at how our broader relationships with friends, partners and even work mates can also contribute to our recipe of Core Belief stew. After all, they too have come from a family with rules, roles, attitudes, behaviours and beliefs. They too, will be trying to recreate their own familiar, safe haven.

Chapter 5

FRIENDS, LOVERS AND...WORKMATES

The meeting of two personalities is like the contact of two chemical substances: if there is any reaction, both are transformed.

C.G. Jung

Man is a knot into which relationships are tied.

Antoine de Saint-Exupéry

Every relationship we have, regardless of importance or intensity will be influenced to some degree by our childhood experiences. Going to nursery or school was when we first learned what it meant to be with non-family members, and how to make friends with people that weren't siblings. How we related to our peers in this new setting came from what we learned at home. Even how we communicated with the new adults around us would have been informed by how we were with our parents and other significant adults, and how they were with us.

This much, at least, is obvious. If you remember the analogy I used earlier in the book about how we are like canvases being painted on by life experience, then you can understand just how complex that canvas becomes once we attend school. There are so many possible permutations it would be impossible to describe them all, but here's just a short list of possible variations: the only child faced with a classroom of other children; the only girl in a family of boys having to deal with other girls; youngest child co-mingling with other youngest children... When you think about it, it's amazing how children navigate their way through these seas of complicated interactions and still manage to have even the slightest sense of self. No wonder some children seem traumatised by the experience of going to school or nursery: they are overwhelmed by sensory input, adjusting and amending their behaviour until such a time as they feel 'at home' in this new environment. Even so, it must be very difficult to make sense of the behaviour and attitudes of others who have been brought up in a different family system, and who have their own unique version of babyhood. Why don't they act the same way as my family? Why do they do this instead of that? Why aren't I getting the response I usually get when I do this or that? Why doesn't teacher put me on her knee and give me a cuddle when I hurt myself?

Jack's Story

Jack was born three months premature. He spent the first two months of his life in the sterile, alien confines of an incubator. His only human contact in his first days of being in the world came from the efficient, professional handling of the doctors and nurses tending to his critical needs. No matter how gentle their touch, it would not have transmitted the same messages of love and belonging as that of his mother (or father). It was two weeks before Jack's parents were allowed to stroke the back of his head for a few minutes each day (as a young child, Jack continued to be comforted, and would fall asleep almost instantly, by having the back of his head stroked).

I can't imagine the anxiety and fear a tiny new born baby – particularly one born months before it was physically ready to join the world – would experience at spending the first few months of its life alone and without the physical loving contact of its parents, and in such an impersonal environment as a hospital incubator. Apart from all the difficulties that would be expected as a result of his very detached and isolated introduction to life, Jack went on to develop problems in making or maintaining close friendships or relationships. His early seclusion resulted in 'faulty wiring' that made it difficult for Jack to form sustainable attachments. His world view is consequently viewed through the filter of someone who's start in life was fraught with stress, anxiety and separation.

As well as having the necessary experience of healthy attachments, making friends is also about finding others whose behaviours and attitudes closely match those of our siblings or parents. If other children are widely different to us, it might be too uncomfortable to fit in with them. Even with the prerequisite foundations in place, it can take years of practice to learn how to adapt our behaviours in order to create lasting friendships: something that not everyone succeeds at. If you're a child who has been over-indulged by doting parents, your every whim acted upon, never having to ask for or earn anything, having gifts, toys, or sweets lavished upon you before you even knew you wanted them, then you're going to find it difficult to operate in a world where those things are not freely given or on-tap whenever you want them. To learn that you have to share toys, treats, even teachers' attention, can be a very difficult lesson to learn.

This child will no doubt grow into an adult that is bored easily and even has a blasé attitude to the gifts given to him by others. This child has never had to wait for gratification, it was always immediate. All of their wants were quickly anticipated by their parents and so they grow up unable to take the initiative and so move from one thing – project, relationship, idea – to another, always seeking that sense of satisfaction that can never last. They very rarely truly appreciate gifts – whether they are material or emotional – as they believe they are entitled and that these things should be given to them automatically. They will expect friends to mirror the behaviour of their parents, to be spoiled and adored at all times. If these things are withheld, then they may equate this with being unloved, as providing presents and constant attention was their parents' way of demonstrating the depth of their love.

The lovers, friends and colleagues of this person will often feel unappreciated. They will feel as if all their efforts amount to nothing of any substance within the relationship. It will be as if they are trying to fill a bottomless pit: no matter how much effort, energy time or emotion they put into it, it will never be enough. This person may show pleasure at receiving a present, but it will be short-lived. They will then need something bigger, brighter, and more expensive if you are to prove that you love and value them. They could just as easily force a smile and a grudging 'thank you', deeming your gift unworthy of them, so used are they to the extravagant displays of love and devotion of their parents.

Then there is the child who has experienced continued punitiveness and criticism. They will believe that they can never get it right; they are worthless, not worth loving, bad, and no good. This child will become adept at deception and lying in order to avoid being punished. They will grow into an adult who is constantly seeking someone else to blame for any minor misdemeanour as a means of deflecting the punishment that the Inner Child believes they have incurred by their 'bad behaviour'. So intrinsic is this trait that they will apportion blame even where no blame is called for. As a child, they may have been the scapegoat; and so, as an adult, deflecting blame becomes, by necessity, second nature to them. It has to be everyone's fault but theirs.

Do As I Say

Did you dawdle as a child? Did you often escape into fantasy and daydreaming? Are you now forgetful or a master procrastinator? If these descriptions fit you, then perhaps you spent your childhood years being constantly directed, supervised, reminded, or coerced by your parents. Over-anxious parents project their fears or their need to be perfect onto their child. This child repeatedly hears, 'get a move on', 'hurry up', 'have you done x or y', 'stop messing about', 'pull your socks up', 'tuck your shirt in', 'comb your hair'... Thus these parents create children who have no other means to assert their own independence – something that is natural and important to the developing child – other than by resisting these continuous commands. How they do this is by deliberately taking their time, becoming easily distracted, playing just that little bit longer after they've been called to come in, staying up as late as they can, and refusing to get up when called.

Naturally, the more this child was coerced and pressured into doing things deemed essential by parents, the more they would stall and dawdle. This in turn would lead to even stronger demands and commands, which would eventually turn into not so subtle threats. As an adult, they resist every suggestion, instruction, idea or request until they become outright demands. Even those you give to yourself would have to be defied and resisted, thus recreating the familiar atmosphere of home where this was a common occurrence. Maybe you're familiar with the words, 'How many times have I told you to?' They may have been spoken to you by a parent who insists you do something such as tidying your room, revising for exams, or applying for jobs. You may even have said those words to your own child as you try to get them to do something that you think is important or necessary.

Another consequence of over-coercion by parents is for the child to become ultra-passive and meek. This child obeys commands without question or resistance. This, they have learned, is how to ensure the continual love and acceptance of their parents. They grow into adults who repeat the behaviour with teachers, colleagues, employers – anyone in authority, in fact.

In his book, *Your Inner Child of the Past*, W. Hugh Missildine, MD, quotes a patient who was a perfectionist that constantly found fault with himself and what he did. He could never be satisfied with his achievements; which, to others, would have been seen as worthy of high praise. This is an excellent example of how our Core Beliefs, given to us by our parents can continue to sabotage us well into adulthood.

> *'Ordinarily I get along fine. If I make an error in grammar or English when I'm speaking to someone, if I use the wrong word, I am ready to die. I can't stand it. I turn red as a beet, my heart pounds; I get so flustered and mad at myself that I can't sleep. Later I wonder how I, of all people, could have made such a boner. Later, I realise nobody cared […] I expect more of myself in that respect than other people do.'*

This man knew that this drive for perfectionism originated with his mother who had been an English teacher and had constantly corrected his grammar and speech. In going into meetings, if he knew that the people there were well educated he would hardly be able to talk for fear that he would make a mistake. Of course, so strong was the pressure he was under to be perfect, he would often make mistakes. This would then become a vicious circle of anxiety, too high expectation and unrealistic demands for perfection.

Having every minute of your day seemingly organised by a parent who believes that they know best, or who just wants you to do what *they* want you to do, how and when *they* want you to do it, will have resulted in you becoming a master of resistance, procrastination, defiance and non-cooperation. Your mantra as a child, teenager and now as an adult will likely be, 'In a minute', or words to that effect. Everything will be done in *your* own time, not anybody else's. And so you will stay up late (later than you probably like) if someone suggests it's time for bed; you will stay on the computer, in the garden, bath, watching TV longer than necessary if someone even hints that you should be doing something else.

As an adult, this person will even struggle to do the things they want to do for themselves – so used are they to resisting instructions or commands. They will complain and make excuses in order to avoid doing something they know needs to be done and become more and more uncomfortable the longer they procrastinate or distract themselves. They have no way of separating out who the command is coming from – a parent or their own desire to do something. It can seem a gargantuan task to untangle whether it is what they themselves want or whether it's residual parental desires and wishes.

If you are in the habit of making lists - written or otherwise - of 'shoulds' and 'need to's', then this might be an area worth exploring. These will be seen as commands by that part of you that was constantly being told what to do and when and how to do it, and so your natural response will be to resist. You will use the same language and tone of voice when deriding yourself for your laziness, worthlessness, uselessness and/or stupidity that your parents may have used as you were growing up. You have taken on their role of dictator in order to recreate that sense of homely familiarity I spoke of earlier. If you can recognise this behaviour in yourself, then you can begin to lessen its control over you by questioning where the directives are coming from and deciding if it is something you want to do or feel you should do.

A childhood spent being rejected, belittled, abused, picked on, shamed, or put down will result in an adult who seeks out partners (and possibly friends) who repeat the pattern. Just as the teenager who provokes anger and threats in the adults trying to care for them, this person will find themselves drawn to someone who is going to hurt them emotionally or physically. They will be attracted to people who treat them with contempt and disdain, who may take every opportunity to belittle them and tell them how pathetic they are. Thus, they are recreating the atmosphere of home and all that is familiar. Even though they do not consciously want this kind of treatment, they will find it almost impossible to break free of the need to experience it.

They will hope for and hang on to the tiniest bit of affection or kindness from their abusive spouse, friend or even boss, just as they did with their parent or parents. Somehow, that tiny glimmer of hope of acceptance and approval makes all the humiliation and rejection worthwhile. They live from moment to moment desperately waiting for the kind word or gentle touch that tells them they are lovable, valued and appreciated. It won't matter that they have people in their lives who do not abuse or disrespect them in any way and may even show affection and regard for them. Ultimately, they are desperate for the approval and acceptance of their parent(s), and so will endeavour to attain this from those whose behaviour mirrors that of their parent(s), otherwise it is meaningless.

Until we break free from these deep-seated commands and directives that govern our beliefs and behaviours as adults, we will continue to be the child in need of parental love, acceptance and approval. We will continue to seek these conditions of self-worth in anyone we have a meaningful or long term relationship with: whether through the love and intimacy of sexual partners, or through the repeated interactions with friends and colleagues.

If, as a child, rejection and abuse were the maps of your life, then you knew how to navigate your way through the storms and deep waters that made up your world. As an adult, you feel out of kilter in calmer waters that demand nothing of you. And yet, that is by far the healthier, happier option. So then, you must tear up the old maps of the world that state categorically that 'here be dragons', and instead draw up a more fulfilling, loving map of your new world. Trust that you can and will create a sense of familiarity within this new world and that you can release yourself from the bonds of childhood needs and cravings.

In Chapter 7, we will explore how family rules and roles contribute to the setting up of our Core Beliefs. At the heart of every Core Belief that we hold is an instruction given to us as children by significant people in our lives. These aren't necessarily spoken commands – perhaps if they were we might have had more chance of refusing to take them in and so allowing them to become the insidious messages that haunt us throughout our adulthood. So subtle were the majority of these directives, we hardly know they are there until we experience discord and discomfort surfacing at certain times in our life. We know something isn't quite right, but it's hard to put our finger on what that 'thing' might be. Hopefully, the list of

Core Beliefs in this chapter will go some way toward helping you to unravel the tangled web of your childhood and so be more able to create a tapestry of life and being of your own choosing.

Before we get to that, however, Chapter 6 focuses on an area that governs all our lives regardless of whether we were born on a housing estate or family estate – money. A thorny subject at the best of times, how we earn, spend, feel and talk about money will have come in the most part from how our parents viewed it: was it the root of all evil? filthy lucre? or something to be got rid of as soon as it came in?

Chapter 6

MONEY MAKES THE WORLD GO AROUND

*I spent a lot of money on booze, birds and fast cars. The rest I
just squandered.*

George Best

*No, not rich. I am a poor man with money, which is not the
same thing.*

Gabriel Garcia Marquez

Are you one of those people who believes that the love of money is the
root of all evil? Or do you ascribe to the view that it's the lack of it that
causes the problems? Whatever your beliefs on making, keeping and
spending money, it will have mostly originated from your parents – as
theirs did from their parents. It is in childhood that we will have first been
acquainted with money - what it means to have it, how it can be gained and
/ or lost, what we believe about the rich or poor, whether we keep it to
ourselves or share it, and do we work hard to get it or is it given to us.

If you came from a family that lived 'hand to mouth', only ever
having just enough (or often not *even* enough) to pay the bills and buy
necessities, then the notion of saving will be something that only those
better off can afford to do. As a child, then, if you were given pocket
money, chances are it burned a hole in your pocket. When I was very little

and my dad gave me my sixpence pocket money on a Friday night, I would race to the shops first thing Saturday morning and spend it all on sweets. As I grew older, my choice of purchases may have changed, but I would still be without a penny come Saturday evening.

I never encountered anyone within my family who saved for anything. If you didn't have the money to pay for it up front, you got it on the 'never-never' and paid weekly for it for years after – or so it seemed. I don't think it ever occurred to anyone to save first and then buy it outright: which amounted to the same thing only the other way round. I suppose it was an early example of learning about instant gratification: something I haven't been able to shake off completely even as an adult. Of course, it was also true that sometimes, household items needed to be replaced, and it would make life difficult if my parents had to save for a year or two before they would have been able to afford it.

As I said in a previous chapter, a child that has it's every wish and desire acted upon immediately - and at times, before they even expressed a wish or desire - would grow up equating receiving gifts and money with love and attention. This has never been more apparent than in today's money oriented culture, where many children grow up knowing the price of everything and the value of nothing. They will continue to measure the love of another by how much they are willing to spend on them and how often. If a parent bemoans the lack of money to pay the bills, it might be difficult for this child to have any real conception of what this means if they have all the constantly replenished designer clothes; up-to-the-minute, super high-tech gadgets; expensive furniture; and an almost daily diet of take-away meals for the whole family. For them, being 'skint' comes to just mean mum or dad has a moan before finally giving in to their demands for more.

It's hard for this person to be in relationships or situations where there truly isn't enough money to spend on luxuries or treats. They will feel unloved and of little value as their Core Belief that money equals love will dominate, making them feel uncomfortable and unable to accept love shown in other, more meaningful and intimate ways. The lure of instant gratification, of having something the moment they decide they want it, will be overwhelming and difficult to ignore. Of course, they may actually put it in terms of 'needing' something as opposed to just wanting it. You may have heard a child say to a parent that they *need* an ice-cream, or even a new phone. We know that what they mean is that they '*want*' it, but in actuality, it is their *Inner Child* (more on this in Part Two) that has the need. So constant is their need for reassurance that they are loved and valued, so linked is instant gratification to that love that they will feel real rejection if the said object is not forthcoming.

As an adult, this person will find it difficult to hold onto money. They will grow bored quickly and move from one pleasure-giving activity to another. They are seeking to recreate that feeling of being loved and valued, but the feeling (which isn't real) quickly fades, which in turn leads to the need to experience it over and over again. They will be addicted to that surge of pleasure they feel on receiving or attaining the coveted item and so will fill their cupboards and their lives with things such as shoes they never wear, bags they never use, gadgets they soon grow tired of, jewellery that quickly loses its sparkle, and relationships that inevitably grow stale. They will flit from lover to lover, friend to friend, job to job and never feel satisfied for longer than it takes for the shine to wear off.

Robbing Peter to Pay Paul

Then there are those who have been brought up in a home where every penny is counted and accounted for. Every item will be priced and measured within the confines of what little money there is to spare and how badly it is needed. In this family, there is real fear of not being able to meet financial demands. 'We can't afford it', is the mantra of this family. So entrenched is the belief that there will always be more going out than coming in, the child within this family grows up terrified to spend money even on necessities. They are convinced that something awful will happen if they do and so feel deep guilt at even considering splashing out on themselves by buying a new coat to replace the old, tatty one they've had for years.

My parents were in their early teens and adulthood respectively when World War Two started. They both experienced, in different ways, the scarcity of staple goods that comes with being at war and the harsh reality of rationing that accompanied it. Theirs was the era of 'make do and mend', and 'making ends meet'. This was something they took with them into their later years and into being parents. As a consequence, we would regularly have left overs that consisted of a variety of food stuffs that didn't quite go together or may even have been well beyond their 'best eaten by' date. My father even went so far as to mix the dregs of tea and coffee cups into a jug so that he could use the foul concoction in the next round of drinks (we could never tell if we were drinking tea or coffee!) It was common for us to be made to sit at the table with our food until every last morsel had been eaten or suffer having it served up the next day mixed in with that evening's fare. This wasn't so much because we were so poor we couldn't afford food, but more because neither of my parents – my father in particular – could bear to waste food, so scarce had it been for them growing up. They held a mutual Core Belief that stated that there will always be scarcity.

Another aspect of this poverty mentality was encouraged through our religion. As Roman Catholic, we lived with the contradiction that money and wealth are evils to be avoided and fought against, but that prosperity and abundance are gifts from God. Growing up, it seemed to me that a good Catholic was, by definition, poor; after all, Jesus was poor and denounced those that had wealth. Every day we were reminded of the saints and how they had lived lives of poverty in order to be closer to their God. And so poverty became linked to spirituality creating another Core Belief that it isn't possible to be spiritual and rich at the same time.

Nor is it possible to be working class and have money, apparently. I would often hear my socialist, Left Wing parents railing against the rich and how they get richer as we poor people get poorer. I was fed on a diet of 'the rich' (it was never explained to me what that actually meant - I was left to figure out for myself that it was anyone with more money than us), being greedy, selfish and totally indifferent to the needs of those less well off than themselves. These Core Beliefs have contributed to my difficult relationship with money. In having money, not only would I be betraying my working class roots, and would therefore risk being considered by my economic peers (i.e, my family and friends) as a heartless, avaricious snob, I would also be denouncing God and any charitable, selfless qualities I might have or aspire to. Now, as an adult who doesn't practice a particular religion and doesn't believe in the God of the bible, I have transferred that belief to my spiritual practices.

It was also this tenet around money and character that caused me to be so discomfited when a woman I didn't know questioned my credentials in my newly opened therapy centre (see Chapter 15, *Finding Your Own King Kong*). I struggled with the concept of charging money to help vulnerable people, believing that I shouldn't profit from their troubles. It's one thing to make a lot of money as a solicitor or private doctor, but something altogether different to make money listening to people talk about their deeply painful, personal issues. Surely charging those people was just taking advantage? Mixed in with these beliefs were my actual experiences of poverty as a child. I clearly remember my mum diligently counting the meagre housekeeping she got from my father (who, despite it being the late 60's, still believed we lived in the 40's as far as the cost of living was concerned!), and trying to spread it around to cover all the bills and still have enough to buy one of us a pair of cheap shoes for school.

For my Vulnerable Child, the memories of privation still linger, but my Core Beliefs around wealth and being the 'salt of the earth' were so strong that I found it difficult to let myself go above a certain income. Consequently, I would sabotage my own efforts to get on. This manifested as not preparing well enough for an interview, not taking the time and trouble to fill out an application form neatly and with enough relevant detail, or just becoming ill at the thought of going for the interview. Part of this was down to my lack of belief in myself and my ability to do certain things. I convinced myself that I wouldn't be good enough, educated enough, or experienced enough - just never enough of anything that I might believe is required for a particular job. If it was a job that would put me in the public eye, then I could be pretty sure I would experience a flare-up of my illness. This was my Vulnerable Child doing its best to keep itself - and me - safe from harm.

As for being self-employed, I am currently working as a freelance therapist (and of course, writing this book!) for the first time since I co-owned the therapy centre with my partner. This is the first time I have allowed myself to consider myself to actually *be* a therapist - therapy was always something I did in tandem with other work. There was a directive working within me that brought the imposter syndrome to the fore so strongly that I could never - until now - allow myself to be something so professional and 'grown-up' as a therapist. As long as I did it on the side, I didn't have to deal with the challenges to my Core Beliefs and I could pretend that I wasn't really a therapist and so no-one could challenge my right to earn a living as one again.

Rags to Riches

For some people, their memories and experiences of lack and scarcity are so strong that they become workaholics in their attempts to out-run poverty. Many great business people and entrepreneurs, who have made a fortune out of nothing, will talk about a childhood of severe deprivation. They can never rest from making money; and for some, their history means they are destined to live a life of austerity and penny-pinching, for to do otherwise would be to betray their family and their roots. They will have spent their younger years listening to parents talk about lack; they will have seen their mother struggling to put three meals a day on the table, and their father working from dawn til dusk to pay the bills. They may also have witnessed a community of people struggling together and supporting each other. They will come to equate poverty with courage, fortitude, self-sacrifice, creativity and selflessness. For them there is great nobility in being poor and making ends meet. They may have resented those with wealth and abundance, perhaps believing them to be parasites without the least bit of interest in the struggles of those less off than them. Of course, these same people could just as easily be great benefactors and philanthropists, bequeathing large amounts of money to charities and projects that help disadvantaged people all over the world.

When you have strong Core Beliefs around money, it can go on to greatly influence your life. Combine those Core Beliefs with low self-worth and you can become an adult that might never be able to ask for a raise, or apply for jobs that offer a higher salary than you're used to, all because you don't think you're worth it or that what you have to offer has any value. You will accept cuts in pay or low wages as if you should be grateful for any morsel thrown your way. For this same reason, if you find yourself in possession of a large sum of money, or happen to land a well-paid job, you will possibly throw your cash around as if it was in some way contaminated and you had to get rid of it as quickly as possible.

Of course, if you have really low self-esteem and self-worth, this might also involve you giving it away to anyone who asks, or buying gifts for people as a way of buying their approval and acceptance. You might even become addicted to gambling. As soon as you win money, you put it right back into the bookies pocket, or buy even more scratch cards. The money that burns a hole in your pocket is truly too hot to handle. Having it for too long can create all kinds of conflicts within you. For you, the Core Beliefs around money may include, 'too much money makes you a bad person', 'giving it to the needy makes you a good person', 'too much money creates false friendships', 'people with money are selfish', etc, etc. How could you possibly hope to make and keep money with these sets of beliefs going on within you?

Fear of Being Poor

Behind each and every attitude to money lies a belief that stems from fear. Every miser, every real-life Scrooge, has the belief that there won't be enough to cover all their expenses, that one day all their money will be gone and they will be left in abject poverty. They may also believe that they don't deserve to live well or to enjoy what money can provide. They will count pennies, become amazingly adept bargain hunters, be conscientious environmentalists (ostensibly with the intention of saving money, rather than the planet), and consume the least amount of food and drink their body can survive on: no treats for them - unless they are free, of course. This is an extreme example – everyone who displays these traits is not necessarily a miser, but they will have a belief that it is wrong to squander money, with the definition of the word 'squander' meaning spending it frivolously.

My set of beliefs makes it difficult for me to spend money on either myself or others. I have a generous nature that is restricted by my fear of there not being enough. I would love to be able to relax and buy the things I know would bring my loved ones pleasure or comfort, but I am unable to throw caution to the wind and use my credit card, thus spending money I don't actually have. This is difficult for me as I am a people pleaser and have a Core Belief that tells me I have to be liked and accepted by everyone if I am to survive. It is the conflict between this and my 'there's never enough money to go around' belief, that keeps me within the confines of my spending limit, i.e. only spending more than I have if it's absolutely necessary, as in to purchase supplements or therapy to help me heal. I know of people who will put themselves in debt in their desperate attempt to please others; in effect, buying the love and loyalty of those they want to keep close. This is the action of a parent who can't say no to their demanding child for fear of being rejected by them or thought badly of. They lavish money, gifts, designer clothes, and the latest gizmo in a bid to keep their child or children on their side.

As a consequence of my beliefs around money, I am not extravagant in my purchases and feel guilty if I spend a 'lot' of money on myself. This measurement varies from person to person: my 'lot' might be no more than £10 on a handbag, say, whilst for someone more accustomed to spending money on themselves or with a higher self-worth, it might be more like £50 or more. Of course, this person could have so much money without any fear of the source drying up, that it's nothing to them to spend that kind of money.

It was this push-me–pull-you, damned if you do, damned if you don't, kind of situation that led me to run my workshops on the Law of Attraction. I was noticing that people – including myself – who subscribed to the tenets behind the Law of Attraction were not exactly rolling in money, glowing with perfect health, or fighting off would-be jobs, suitors or friends. I knew that what we believe about those areas of our lives is what we will see played out in them, regardless of how many affirmations we say, or how many times we tell ourselves that we deserve to have x, y, or z. And so my first set of workshops explored the true beliefs that were getting in the way of people being able to manifest the life of their dreams, the life that the LoA promises is theirs for the asking.

However, in doing these workshops, I soon discovered that the values participants had around money, health, relationships, work etc, went far deeper than just holding two conflicting beliefs. That in fact, the beliefs that we exposed and then explored were literally the tip of the iceberg. It was like peeling back the layers of an onion – a very big, multi-skinned onion. You think you're getting to the crux of the situation, only to find more and more layers that need uncovering as you go deeper and deeper into the origins of the beliefs.

From this understanding I designed my Core Belief workshops. I did this as much with the intention of helping LoA followers to achieve their dream life, self, or world, as anything else. What actually happened was that groups of people discovered who they were and what made them tick at the deepest level. Now they knew what it was that kept them from making and keeping money on a hitherto, profound and complex level. Now they could truly understand why they felt uncomfortable being spiritual people who charged for their services. Now they had the means of letting go of those outdated values and attitudes that had never belonged to them in the first place. Now they could choose how they felt about money, about spending it or keeping it or giving it away.

In the next chapter, we will explore Core Beliefs in more detail. We will name and shame them out of hiding and into the light where they can be exorcised and laid to rest: or, where they can be integrated and adapted to suit the needs of adults who know how to function in an adult world.

Chapter 7

IDENTIFYING CORE BELIEFS

*Never be afraid to fall apart because it is an opportunity to
rebuild yourself the way you wish you had been all along.*

Rae Smith

*Yesterday, I was clever, so I wanted to change the world.
Today, I am wise, so I am changing myself.*

Unknown

At the beginning of this book I described the creation of my own personal
army of Core Beliefs. To re-cap, I was the product of a pregnancy that
should have resulted in the birth of my joyfully anticipated and literally
dreamed of younger brother. I spent the most formative years of my life
(excluding my teenage years) in direct competition with my brother for our
mother's love and attention. Sometime around the age of 4, I was taken on
an extended bike ride by a neighbour, who also happened to be my friend.
He took me somewhere secluded and raped me. On the way home he
kissed me even though I'd told him I didn't want him to.

Now to add a bit more to the formidable mix of complex Core
Beliefs: When I was twelve and my brother was ten, our father was killed

in a car accident. He left the house one Saturday afternoon in his brother's car and never came back. After a week in a coma in intensive care, he finally let go and passed over. My mother went into mourning in such a way that she could barely function in any real sense. As well as spending the best part of a year immersed in an alcoholic fugue to ease her pain, she became addicted to prescription drugs. Valium and Mogodon were the drugs given indiscriminately for an indefinite period to any woman suffering from depression at that time. Immediately after the death of her husband, my mother transferred all of her love and affection on to my younger brother. He reacted quite badly to our father's death and would keep vigil at his bedroom window every time mum left the house. He was terrified that, like dad, she might not return home again.

My mother's reaction to her grief and my brother's fears, resulted in her total pre-occupation with his care, to the extent that I felt my own needs and grief were of lesser importance to that of my brother. As I reached puberty I, like all teenagers, entered a world where only my pain and needs mattered. I believed the world revolved around me and my thoughts, hopes and fears. It's hard enough for a parent to navigate their way through this tumultuous phase of a child's life without the added hardship of also being in a profound state of grief, poverty and addiction, as well as being the single parent to the four children that still lived at home.

As an adult, I know that my brother's needs were equally as valid as my own (and, in some ways, perhaps more so), and I am also aware that in my egocentric adolescent state, I had no idea how my other siblings were coping - or not - with their grief and our mother's seeming abandonment in favour of our younger brother. They will no doubt have their own stories to tell and their own King Kong's to deal with: I can only speak from my own experience.

And so now you have a fuller picture of the birth place of my personal King Kong. With all this in mind, I will take you on an abridged version (for it spans many years of introspection, self-development and self-challenge) of how I discovered, identified, confronted and approached working with my Core Beliefs. At the time of writing I still have more layers of the onion to peel away as I still see evidence of their existence on a regular basis. As I continue to exhibit certain symptoms and bodily reactions, I know that they are still operating somewhere in the background. What I also know is that they are not as fully operational as they once were; and that perhaps a time will come when I will have successfully slayed my dragons, exorcised my demons and tamed my King Kong.

As I touch on each moment or stage of creation, I will put them into a broader context: one in which you may see aspects of yourself and your behaviours. In this way, you may be able to begin delving into your own past in a positive and productive way. If you recognise yourself in any of my adult responses to my childhood aspects, then perhaps you can use that as a starting point for your own exploration into what may have triggered or established similar behaviours in you.

Given the physical and emotional hardships I have encountered in my life, and supposing that I knew 'psychically' that I wasn't what my mother wanted or expected, I feel that, at the time of my birth, my spiritual-self may have panicked and had a change of mind. I now believe that in choosing to be born into that particular set of circumstances (background, gender, period, location, etc.) - circumstances I may have felt would be of benefit to me spiritually - I realised I had bitten off more than I could physically chew and wanted to reconsider the life experiences that possibly lay ahead for me.

Of course, we all have free will, and it wasn't absolutely inevitable (only probable) that I would go on to have the experiences I had deemed beneficial in order to further my spiritual development. Even so, I would also have known that the hardest, most painful experiences bring the greatest opportunities for growth and development, and so my spirit-self would have suspected that I might not opt-out once I got going.

And so my first experiences of life from 0-3 years instilled the following set of Core Beliefs:

*   *I am an imposter*
*   *I have no right to take up space*
*   *I am unlovable*
*   *I shouldn't be here*
*   *I am a mistake - a mistake that I have to make right*
*   *Love has to be earned*
*   *I am not worthy*
*   *If I'm not 'good', love will be withheld*

All of these beliefs combined to create a philosophy that dictated the central theme of my personality. As I was a mistake, a usurper and an imposter, I would have to earn my right to take up space – especially as it was supposed to be someone else's. I was only here by default and if I wanted to be allowed to stay, I would have to win people over by making them happy and getting them to like having me around. I learned quickly to behave in ways that were acceptable and agreeable to whomever I was with at any given time. This would mean adapting at a moment's notice by subjugating my own desires and opinions in favour of those of another. I became a chameleon.

You may not have been made aware that you were not planned (or wanted) as a child, but often our relationships with our parent(s) or siblings can influence our sense of belonging in profound ways. Whenever we won the approval of a parent (or anyone charged with our regular care), we would be overjoyed at the feeling of belonging that this would engender within us. Naturally, we're going to seek out more of the same and so develop a catalogue of behaviours that we can rely on to produce this approval. Conversely, when our behaviour meets with disapproval, we quickly learn to change it as it doesn't produce the desired effect.

I was a mature adult before I realised I had become so good at adapting my behaviour and desires to fit in with the people around me that I truly didn't know my own mind, and would constantly defer to the wishes of others. When asked, 'What shall we do?' I would respond with, 'I don't know', or, 'I don't mind, what do you want to do?' The sad thing is, I believed that I was being open to suggestion and easy-going; when in fact, deep down, I was afraid of causing upset and losing favour with people.

Take a moment to think about how you respond to questions aimed at getting your opinion. Do you hesitate before answering? Do you wonder what would be an acceptable answer? Do you instinctively consider the other person's needs and then mould your answer to fit with that? Do you say you don't mind either way, believing that the outcome doesn't really matter to you? You may have convinced yourself that your altruistic response is really healthy. You don't force your wishes on others. You selflessly take into consideration the needs of those around you. You really don't mind one way or the other, you'll be happy if they're happy. You're such an easy-going person and so easy to be with. After all, anyone who expresses a different idea to that of the majority is just being awkward or stubborn, aren't they?

If forced to really think about what it is *you* might want, you will probably struggle to figure it out, and find it very difficult to come up with an answer. You learned a long time ago that it's dangerous to have your own opinions, that in order to be accepted and ok, you needed to suppress your wants in order for someone more important than you (and that would be just about anybody and everybody) to get their needs met. You may even believe that you genuinely have the same desires as your partner or mother or sibling or whomever. Like Michael in our earlier example, you might even become completely overwhelmed when pushed to voice your own thoughts when making a decision. Whenever we say 'it doesn't matter' or 'it's not important', in response to a question or statement about how we feel or what we want, what we're really saying is '*I* don't matter', '*I'm* not important'.

If you recognise yourself in even a small way in any of these examples, then have a think back to your childhood. Try to remember how your parents or care-givers responded whenever your desires or wishes contradicted theirs. What happened when you assertively expressed your feelings on a subject? How was it made implicit that what you wanted didn't matter and that you were to keep your ideas to yourself?

Early Trauma

Being hurt by someone I considered to be my friend constituted a major turning point for me at a crucial stage in my development. This was when my biggest Core Beliefs were created and instilled deep within me. This man had made me feel special, worthy of the attention of grown-ups. It goes without saying that I trusted him, as did my family. Within the space of less than an hour, my view of the world I lived in had been completely transformed. This is what I was left with:

* *The world is an unpredictable place*
* *Friends and adults (men in particular) are not to be trusted*
* *Being loved hurts physically*
* *Love means sex means love*
* *Adults control everything*
* *Being special is dangerous: bad things happen when you're special*
* *No-one will come to save me; no-one can protect me*
* *I did something bad – I must be a bad person*
* *Being visible is dangerous – I must make myself invisible*

No-one ever said that what happened was my fault or that I'd done something bad - not as far as I can remember, anyway. But I do have a sense of how the adults in my family reacted. I'm pretty sure that my Nan, who used to tell me off for putting my legs up on the settee which resulted in me inadvertently showing my knickers, would have pursed her lips and tutted - maybe not at me, but at the situation. My mum, understandably, was shocked and upset. It was she who took me to the police station, and then to the courts where my one time friend was being tried.

I don't remember my father being involved in any of these events. I have no idea if he was angry, if he wanted to beat the neighbour to a pulp for hurting his little girl, or if he just couldn't handle the shame or guilt and so closed down emotionally. Judging by people's reactions (viewed through the filter of a four-year-old), I would have believed *I* was responsible for causing so much anguish, pain and uncomfortable silence in my family, and possibly the withdrawal of my father's affection. How could I not have been a bad person for causing all that?

I'm sure you can imagine the ways in which my perspective on love, sex and friendship (particularly with the opposite sex) was affected: they are the natural, more conscious experiences of someone who has been abused in some way. The formation of Core Beliefs is what is relevant here, and how they worked in my defence from that time on until I finally, one day, lay them to rest and convince them to take permanent retirement. Maybe I won't get to benefit from these changes and new ways of being in *this* life experience, but I'm sure that some version of me in another life will appreciate the freedom and expansion.

One of the outcomes of this event in my life was my desperate need to be in control. My partner often tells me that, although I might not be a complete control freak, I do have a tendency to need to be in charge most of the time. I saw this as evidence that I was being an assertive feminist woman. It's only in the last few years that I've actually come to link this need to be in charge with my lack of control as a child in that traumatic situation. *Understandably, I'm not going to let a man get the upper hand and tell me what to do and how to do it. Obviously, I'm going to seek out sensitive, gentle men as partners. Naturally, I'm going to try to dominate the relationship and get my own way as often as I can.* All of these attitudes and behaviours seem logical now in light of what I've uncovered about my Core Beliefs. I thought I had it sorted and knew what I was dealing with and how it manifested in my life. Surely there couldn't be anything else I hadn't looked at from all sides – including inside and out?

Stick to the Path

One aspect of my personality literally stood out in the light of this new awareness and understanding. At the time, I was in the habit of constantly considering ways in which my Core Beliefs could be operating in the background. One day, my partner and I went for a walk around the village where we live. As usual, and due to the fact that I was once again recovering from a flare-up of my chronic illness (more on that later), I wanted to know what route he was planning on taking, just in case I thought it was a bit too much of a challenge for me. He told me what he had in mind and I agreed it would be manageable. My needing to know the route in advance is, in itself, evidence of the subtle ways in which Core Beliefs can influence our decisions and actions - making us believe it's something else entirely and so not suspect their involvement.

We set off for our short jaunt around the village, enjoying the late evening sunshine and the opportunity to discuss the workshop we were designing on Core Beliefs. As we talked, my partner began to cross the road. This wasn't the way he'd said we were going, what was he doing going in a different direction? I stopped and asked him as much, my voice slightly louder than necessary and perhaps even a little shrill. I was surprised at the strong emotion I felt at his sudden change in direction. He was baffled at how irritated I was that he'd innocently changed his mind about the route of our walk. So was I. All I knew was that I was very angry with him for changing direction without even discussing it with me.

I'm sure after reading this account of my minor meltdown, that it's obvious to you what was really happening. It's scary to think that I'd been behaving 'irrationally' around that kind of thing for years and never once suspected it was anything other than my need to be in charge. This is such a strong compulsion that on walks when several people are involved, I always stride out in front. I thought it was because I was impatient to get where we were going or to just get the walk over with (I'm not a big fan of rambling!). If I hadn't spent the previous couple of months re-visiting the rape and looking at it in light of what I'd learned about Core Beliefs, I would never have made the association. My partner and I would have continued to have fights over who is in charge and planned and unplanned routes on walks, oblivious to the fact that there was a frightened little girl inside me who was terrified she would be taken somewhere secluded and hurt.

Think about those times when you may have over-reacted in a situation. Perhaps you shouted at someone over an unimportant incident. You may have just had a bad day and don't have a cat to kick when you get home (not that I would ever advocate kicking any animal!), but on thinking about it, you always seem to get angry in that particular kind of situation. I'm not suggesting that there is a hidden event in your life, or a forgotten trauma, but perhaps you've been trained to react in that way because of the messages you were given as a child.

It could be something as simple as hating to leave food on your plate. There's no obvious explanation for this compulsion to eat every morsel even if you're really full. You insist that you just don't like waste. If you were to really think about it, you may discover that as a child you were forced to eat everything on your plate: not just because it would be wasteful, but because your family couldn't afford to waste food. My siblings and I had it drummed into us that leaving food on our plates somehow made us responsible for all the starving children in Africa! Of course, I realise now that my father (who was the main advocate of this doctrine), had suffered deprivation as a child and then strict rationing as a teenager, no wonder he had issues around waste.

Anna's Story

When Anna was a little girl, she learned that in order to not incur the wrath of her father -something she witnessed happening to her brother - she had to eat everything on her plate. In competition with her brother for her father's attention, this need to show her dad what a good girl she was, contributed to her going on to develop an eating disorder. Whenever Anna feels alone, rejected, unloved or unapproved of, she wants to eat more than she would really like. What's happening is the younger version of Anna needs the comfort and reassurance of her parents - her father in particular. As an adult, she isn't aware of this need; and, as the need stems from her Inner Child, she wouldn't be able to get it even if she was. Consequently, even though Anna feeds this craving for affection and/or attention by eating, she never feels satisfied and so will often go back for more.

The Core Beliefs around food and control can easily get overlooked when dealing with weight and eating disorders. Anorexia and Bulimia are major emotional and psychological issues that often need intensive therapy if they are to be overcome. In my experience, the person with an eating disorder is not the only one in the family with the problem: they're just the one manifesting it. As for weight issues, Core Beliefs are why so many people yo-yo on often futile, expensive, emotionally draining diets. It is pointless dieting if the Core Beliefs behind the need to eat - to be bigger and so be protected by extra weight, for example - have not been addressed. It's not enough to instil more discipline or to restrict your calorie intake if your need to eat originates from low self-worth or the need to stuff down what you believe to be unacceptable or overwhelming emotions.

Again, this whole area of life and living is tied to our experiences as a baby. We come into this world with only one instinct, and that is to suckle. It doesn't matter to us from a survival perspective whether this need is met by suckling on our mother's nipple or the teat of a bottle (I do believe it might have an emotional effect, however). We need to take in food to survive, and this is the only means available to us. Imagine, then, the relationship we have with our mouth and what passes through our lips.

Eating (and drinking) is our strongest connection to life and survival and it becomes synonymous with love, nurturing, safety and warmth. And so, understandably, as we grow older we will continue to attempt to recreate this experience. Adults experiencing emotional pain, low self-esteem and self-worth, would seek to recreate the sense of comfort and security felt whenever they were fed - and therefore held - as babies. They would naturally try to make themselves feel better by putting things to and in their mouth: hence oral fixated addictions such as smoking, drinking, eating, biting our nails, and even sex. When we feel good about ourselves and the immediate world we occupy, our need to derive comfort from orally focussed activities decreases. Add to that the way children are rewarded, coaxed or placated with sweet treats and snacks, then you get a better idea of why a lot of people crave sugary things and struggle to curb their cravings for biscuits, cakes, crisps etc. - particularly at night when they might be alone or actually still for the first time that day, giving them time to dwell on those areas of their life where they might not be happy.

This whole area of Core Beliefs and their relationship to food and eating is a book in its own right. However, if you're struggling with any kind of food / eating disorder, then working on your Core Beliefs would go a long way to helping you figure out why. I go into this in more depth in *Deeper Travels Within* in Part Two.

Keeping Below the Parapet

My seemingly irrational anger at being taken off the agreed route is a prime example of my King Kong coming into action, beating his chest and roaring into the air - and that was just over a change in direction on a pleasant walk with my partner! Imagine how he reacts when I'm faced with something far more threatening to my survival: being visible and being special.

It would take too long to explain just how my need to avoid 'being special' has affected my life. In the last few years, and since I've consciously been in touch with my Higher Self and guides, I have been reminded that I am special. This freaked me out to begin with as, apart from the obvious link to being considered 'special' as a child (by the man who raped me), I didn't like the possibility of developing a huge ego that wanted guru status. I insisted that everyone is special; which, of course, is exactly right. The problem was, I just couldn't handle the bit about *me* being special. I argued with my guides or just dismissed their questions about why I didn't believe I was special. I was convinced that these words of wisdom and confidence building were actually the work of an errant ego coming from the need to feel somehow better than everyone else. I completely missed the fact that I could not allow myself to be special as I had learned to equate that with being hurt.

As for not standing out from the crowd and so staying invisible, that is an issue that has plagued my life for over twenty years. I know now that I have Core Beliefs whose sole purpose was to keep me safe. Thinking about it, I am amazed at how ingenious they have been in creating the means of fulfilling their mission. Unfortunately, they also succeeded in making my life an utter misery and almost resulted in me having major, irreversible surgery. They managed to keep me safe all right, but in doing so, I experienced incredible humiliation, shame and despair. And they're the good guys!

Back in the early nineties I was a professional actor. I mostly worked with Physical Theatre in Education companies touring issue-based productions around schools in Britain. I had been working as a professional for all of a year when I developed *Ulcerative Colitis*: just one version of inflammatory bowel disease. For the next several years of my life I was hospitalised many times and given intravenous steroids and countless blood transfusions. At one point, my consultant despaired of me ever leading a normal life and suggested, or should I say, strongly encouraged, me to have my large intestine removed. I was horrified at the thought and so refused to have the surgery. I disregarded the well-meaning if misplaced advice and set out to cure myself of this debilitating disease as naturally as I could.

I was a few years into the illness and sick of being flooded with steroids when I rejected conventional medicine and treatment in favour of complimentary therapies and personal development. Over time, I developed strong convictions that I had this chronic illness for a reason other than the failure of my bowel to do its job properly. I also strongly believed that my body was not my enemy and that any dis-ease or physical problem that manifested within it was my subconscious or Higher Self trying to bring my attention to a belief or attitude that needed addressing. I started to explore why I might have developed this particular disease. And so began a long journey into self-discovery, self-analysis and deep inner work - some of which was useful and some misdirection of sorts. Not that I didn't learn from barking up the wrong tree: I learned plenty, if only that the tree I should have been barking up was in an entirely different neck of the woods.

Bear in mind that my Core Beliefs had created the *Ulcerative Colitis* to keep me safe. I was on the verge of becoming a successful actor and so would be extremely visible in every sense of the word. This could not be allowed. If I was visible, I was in danger of being hurt very badly. If I didn't choose to keep a low profile, then my body would have to be brought in to see that I complied. Sounds radical and totally unreasonable, but not for one moment am I saying that my body rose up against me and deliberately wanted to cause me pain and suffering. There was a very complex set of actions being put into place that would serve many purposes. With such a debilitating illness, I would have to spend much of my time at home. I needed to stay hidden and this was the best way my Core Beliefs could come up with - and very affective it was, too. (There is a lot more to the creation of such a chronic physical illness, and I will go into this in Chapter 16, *Heal-thy Mind, Heal-thy Body.*)

I was eventually forced to give up my much wanted and dreamed of career and take up a position as administrator to the theatre company I had spent several years working for as an actor. I must admit that a large part of that decision came out of the fact that I found it extremely difficult to leave my two young children every time we went on tour. I would pine for them constantly and it broke my heart to hear them crying on the phone for me to come home.

My very conscious need to be with my children, combined with my unconscious need to stay hidden, undoubtedly contributed to the creation of my illness. I had spent many years training to be an actor and had committed myself to working for the theatre company. The nature of the work meant I spent every school holiday with my children. Except when on tour in other parts of the UK, (two to four weeks for each new production), I was home very soon after my children got in from school - I was even able to pick them up on occasion. I knew that they would be fine, especially as they had such a doting father. Even so, being away from them for even just a couple of weeks now and again, tore at my heart. Unfortunately, the Core Beliefs did too much of a good job helping me to find a 'legitimate' reason for staying at home and I would often have to spend weeks in hospital!

By now, you hopefully have a good idea about what a Core Belief is, how they are created and how they can operate out of awareness. The more you look for them, the easier they are to spot. If you watch any of the films detailed in Part 3, you will find that the Core Beliefs of the characters pretty much jump out at you - especially if you read the accompanying chapter for each film first.

Once you have a good idea of what your Core Beliefs are and why your own King Kong might still be trying to protect you, you will be in a good place to start modifying them or, hopefully, getting rid of them completely. Now that I know what's going on under the surface whenever I get upset at my partner changing our route on a simple walk, I can consciously take control of my feelings. I can placate my King Kong and remind it who's boss and why. I'll cover more of this in Part Two, where I will look at several ways of identifying and transforming Core Beliefs from being something that works *for* you rather than *against* you. Knowledge is power, as they say, and the knowledge you now have about your own Core Beliefs can truly aid you in getting them to relinquish control of your life.

Chapter 8

OUT OF THE SHADOWS

*When you know yourself, you are empowered. When you
accept yourself, you are invincible.*

Tina Lifford

*Make it thy business to know thyself, which is the most
difficult lesson in the world.*

Miguel de Cervantes

In the following chapters we are going to visit and explore a range of
approaches you could use in order to work with your own King Kong. We
will cover a selection of methods and techniques you can adopt in order to
begin freeing yourself of your limiting beliefs.

Once I had a clearer understanding of why I had *Ulcerative Colitis*,
I was better placed to really begin the work of re-programming and shifting
the Core Beliefs that created it on my behalf. For most people, there is no
overnight cure or magic spell that can delete the programming within them
at that level. There are, however, various approaches that can work
wonders and, in some cases, have relieved people of the limiting beliefs
that plague them. I'm not going to come out on the side of any one

treatment, approach or therapy because I do not believe that such a panacea exists. If it did, whoever discovered, developed, delivered, administered or used it in their practice would be extremely rich and would be inundated with requests for training, treatment, books, articles, talks, seminars... In short, it would be a miracle cure and everyone on the planet would be lining up to get some for whatever ails them.

Just as we create illness and physical conditions, or limiting behaviours and attitudes, for a reason, so we hold on to that illness etc. for a reason. As we saw in the preceding chapter, our King Kong serves an important purpose in our lives. It's not likely that it will give up its role in keeping us safe without good reason and possibly without a fight. In order to completely rid ourselves of our limiting beliefs, we need first to establish if there is still a credible reason for them to continue to exist and exert power and control over our lives. As you will see in the following chapters, even those that claim to be able to rid you of them in one fell swoop as in Kinesiology), will still begin the process by asking for permission to remove the belief. Who do they ask? Not you, the client: or at least not the conscious part of you. They ask the subconscious - or, in my terms, that clients' King Kong - if it is ready to relinquish control. What they're doing is checking out that the reason for its existence has run its course and that what they are dealing with is a set of beliefs that are running on automatic pilot behind the scenes.

If we do manage to find a way to remove something in our body or a behaviour that was the result of a Core Belief, and it *is* still serving a purpose, then you can guarantee that something else, possibly more debilitating, will come along to take its place. Getting rid of the symptom doesn't automatically mean you've rid yourself of the cause. If the original reason for the Core Belief hasn't been dealt with, then it will keep recurring or coming up in various guises until its *raison d'etre* has been identified and addressed. It might be worth pointing out at this stage that not all illnesses or physical conditions are the result of Core Beliefs. When working with my own set of Core Beliefs that set up the *Ulcerative Colitis*, I also encountered something within its existence that related more to my spiritual and personal development as opposed to just my inherent, perceived need to be safe and protected. I will go into this in more detail in the Chapter 16, *Heal-thy Mind – Heal-thy Body*.

Also at work is the power of belief in its own right. You might hear of someone who has had a particular treatment for something that you also suffer with. This person swears by the efficacy of that treatment, proclaiming that they were relieved of symptoms either completely or enough to give them respite for a good length of time. Perhaps you've heard of this treatment but always thought it was a bit too good to be true. You might think it seems incredible that something seemingly as simple as say, taking a herbal supplement or having someone apply gentle pressure to your head, could result in either a cure or something that can afford you relief from suffering so much. Desperate to try anything however outlandish it seems, you order the capsules or book an appointment with the therapist. However, you're still not convinced this thing will work for you. Perhaps you might be quite doubtful of the whole alternative remedy approach to healing, but you've been to the doctor who can find no reason for your malady and can only prescribe something to alleviate the discomfort.

You take the supplements (shaking your head at how a plant extract can relieve the itching of your skin), or you abstain from eating sugar (something you resent as you like sweet things and so feel you're being punished in some way for being ill), or you attend the appointment with a reflexologist (for example), but you can't see how somebody applying pressure to certain parts of your feet could fix the problem with your skin.

Suffice to say, it might turn out that regardless of whichever approach you try, it has little or no effect on your condition. It might have afforded you a modicum of relief, but maybe it didn't last long. This isn't because the supplement, treatment or diet you used was ineffectual (although you will by now undoubtedly be more convinced than ever that it is), or that the therapist was a quack and their therapy a sham (something else you will probably be convinced of), or because there's no point in cutting something out of your diet (unless you believe it's something that would help you to lose weight, of course). You might even have had the problem for so long that it's hard for you to imagine life without it. Perhaps your medical practitioner told you that this is a lifelong illness/condition and that any idea of complete healing is out of the question and all you can do is hope for a reasonably pain free life. One of the reasons that these treatments can be so ineffectual is because deep down, you didn't believe they would or even could work.

Potions, Pills and Placebos

In the West, we have been brainwashed into thinking that if we get ill we need to see a doctor and then take whatever medication they prescribe. At the first sign of illness we consult our GP. Something has gone wrong with the machine we call a body, and the GP - or body mechanic - can and will put it right with the correct drugs or tools. When we have an infection and our GP prescribes antibiotics, we don't usually even think of its efficacy as we fully expect the drug to work; and, more often than not, it does.

However, countless placebo-controlled clinical trials show that just believing in the treatment being given by doctors works more effectively than most of the chemical based medical treatments.

In a placebo trial, a group of participants receive either the drug being studied or a placebo (a placebo is defined as: a medicine or procedure prescribed for the psychological benefit to the patient rather than for any physiological effect). The placebo (from Latin, literally 'I shall be acceptable or pleasing'), is often referred to as a 'sugar-pill' and has no active, medicinal ingredients. In 'double-blind, placebo-controlled' research, the professionals working directly with patients in the study will not know which group their patients are in. Only members of the research team not involved in providing day-to-day clinical care will know which patients are receiving an active treatment or a placebo.

Placebos have been used for many years, but it's only since the development of brain imaging techniques that we've been able to measure their physical effect. We now know that the brain is altered physiologically by placebos. These can include changes in heart rate and blood pressure to chemical activity in the brain that can influence such things as depression, anxiety, pain and fatigue. In some instances, the effect is more subjective, as when the patient reports improvement despite no physiological change in the underlying condition. However, the NHS won't be sanctioning the overall use of placebos anytime soon as medical practationers aren't too comfortable with the commonly held belief that placebos rely on the doctor prescribing them deceiving the patient. They also believe they are unreliable and unpredictable. However, a clinical trial carried out in 2010, using what's called an 'open-label' placebo (where the patient is aware that they have been given a placebo), showed that it isn't necessary to deceive a patient about what it is they are taking.

This particular trial used a random group of IBS patients split between those taking the placebo and a control group who were receiving no treatment other than seeing a doctor or nurse practitioner. The placebo taking group were informed that they were taking 'something like sugar pills, without any medication in it' that had been shown to produce, 'significant mind-body self-healing processes'. (All patients were told to continue with their IBS medication as normal.) In their conclusion, the researchers stated that, 'patients given open-label placebo in the context of a supportive patient-practitioner relationship and a persuasive rationale had clinically meaningful symptom improvement that was significantly better than a no-treatment control group with matched patient-provider interaction.'

This study shows that the relationship between practitioner and patient is extremely important if healing is to take place. What it doesn't show is something that can never really be measured scientifically, and that is the depth of belief a person has in their treatment. In part, belief in treatment success is fostered by the emotional support given by the practitioner or therapist. This can be greatly increased if the person delivering the healing, in whatever form, completely believes in the efficacy of what it is they are prescribing or providing, and the patient trusts the person administering it.

In another study, the actual physician was described as a placebo, particularly when they use positive reinforcement such as, 'you'll start to feel better in a few days', or 'this treatment I'm giving you is very effective'. What this means is that the patients' belief in the treatment is added to by the physician / therapists belief in it. In order for any treatment to be effective, it's imperative that trust in the substance being taken or the therapy being received is strong and unwavering.

Doubt is the most pernicious obstacle to achieving true and lasting healing. This is why, at the beginning of this introduction I stated that I could not recommend one therapy or treatment over another. I have tried many over the years, both chemical and natural, and have yet to discover one that provided healing or even lasting improvement. I ascribe this to the fact that I either didn't fully believe in what I was receiving, or had yet to discover the true cause or purpose of the condition. I do believe, however, that if we were encouraged to take the time and the trouble to uncover our Core Beliefs and to explore physical issues with a view to determining the message behind the condition, then we would save ourselves a lot of time and money spent on treatments, supplements, drugs and possibly even surgery. By getting to the root cause of our physical problems we can cut out the middle-man, thus standing a better chance of healing ourselves naturally and healthily - especially when you consider the plethora of nasty, equally debilitating side-effects that often accompany prescription drugs such as antibiotics or steroids.

Illness as Metaphor and Guide

In their challenging and often controversial book, *The Healing Power of Illness*, Thorwald Dethlefsen and Rudiger Dahlke, go even further in their appraisal of the meaning of illness. They believe that symptoms and illness are signals that carry vital information. The illness causes us to stop and give it our attention. This pause in life, however, is meant to cause us to examine our lives very closely: from the language we use to the way we feel about certain situations. This approach is similar, in part, to other books available on the subject of the mind-body connection in health and healing, such as those by Louise L Hay, or Debbie Shapiro.

What makes this book different is their unyielding belief that every illness and condition, every virus or infection we 'get', is not there because of something external getting in (germs, virus' etc.) or internal problems showing up (genetics, faulty organs, etc.). The only reason we experience illness is in order for us to become whole. The illness points to an inner, psychological imbalance that, once discovered and addressed on *that* level (as opposed to trying to defeat the symptoms with physical treatments and medication - including natural remedies), can then be released from the body. If we try to eliminate the problem without looking for the reason for it being there in the first place, we will simply create a *symptom-shift* and the inner issue will be forced to manifest elsewhere in the body.

In this way, conditions within the body are, in part, messages from our Greater Self to help us grow, learn and develop. If we agree with the premise that illness is a call to action, a signal for us to begin the process of self-discovery and examination of negative attitudes and behaviours, then it is counter-productive to attempt to eradicate it with pills, treatments, surgery, etc. In so doing, we're forcing our Greater Self to use other means to get the message across resulting in us developing yet another illness or condition. This cycle of symptom suppression, re-emergence somewhere else, suppression, re-emergence, will continue until we start paying attention to the message and stop destroying or removing the messenger.

The Gift Disguised as Threat

The reason why *The Healing Power of Illness,* is often challenging, lies in the fact that the authors don't pull their punches by wrapping their interpretations in gentle, euphemistic suggestions. They go straight for the jugular. As I've already discussed the likely cause(s) of the *Ulcerative Colitis* I've struggled with for so long, I'll use that as an example here.

In her book, *You Can Heal Your Life*, Louise L Hay has this to say about the likely cause of *Colitis*: 'Over-exacting parents. Feeling of oppression and defeat. Great need for affection.' Neither of my parents exerted any overt control or high expectations over me or my siblings. Similarly, as someone from a Socialist, working-class background, my whole childhood was experienced through a sense of oppression! The 'great need for affection', is clearly very true. She then goes on to give an affirmation in order to establish self-approval and joy.

In, *Your Body Speaks Your Mind*, Debbie Shapiro describes the condition and then offers areas of exploration and questions to ask yourself about the various issues to which it may be connected. *Colitis*, then, is described as coming from 'intense irritation and frustration about what is happening and an inability to digest or fully absorb events. [...] Inflammation is associated with anger. So, is rage being internalized rather than expressed?' I find this approach more helpful, as echoing the language we use to describe certain issues etc, gives me insight into the possible causes of the issue. These *double entendre* and puns, give us the ulterior meanings of our symptoms. Thus, if you're *pissed off*, you might experience that emotion manifesting in the bladder as *Cystitis*.

In *The Healing Power of Illness*, the sufferers of *Ulcerative Colitis* are left with nowhere to run in terms of facing the behaviours and attitudes that may have gone into its creation. This was the hardest *raison d'etre* for me to accept or even consider.

'Ulcerative Colitis…is accompanied by [...] blood and slime (mucus) in the stools. Here again common parlance reveals deep psychosomatic knowledge. We all know people who are 'slimy'. They are people who are prepared to 'lick our arses' in order to ingratiate themselves with us.'

Like I said - straight for the jugular. No tip-toeing around with good old, easy-peasy things like rage or anger. Oh no, according to the authors, people with *Ulcerative Colitis* are grade one brown noses, sucking up to anyone and everyone in order to win their approval! And guess what? They're right. As hard and unpalatable as it is for my ego to accept, I have been a creep for most of my life. How else would someone who intrinsically believes that they have to prove their value and worth achieve this if not by desperately trying to ingratiate themselves? I have been a chameleon, constantly shifting and changing my colours in order to fit in with the crowd (or even individual). I have expended untold energy in adapting my behaviour in order to be seen as likable and worth having around. Everything I did as a young (and not so young) adult was with one aim in mind, to be liked, accepted and approved of. So yes, I have been an *'arse licker'* - as repugnant, unpleasant and shameful as that sounds.

And therein lies the beauty of their book: it challenges you to be honest with yourself. Illness is brutal in its honest, no holds barred, challenge to the ego and carefully constructed beliefs about the self. More honest than even the most truthful friend or family member: which is why our enemies can often be more helpful to us than our truest friends - they don't hold back, they let you have it with both barrels. As difficult as this appraisal of your personality might be, and as hard as it is to swallow, it just might be the closest you get to uncovering negative traits before they become manifest in your body.

In the following chapter, I explain how illness is often not just a means of learning about our behaviours and attitudes, but how it can also be a guilt-free tool for avoiding all sorts of things, including full participation in life.

Chapter 9

THE HIDDEN BENEFITS

Illness is a part of every human being's experience. It enhances our perceptions and reduces self-consciousness. It is the great confessional; things are said, truths are blurted out which health conceals.

Virginia Woolf

Without anxiety and illness I should have been like a ship without a rudder.

Edward Munch

Not all Core Beliefs are destined to cause us pain and anguish. Some are actually beneficial, but only as long as we are aware of them and how they operate in our lives. Then we can use them to our advantage, making them work for us instead of against us. However, even the most damaging of beliefs can be of use. We learn at an early age the law of cause and effect: if I do or have X, then Y happens. The X can become a very important, almost indispensable part of our lives – even when it's a serious or chronic illness.

In this chapter, I explain the pay-offs we can get from being ill, helpless, not being taken seriously, impatient, grouchy... All the traits that on the surface appear to be either unpleasant or unwelcome, but that deep down, provide a much needed service that can be difficult to admit to let alone be willing to give up.

This was a difficult chapter for me to write, but it might prove to be even more difficult for you to read and accept. It's one thing to think we have manifested illness as a result of our Core Beliefs wanting to keep us safe, it's another to think that we might be creating or perpetuating an unpleasant situation deliberately. Which is why I have to be very careful how I word what's about to follow. If I pitch it wrong, you might turn off to what I'm trying to say and dismiss it - and the rest of the book - as a load of hokum. But bear with me. You've come this far so why not stay with me a while longer? Suspend your disbelief and the possible need to defend yourself by insisting that your uncomfortable situation - be it an illness or a limiting behaviour - is not in your control.

This isn't about blaming, shaming or judging. It's about approaching a difficult situation from a different perspective: one that you may not have considered before. It's about challenging yourself, giving yourself the chance to look at things in a new light. After all, that's what this book is all about - shining the light of awareness on the shadowy realms of limiting habits and behaviours, seeing them for what they are and making a choice about whether they are rightfully yours or those that you acquired along the way. So if you recognise yourself in any of what follows, don't feel bad or beat yourself up. Be happy that you have seen behind the scenes, as it were, and now have a chance to re-write more of the script of your life.

In this chapter, I'm going to ask you to consider the possibility that whatever ails you provides you with a positive service - in some way(s). In her book 'Why People Don't Heal and How They Can', Caroline Myss suggests that illness can be the answer to a prayer. Obviously, there's nothing positive about pain, in and of itself. However, if you look closely enough, you may find that there are benefits, hidden deep below all the surface stuff you don't like or want as part of your life. That pain or illness might actually help you in some way: the problem is, the help isn't always beneficial. This chapter will take you deep into the layers of why you now, as an adult - years after their creation was first deemed necessary by your King Kong as a means of protection - still have those limiting behaviours, debilitating illness, and outmoded attitudes that cause you discomfort, pain, sadness, etc, etc.

I enjoy convalescence. It is the part that makes the illness worthwhile.

George Bernard Shaw

Several years ago, I was working with a group of adults who all suffered with anxiety and/or depression. When I asked them what positive aspects there were to their respective situations, they were shocked and appalled that I would even suggest such a thing. 'Why', they asked, 'would anyone hold on to an illness or mental health problem? How is it possible to get something positive from being ill, anxious or depressed?' It took a lot of persuading to get them to even consider the possibility that there were payoffs to their being ill. The most difficult question I asked (for them) was what would happen in their lives if they woke up healthy the next day with no sign of anxiety or depression.

At first they all - almost in unison - said they would have their lives back, be happy, be able to go out, socialise, and enjoy themselves more easily: all of which may have been true. Then I asked them if that were to happen, would they be able to stay on DHSS benefits, or would they have to go back to work. Suddenly, the room went quiet. A few brave ones admitted that they wouldn't be able to manage without their benefits, or that they had no skills to re-enter the workplace and considered themselves too old to re-train. For some, the thought of entering the work force again, filled them with dread.

For all of them, the financial rewards for being on long-term benefits, with no real possibility of that changing, turned out to be a huge incentive for staying ill. As much as the majority of them hated being on benefits, they were too scared to come off them to even contemplate it. Even with this obvious possible payoff to being ill, many of them could not entertain the possibility that it might have anything to do with their not being able to get well.

Then I asked them about how members of their family treated them. Again, many admitted that they were given an easy time of it at home. That they were made a fuss of, or if they were having a particularly bad day, they were let-off from attending family outings, or having to deal with difficult situations. Everyone knew they were anxious and so cut them a lot of slack. For some, this had become a habit for everyone in the family and was no longer questioned or challenged.

Most children learn at a very young age that having a stomach ache or headache gets them out of going to school, or to visit an elderly relative they don't like, or perhaps they would just prefer to stay at home on the computer, or get to spend quality one-to-one time with mum or dad.

It's no different when we're older. We carry on avoiding things we don't want to do, but don't have the assertiveness or confidence to be able to just say no. It's hard to tell a friend or relative that we're not going to drive them into town as we would rather stay in and read or do a bit of gardening. It seems selfish (and unacceptable) to say no because we want to do our own thing rather than help them out. It's much easier to tell them we're having a bad day and don't feel well enough to go out. This provides us with two pay-offs: we get to stay in, guilt free, and we might even get a bit of sympathy.

Victims of Success

The benefits of not being successful could probably fill a chapter on its own. Think about what it might mean to be a success. We would have less time to do the things we enjoy or to spend time with our loved ones. We would have to make big decisions about all sorts of things from finding an accountant, paying VAT, paying more tax, employing staff... This is without any consideration as to how it might affect our values. I was raised in a working class home with parents who had socialist ideals. I would often hear my mother berate those who had money and status. It was a world of the haves and have not's. We didn't have much of anything and I was instilled with a sense of pride in our salt of the earth attitudes and beliefs.

I was given strong if covert messages that the rich (anyone in white collar employment up) were usually greedy, untrustworthy, out of touch with the real world, selfish, snobs... With these sets of Core Beliefs well and truly ingrained in my very being from an early age, is it any wonder I have difficulty earning above a certain level of income? In doing so, I would be betraying my roots and my parents (even though they have both been dead for many years, and would actually want me to succeed and be financially secure).

Paul's Story

Paul was a gifted singer and guitarist. He had everything necessary to be a professional musician making a successful living doing what he loved -

singing and playing music. He had such an amazing voice, he could have made it as a recording artist with a huge fan base, touring around the world and making hit records. Instead, he settled for being a gigging lead singer with numerous cabaret bands, playing in social clubs and pubs. He'd had a little bit of work as a session singer and his distinctive voice could even be heard on a couple of television commercials. He also had the opportunity to go on small tours in Europe.

Part of the set-up of being a gigging musician, even at that modest level, involves spending weekends in clubs and pubs where it's the done thing to drink as you're setting up; drink as you wait to go on; drink in-between sets (and often during them); and drink as you pack up - all easily done if you have a roadie to do the driving. Inevitably, Paul developed alcohol dependency whilst in his early 20's, and it was the alcohol that eventually ruined every aspect of his life and health. By the time he reached his mid-forties, he had been hospitalised twice and was warned that if he didn't stop drinking he would die. He didn't stop, and did eventually die of alcohol related illness. It was also the alcohol that helped him to stay small and to avoid success on a greater scale.

As a working-class lad from a rough neighbourhood, it was scary for him to contemplate a life away from the home he shared with his wife and two children. Success would have taken him away from all that he was familiar with – his family, his neighbourhood, his friends. The demands on a lead singer in a cabaret band are small compared to a big-name band touring the country. A cabaret singer doesn't have to please an ever-demanding manager, tour operators, or fans; they don't have to worry about ticket sales, publicity, radio play, or their image. They mostly get to sleep in their own bed at night and wake up in their own home. There isn't the pressure to produce more and more hits. If they have a bad night and sound a bit rough, no-one really notices or even cares - the audience hasn't made a special journey to see them, nor have they paid a lot of money for the pleasure of doing so. Most people in social clubs don't even listen to the band playing, and when they do pay attention (usually at the end of the night), it's only because they want to be able to dance to the music they're playing.

Paul's life would have been altered beyond recognition had he made it as a musician. The day-to-day choices and demands even for a small-time star would have had been major compared to that of a jobbing cabaret artist.

Seeing how he came alive whenever he played his guitar and sang, Paul's family and friends couldn't understand why he never got further than he did even as a session singer or why he didn't pursue the opportunities offered to him to travel and play his music in other countries. They would berate him for his missed opportunities. Not quite believing the excuses he made to not see it through to another level. He would have an appointment that he couldn't change, or suddenly find himself with a bad cold and have to cancel. He would often claim that his wife didn't want him travelling away from home and would give him a bad time for leaving her with the children.

Paul dearly loved his wife and doted on his children, but he could never admit to his friends that it was *him* who couldn't bear to be parted from *them*. He would have felt unexplainable discomfort and anxiety at the thought of touring in another country, or of getting steady work as a session singer – especially if it involved travelling to London to do it. Perhaps he was afraid of discovering that he couldn't hack it as a small fish in a big pond. Whatever the reason, it was easier for him to stay small, stay home, stay safe.

Who's the Boss of You?

Most people don't have that willingness to break bad
habits. They make a lot of excuses and they talk like
victims.

Carlos Santana

As we have already seen, as children we will develop or create a set of defence systems - our own King Kong - that protects us from the big scary world. It is this part of us, this scared child, which creates ways of sabotaging our attempts to succeed as adults. Paul could easily have developed a chronic illness or disability in order to avoid success and/or failure. His story could be a template for so many of us that consciously want something very badly, and yet unconsciously do everything we can to ensure we don't get it. Unless we uncover those hidden motives or fears, we are doomed to repeat our failures: allowing ourselves to get only so far before we find a way to stop ourselves from going further.

Until and unless you take the time to truly explore your limiting behaviours, you will believe that you are a victim of circumstance and external agencies that are beyond your control. If you have an illness or find yourself in situations that consistently prevent you from achieving the things you want, the chances are there is a hidden pay-off keeping your King Kong in operation way beyond its original purpose. By identifying the possible benefits to be gained by staying as you are, you give yourself the power and means to make the choices that can set you free.

You can't fix something if you don't know it's broken. When you accept that the damage exists, then you can do something about it. You might decide that you don't want to let go of something because you're not ready to deal with the consequences, such as having to be assertive instead of making excuses. You might find that in uncovering the reason behind your pain, failure, illness etc., you realise you don't want to let it go, but at least you've made an informed decision. You take control when you have the ability to choose. The alternative is to aimlessly bob about like a passenger in a boat without a rudder, with no compass to point the way and no understanding of constellations to guide you. Some people don't want to take control: they would prefer to be swept along by the current instead of taking responsibility and choosing a direction or a course of action. It takes courage to take control and responsibility for our lives. This is why so many people prefer to think they are helpless victims on the receiving end of illness, disease, germs, accidents, even other people. 'It's not my fault', they say, 'it just happened that way'.

Again, it's important to realise that this process isn't about apportioning blame – to yourself or anyone else. It's about recognising the beliefs that are operating behind the scenes out of your awareness and therefore out of the realm of your control, and so acknowledging their power to influence your behaviour, attitudes and feelings. Claiming or owning your power is crucial if you are to move forward into a future of positive growth and development. Ignorance of those things from the past that affect who we are in the present will undoubtedly create a future filled with more pain, discomfort and stagnation.

Sharing Your Life with Another

In this chapter, I've only explored a couple of examples of behaviour or illness that can keep us stuck, keep us safe, but you could apply those examples to any aspect of your life that isn't serving you positively. You may be someone who is lonely and longs for companionship, for someone to share your life with in an intimate, meaningful way. You might have spent a long time on your own: independent, totally in charge of every aspect of your day-to-day life, answerable to no-one but yourself. You do what you like, when you like. You choose when to watch TV or listen to music - choosing the channel, radio station or CD according to your mood. You might value time alone to meditate or practice something like Yoga.

What might it mean to you to let another into your life? Someone who would have their own expectations, desires and goals that might conflict with yours? How they go about their life in the home will be completely different from your way of doing things. On the surface, you might say you'd be happy to allow another into your life and that you would gladly adapt and compromise if the right person came along. Deep down, however, you might not want to let go of your independence. You might be afraid of the demands and uncertainty of a new relationship. You might even, unconsciously, have arranged your life in such a way as to not allow room for another to take up space. Perhaps you love the comfort, security and tranquillity that your bed offers you each night, and would be loath to give that up to share it with another: someone who takes up all the bed, hogs the duvet, snores, fidgets in their sleep... You can see how it might be that you set yourself up to sabotage any possibility of meeting someone you would be willing to allow to come into your life.

Some of these preferences will not have much to do with your Core Beliefs, but they are beliefs nonetheless, and they will operate in the same way: in the background out of awareness. If you don't take the time to examine every aspect of what it is you want, on every level, the covert limiting beliefs will continue to exert power and control over your life without you even realising it. Understandably, you will blame all sorts of things for your inability to find a loving partner, from lack of time to socialise to believing all the good ones are already taken. By making excuses - as convincing as they may seem - you cut yourself off from awareness of what is really going on, and so deny yourself the chance to experience the joys and challenges of sharing your life with another.

Now you have gone some way in uncovering your hidden, limiting beliefs, in Part Two, we begin the process of working through and with them. We will explore various methods and approaches designed to take you to the heart of your Core Beliefs and confront your own inner King Kong.

PART TWO

YOUR INNER WORLD

Chapter 10

WHAT DREAMS MAY COME

The only journey is the journey within.

Rainer Maria Rilke

*One level of dream life deals particularly with the biological
condition of the body, giving you not just hints of health
difficulties, but the reasons for them and the ways to
circumvent them.*

Seth

When we dream, not only do we access a treasure trove of information, insights and guidance, but our energy body visits a place of all time where it gathers experience, understanding and awareness about who we truly are. During our sleeping hours we explore other realms where we are assisted in our development and where we might even be the ones assisting those who have made their transition and passed on. In sleeping we provide the body, not only with much needed rest, but also with the opportunity to heal and re-energise. On waking, we have only to pay attention to what we recall, practice interpreting the symbolism of our own 'dream' world, and act on the guidance we receive, in order to regularly benefit from our nightly excursions.

Even if you find it difficult to believe that you have such a rich and spiritual experience whenever you sleep, looking closely at your dream content can greatly improve your waking life in many ways. Some people are convinced that they don't dream. However, everyone dreams every night - no exceptions - it's just that we don't always remember them. This could be for several reasons:

* *We don't make a habit of trying to remember our dreams*
* *On waking, our minds instantly fill with thoughts of daily activities to be done*
* *Our sleep is affected by drugs, alcohol or stress*
* *We are so busy or stressed that our subconscious decides not to add to that weight and so dreams fade away as soon as we wake*

The subconscious is a very special part of us. It speaks to us in lots of different ways -through our dreams; creative expression like music, art, and writing; or through day-dreams. While our conscious mind is busy getting us through each day on a practical level, the subconscious helps us to process these day to day occurrences and gives us back the most important aspects of them in our dreams like nuggets of gold buried deep within. If we take the time and effort to dig down, to decipher the symbols, metaphors and puns of our dreams, we can always find inspiration, understanding and deep self-knowledge.

When you do start to pay attention to your dreams and value them as the amazing resource that they are, you will find yourself not only remembering more of your dreams, but remembering them in more detail. It's as though the subconscious is celebrating the fact that you are at last appreciating its efforts, and so wants to give you more and more of its precious treasure. Not only that, but your dreams will change, becoming more meaningful, and seeming less confusing and random.

If you regularly experience nightmares or recurring dreams, it's best not to ignore them in the hope they will stop or go away. The subconscious, desperately trying to get a message through, has possibly had to resort to either repetition or shock tactics to get you to pay attention, or you may even be giving yourself the opportunity to face and overcome fears. Every aspect of your dream comes from you, so you can never be harmed by its content. The nightmare might be trying to draw your attention to something that is causing you concern in your waking life. By looking at what the nightmare might be trying to tell you and then acting on that guidance, it will either stop or change in some way, as the subconscious will no longer need to bang you over the head to get you to listen.

In this chapter we are going to explore dreams to see how they can help you solve daily problems, gain insight into difficult situations, and provide you with your own personal development material and processes. What, you might be thinking, have dreams to do with understanding Core Beliefs? Well, they can and probably already do, give you hints about how to recognise your Core Beliefs and how to deal with them - as shall be seen in a later example.

When I have been ill, I have often had dreams that in some way gave me a new perspective on the illness or the treatment, or gave me insight into what might be causing the problem and how I can go about resolving it. Without exception, these dreams have provided me with invaluable guidance on what's going on within my body without the need for visits to the hospital for invasive and often unpleasant tests and procedures. I'm not suggesting that you forgo any kind of allopathic treatment. If you believe in a conventional approach to healing then it's important to keep to that method. As we've already seen, everything - even healing - ultimately comes down to belief.

Why Sharing Your Dreams Can Be Beneficial

The Senoi are a tribe of aboriginal people who live in the jungle highlands of Malaysia. They live near rivers in loose-knit settlements of fifteen to 100 people and are characterized as an easy-going and nonviolent people. They are believed to be among the healthiest and happiest people in the world. According to Kilton Stewart, who wrote about the Senoi in his 1948 doctoral thesis and his 1954 popular book *Pygmies and Dream Giants*, 'The Senoi make their dreams the major focus of their intellectual and social interest, and have solved the problem of violent crime and destructive economic conflict, and largely eliminated insanity, neurosis, and psychogenic illness.' Apparently, the Senoi begin each day by sitting together and sharing their dreams. They take their dreams very seriously and view them as a connection to their inner life: a connection they believe is there to help them function both as a people and as individuals.

As you can see from this, we can gain more from our dreams than just a momentary bit of fun. Taking the time and trouble to value, explore and take notice of our dreams can culminate in a meaningful relationship and connection with our inner life and greater being. And by sharing them with others in a respectful and appreciative manner, we can strengthen bonds and so create a more harmonious community. Maybe it's something that should be considered as part of the morning activities in classrooms?

I had the following dream during one of the worst *Colitis* flare-ups I've had in a long time. Although the symptoms weren't as bad as they had been in the past, I was finding it extremely difficult to overcome the flare-up and thought I was beyond healing naturally and might have to resort to more orthodox methods - something I hadn't done for over twelve years. Every day was a struggle and it became increasingly difficult for me to stay positive and trust that my body was doing its best to heal.

As a result of the work I had been doing on my own Core Beliefs, I knew that the rape had not only created some new Core Beliefs, but it had also re-enforced those created by the circumstances around my birth. I also knew that the *Colitis* came about partly as a result of those Core Beliefs.

Slug Dream

I am on an expedition with a friend 'David'. We are somewhere in the countryside and are returning from a walk or a hike. I have a sense of completion or achievement. We approach his/our Land Rover and stop to chat at the back of it. David stands against the doors with me facing him.

As we talk, a large, black slimy slug-like creature emerges from between our things on the roof rack, hooks over the top of the Land Rover and attaches itself to his right shoulder. It has sharp needle-like teeth, and I watch in horror as it uses them to puncture him quickly before slithering back into its hiding place. David looks at his shoulder and casually says, 'I've been bitten'.

We move around to the side of the vehicle which has now transformed into a sort of camper van with a sliding door. Another man is seated inside the van. We tell him what happened and describe the thing that bit David. He gets his computer out and tries to find out what it was that did it. I do the same only with my phone. This is all done in a matter of fact fashion. It is as if we are more interested in figuring out what it was than concerned about David's wound.

I go around to the other side of the van and find a large, quite deep L-shaped trench dug in the ground. Lying at the bottom and along the length of the trench is the slug, which almost fills the trench. I am slightly repulsed by the sight of it and intend to get something with which to kill it.

As I think this, the slug communicates with me 'telepathically'. It pleads with me not to kill it. I realise that it didn't act out of malice when it bit David. It tells me that it was only doing what it was created to do and meant no harm, and that it shouldn't be punished for doing what it was created to do. I feel sympathy for it and so decide not to kill it.

For me, the most important part of this dream is the end. It helped me to realise something that is so crucial in working with Core Beliefs - the acceptance that they exist for a specific purpose and that they are loyally carrying out their instructions with utter determination and commitment. They are not our enemy any more than our body is. We need to send them love and appreciation for what they are trying to do, just as we need to send any ailing part of our body gratitude for how hard it's trying to put things right, to restore homeostasis and balance.

Dream Interpretation

When working with dreams, background information is as important as the various elements within the dream. Absolutely *everything*, no matter how small or seemingly irrelevant or unimportant, is there for a reason. There is nothing in dreams (as with movies) that is unnecessary or insignificant. I will explain how to work with dreams - either alone or with a partner – later; for now, we will look at my *Slug* dream, and how it related to my life at the time. When working with my dreams, I let myself free-associate. It doesn't matter how someone else might describe a Land Rover or a trench:

it's my dream and therefore it's my interpretation that matters. Although I went into this dream in a lot of detail in my dream journal (something I strongly suggest you begin to keep for yourself), I will keep this account to those aspects that are more relevant to this book.

'David'

His part in the dream was to prepare me for what was to follow. He is a very professional, rational man, and so he represented the part of me that has handled the memory of the experience of being raped: I was always detached when I spoke of it, as if it happened to someone else, or was a storyline in a soap opera.

Emotions

* David and I are in good spirits when we return. I have a sense of accomplishment and satisfaction with our trip.
* When David is bitten, neither of us seems very concerned: David remarks on this very casually as if he has noticed a small mark on his shirt.
* Our companion is also unconcerned. None of us pay much attention or give much thought as to what might happen to David as a result of the bite.
* I am repulsed by the slug and want to do it harm.
* The slug can't understand why I want to kill it for doing its job.
* I feel pity for the slug.

Objects

The **Computer and Mobile Phone** that are used to research what the slug is, represent the way I often detach and distance myself from my emotions and from experiencing the real world. The Web and cyberspace is the world of virtual experiences. It's hard to convey any depth of emotion over the internet. I/we only have words and graphic 'emoticons' to describe how I am/we are experiencing others or the world.

Story

*   *We none of us pay much attention to David's wound.* No-one attempts to dress or examine it in any way. No-one, including David, is concerned about how his health will be affected by the bite. Even though I have explored the rape several times over the past few years, I never actually connected with it emotionally. I looked at it as though one step removed, examining it as if it were a mystery to be solved rather than a painful, traumatic aspect of my life that needed to be integrated and healed. I was very much approaching it from a clinical perspective, like a scientist in a laboratory.

*   *Separating from my friends, I go to the other side of the Camper Van.* I've begun the journey to connecting with my emotions which are on the other side from logic (the Land Rover). I suppose you could say I move from my left-brain hemisphere, responsible for analytical, problem solving, to the right-brain hemisphere which is responsible for intuition, creativity and imagination.

*   *The slug, now much bigger, lies inside an 'L' shaped trench.* My partner gave me some very useful insight when he said it was 'en-trenched'! The shape of the trench mirrors the colon, with the slug in the part that is affected by the *Ulcerative Colitis*. This meant the slug represented an experience that is also responsible for my chronic health condition. Its creation and existence is connected in some way with my gut.

* *I am repulsed by the slug.* If you know anything about *Ulcerative Colitis*, you will know that it is not the most attractive of diseases! I have spent many years 'repulsed' by my own bodily functions which, during an acute flare-up, often go into massive overdrive. This for me was the hardest aspect of loving and accepting every part of my body, no matter how it looks or behaves.

* *My intention is to kill the slug, but it speaks to me 'telepathically' asking me not to kill it.* It tells me it was only doing what it was created for. This is such a clear description of Core Beliefs! Not all my dreams are this 'on the nose', and I'm grateful that this one was so easy to understand.

* *I take pity on the slug and let it live.* When the slug explains that it was not acting out of malice or malevolence - that in fact, it was performing its function to the best of its ability - I realise that to kill it would be senseless. If you stand on a dogs tail while it's sleeping (even by accident), and it turns on you, you don't immediately blame the dog and think it had malevolent intent. You know it was reacting instinctively to pain - just as we do. The slug, when it bit David, was only doing what it was created to do.

You don't have to be a dream therapist to appreciate the messages within this dream. I was actively working on my Core Beliefs at the time I had it and my subconscious, or Greater Self, provided the dream in order to give me deeper insight into the work I was doing. By having this dream, I was able to go to other levels of understanding and acceptance of my Core Beliefs and what they were trying to accomplish. As a result, I was not only kinder to them, but to those parts of myself that had created them.

The slug returned in a later dream, only this time it was very different to the original slug. In this dream, I was aware of what felt like a bony finger scratching up the left side of my body and then digging its nail into my shoulder. A strange conversation took place between me and the finger. I don't remember what was said, but I sensed that the 'finger' was an aspect of the slug.

What I learned from this was that although it was still operational in some way, it was much smaller than the original slug and therefore not so 'dangerous'. Also, instead of a 'mouth' full of barb-like teeth, it had only one 'nail'. I felt this to be very positive, especially as I felt I was actually awake during some of this experience, and was left feeling very calm and reassured about my state of health at that time.

Sometime later, I had a dream in which I am lying on a beach coaxing a dark creature towards me. The creature is on my left (which is side affected by the *Ulcerative Colitis*). As I continue to tease it, it transforms into a child. I feel guilty about teasing it and so pull it up onto my belly. I give it some food and it seems quite content, chatting to me in a foreign language.

I won't explore in detail each aspect of these dreams - or dream-like experiences - as I did with the Slug dream. However, what I understood from these experiences was that there has been some type of transformation of the 'Slug'. This shows that the work I have done since having the original dream has had a dramatic effect on its power and influence in my life. I now have a relationship with it that is nurturing and supportive - something that we can both benefit from.

As these are my dreams, and so personal to me, the symbolism will be more in keeping with my own way of interpreting them. A camper van to me, in the Slug dream, may not have the same meaning to you if one appeared in your dreams, or indeed, to me in another dream. I can remember my mum telling me that to dream of fire meant you would soon hear hasty news. In one dream book I consulted, to dream of fire means that prosperity will warm your life, even if it's engulfing your home. In another, fire represents passion, sexuality, anger and desire. I think of fire as something that clears the space (as in controlled forest fires), energy is transformed through fire, or it may even be a sign that there is a fever of activity within the body. I use this example to show that there are many possible interpretations of any element of a dream.

Lots of people use some kind of dream dictionary when faced with a perplexing dream experience. I've never been a great fan of them as I don't believe that one size fits all, but there are some decent ones available. I have provided a basic bibliography in order to give you some idea of the kind of books that have been of value to me in my personal and/or spiritual development. As well as good books on dream interpretation, I will also include a couple of dream dictionaries that I believe to be more aware of the uniqueness of dream content and symbolism.

When we think of the origin of problematic issues and consider the possibility that they are emanating from earlier versions of ourselves, it gives us the clues we need in order to know where to begin and how to proceed with putting those issues right. In the following chapter, I will introduce you to the world of your *Inner Child*. This is yet another way of looking at your own inner King Kong - one that doesn't have such aggressive and overpowering connotations, but can still cause problems for any adult who doesn't acknowledge its existence.

Chapter 11

THE CHILD WITHIN

Only when I make room for the voice of the child within me do I feel myself to be genuine and creative.

Alice Miller

The inner child is a powerful presence. It dwells at the core of our being.

Lucia Capacchione

Who were you as a child? Even if you grew up in a troubled, painful, dysfunctional family, you will still have had times when you were truly free to be a child. Perhaps it was at school, or when you visited a friend's or relative's house, or just those times when you were able to be by yourself to play and have fun. Imagine how carefree you were as a small child. No matter how awful their life is, children have an amazing (possibly life-saving) ability to be completely in the moment, no distractions, and no doubts that their world of make-believe isn't any less real than the 'reality' of their life. They are able to totally immerse themselves in their games and their fantasy worlds.

Children have a capacity to seek refuge from painful experiences by escaping within the shelter of their imagination. It is this aspect of the child that remains with us into adulthood and continues as a survival strategy at times of threat or anxiety. Commonly known as the Inner Child, it, like any physical child, loves to be spontaneous, needs nurturing, loves to play and explore, and thrives on being in the present.

As I've already mentioned, adults possibly seem like giants or ogres to small children. It is for this reason that fairy tales are so popular, and why children love to have familiar stories repeated over and over. They speak to the child within us all and reflect the awe and terror we felt imagining ourselves as Hansel, Gretel, or Jack, as they pit their wits and resourcefulness against their adversaries. Every time the hero or heroine succeeds in out-smarting the villain, the child feels it is they who will live to fight another day and that they too can survive in a world full of giants and danger.

When this sadly doesn't prove to be true, and the small child realises that the giants and tyrants that populate its world are immune to magic potions and spells, it is left to the Inner Child to seek refuge behind its own protector. These then are the Core Beliefs, its very own King Kong, the warrior within us all. As we have seen, this force of nature is absolutely focused on its mission. It has a purpose, is single-minded and will not easily be swayed from its task.

Act your Age, Not Your Shoe Size

Adults, particularly parents, feel duty bound to *socialise* children, to teach them how to behave in a socially acceptable way, whether in company or at school (where, with timetables and strict routine, they are taught how to be anything but spontaneous). With every demand for more and more 'adult-like behaviour', the child loses more and more of its naturalness as it learns to conform to the expectations of grown-ups - or else. From a pre-verbal age, children are able to intuitively pick up on the feelings and intentions of those around it, especially those it is closest to. Since the primary care-giver - most often the mother - is also the child's primary means of survival, she will do all she can to please, fearing disapproval and abandonment that might come from not getting it right. Thus, the child sublimates her needs for those of her parent(s). In order to survive, the growing child must learn to conceal and suppress her playful, enthusiastic spirit, locking it away where it can no longer be damaged or mistreated.

The Inner Child learns how to lie when it realises that adults generally are not comfortable with, or more likely, don't believe in talk of special friends that no-one else can see: magical places at the bottom of the garden or under the bed, or the belief that wishes do come true. But the Inner Child never grows up and never goes away. It's there within us always. It's a part of us that is desperate to be acknowledged and nurtured. Every time a child is told not to cry, or told to be quiet, not to make a mess, or to calm down, their Inner Child retreats further and further into a safe and/or magical haven deep within.

And so we grow up having denied our feeling-self in order to survive. We become adults who, on the most part, operate predominantly from our left-brain. We spend the majority of our adult lives locked in our heads, so far removed from our bodies and natural impulses that we have effectively abandoned our child within. When the needs - such as love, attention, guidance, nurturing - of this Inner Child are not met, we create an environment rife with physical, emotional and psychological problems. It's at these times the Core Beliefs within us come to the fore. Our Inner Child now needs firm guidance as its need for love and attention can so easily be misinterpreted. In her book, *Recovery of Your Inner Child*, Lucia Capacchione warns that instead of listening to the feelings of the Inner Child, 'we feed it too much food. Instead of playtime, we give it drugs.

Instead of self-love, we give it sex at the wrong time or with inappropriate partners.'

As well as physical addictions, over-protective Core Beliefs combined with an abandoned Inner Child can also hide out in emotional compulsions and obsessions. As we saw earlier with Jean, OCD is a common manifestation of Core Beliefs out of control. Obsessive worry, fear, rage, accident proneness, or lack of self-interest, are all signs of a neglected or ignored Inner Child.

During her extensive research and many years of experience of working with individuals and groups, Lucia Capacchione came to realise that there are several aspects to the Inner Child, which can include the Vulnerable Child, and the Angry Child. According to Capacchione, it is the Vulnerable Child that manifests illness – both mental and physical. These symptoms can be anything from aches and pains, through to serious illness and chronic disease. When a child is feeling scared or vulnerable, their instinctive response is to hide – even if it's just by covering their eyes – or to run away.

As adults, these strong urges to flee or become invisible in times of stress and anxiety - particularly if we're not able to make it happen - can manifest as restless legs, eyesight problems, stooping shoulders, as well as a myriad of skin and joint complaints. This is the Vulnerable Child desperately trying to disappear or escape from the uncomfortable situation. As an adult, you may well be more than capable of giving a speech or dealing with authority, but if you have a Vulnerable Child within your Core Beliefs that equates being visible with danger, then you will struggle to physically get through the ordeal.

In my work as a therapist, I have come to realise just how prevalent the Child Within is when working with people with issues around food. Many of my clients with eating disorders (and by that I don't just mean Anorexia or Bulimia - it increasingly includes Orthorexia) have shown that food is a way for the Vulnerable Child to obtain the nurturing comfort they need. When, as an adult you are feeling unhappy, rejected, lonely, inadequate, even ugly, the vulnerable child within comes to the fore to make itself feel better by doing what their loved ones would have done at those times when they were a child. They would cheer you up by providing you with comfort and reassurance in the form of cakes, ice-cream, chocolate and sweets, crisps etc; and, for a while, it might work. Just for a little while you might feel better, like the world isn't such a horrible, lonely place to be. As a child, you would no doubt be distracted from your sadness long enough for you to find something else to occupy your mind - playing games, watching TV, etc. Jump ahead to that child as an adult feeling sad and alone and needing comfort and reassurance: is it any wonder we go to the cupboard for biscuits and treats, or the fridge for ice-cream?

Most of the self-awareness I've written about in previous chapters could be likened to Inner Child work, especially my realising why I needed to be in control on walks with my partner. It was my scared and Vulnerable Child that didn't want to deviate from the designated route as she was afraid I would be hurt at the end of it. She didn't realise I was with a man I could trust completely, a man that loves and cherishes me and would never do anything to harm me. All she knew was that I was being taken somewhere I didn't know and so brought my inner King Kong to the fore to protect me.

Since coming to this understanding, I have been able to just go with the flow far more easily when out and about on walks or bike rides. Had I not already had an understanding and awareness of my Inner Child and her fears and concerns, I might never have got to the bottom of why I needed so desperately to maintain control in those circumstances, and my partner and I would have continued to believe I was just an irrational control freak for no other reason than I like it!

Marie

Marie, she had been self-harming for several years. As previously mentioned, one of her physical problems had been difficulty sleeping - either going off to sleep or staying asleep. Her psychiatrist had prescribed Prozac, but Marie had a reaction to them and so this powerful anti-depressant was replaced with Melatonin.

Marie's parents are separated and, at that time, her father was struggling with alcoholism. Marie and her father are very close and, when she was 13 years old (which, significantly, was around the time she began self-harming), she would often stay with her dad, sleeping on his couch in the front room. She would regularly wake to find him drunk and passed-out on the floor. Nothing she did could rouse him and so she would lie back down on the couch and try to sleep despite being afraid he might not wake up. Sometime later, she would hear her dad moving around; and, although relieved he was alive, she would pretend to be asleep as she listened to him stagger off to bed.

When I first started working with Marie, I was appalled to learn that several mental health practitioners (including her psychiatrist) had ignored or simply been ignorant of the connection between her past experiences and her physical issues. What shocked me most about her medical treatment was the fact that at no time did her psychiatrist ask her when she had started to experience sleep difficulties. It seemed he simply put it down to being an understandable symptom of her anxiety and stress and so prescribed something to help her sleep instead of getting to the actual cause of why she was unable to sleep.

All of the practitioners who had been working with Marie were aware that her father had alcohol issues and that this would naturally have had something to do with her emotional/mental health. When we discussed her sleeping problems, she told me that she had trouble sleeping even when she felt exhausted. She went on to explain that it wasn't always intrusive thoughts or worry that kept her awake at night, and it certainly wasn't intrusive thoughts that woke her up a few hours after finally falling asleep. Her body was complying with a deep-seated command from her subconscious and I believed it was necessary to uncover this instruction in order to remove it, rather than to mask it with drugs.

In one of our first sessions together, I explained that for some people, going to sleep is fraught with fear on a deep subconscious level: and that often what they fear is death. I told her the Edgar Allan Poe quote referring to sleep as, 'those little slices of death'. I went on to explain how sleeping very deeply and then perhaps not remembering your dreams, might even make some people feel as if they had been dead during that time - we often refer to being in a deep sleep as being 'dead to the world'. I also explained how some people are afraid to go to sleep because they are not in control during that time and sometimes bad things can happen when we're in that state. At the time, I didn't know a lot about Marie's experiences at home or as a small child, but I thought that as she was young, was in the care of a psychiatrist and self-harmed as a way of managing strong, overwhelming emotions, it was safe to assume her fears around not having control might have something to do with her inability to sleep.

It was then that she told me about what it was like when she stayed over at her dads. For a 13 year old, it's a terrifying experience to see your dad - who is supposed to be your protector and the one responsible for making grown-up decisions - unconscious on the floor. No wonder she had lost the ability to sleep, she had a 13yr old girl inside her that was terrified to sleep. For that younger self, whenever she slept bad things would happen, and so she felt it was imperative that she kept vigil - perhaps that would prevent her dad from passing out. But when she did sleep, she would wake to find that he was literally unconscious and couldn't be roused: again, a terrifying thing for a young person to have to deal with.

What her younger self learned from these experiences was that it isn't safe to sleep. After I had finished describing these things as a possible reason for her difficulties sleeping, a tentative smile spread across her face. She now had an explanation that fitted with her experience. Before we tackled anything else, I wanted to help her feel safe enough to sleep naturally. This meant doing Inner Child work in order to meet and acknowledge the frightened little girl within her that needed reassurance.

This proved to be a powerful experience for Marie. Discussing the written dialogue and drawings she had done during an Inner Child session, gave her a new perspective on her current behaviours and fears. She was able to reassure her Inner Child that she was safe and that she could relinquish some of the control she'd been exerting on Marie - control that had interfered with her ability to relax and sleep naturally.

At eighteen, Marie is no longer in therapy. It's been months since she felt the need to self-harm in order to cope with overwhelming emotions. she is better able to cope with any strong emotions and no longer feels overwhelmed by them. She has overcome her debilitating social phobia, has a boyfriend and a good group of close friends; and, having recently returned from travelling in America for 6 weeks, she will be moving out of her home town to begin studying for a degree in Psychology and Counselling.

Getting To Know Your Inner Child

What follows is a brief over-view of Inner Child work and how you can do it for yourself. Of course, nothing beats being with a gifted therapist when accessing such hidden, vulnerable parts of ourselves: someone who can support you as you process what comes up. You could share this inner work with a good friend or someone you trust, but you may find it difficult to truly go into the places where your Inner Child might hide out for fear of being belittled, shamed, hurt, dismissed or embarrassed. With a therapist, you can really allow yourself to open up to deep, scary emotions, knowing that whatever surfaces will be met with understanding, acceptance and compassion. A therapist will be able to answer your questions about the work you do together and certainly won't have any judgements about what emerges. They would, however, help you to put it into some kind of context so that you would be able to transfer that new learning and awareness into your everyday life.

That said, there's nothing wrong with doing some Inner Child work by yourself, and there are many excellent books on the subject (I've included some that in the Recommended Reading section), that are designed to help you go through the process and interpret what you might be discovering.

PREPARATION

You will need:

* **Paper** - A4 will do but you will have more scope if you use A3. White is usually best.
* **Crayons** - any size will do, but I like using chunky ones as they make my hand seem small like a child's!
* **Peace and Quiet** - try to do this when you know you won't be disturbed. Turn off your phone and close the door if you're not entirely alone in the house.
* **Time** - give yourself at least an hour to do this valuable work. Remember, you are honouring yourself and your Inner Child, so give her / him your undivided attention.
* **Trust** - allow yourself to let go of any doubts about what takes place. Try not to judge or dismiss what comes up.
* **Compassion** - be prepared to shower your Inner Child with love and affection. Let them know you truly care about them and what they're trying to convey to you.
* **A Journal** - you might want to do this several times so it's good to keep a record of how you felt each time before, during and after. It's also good to record these things for future reference.

BEGINNING

1.   Lay your paper and crayons out on a clean flat surface. You can do this on the floor (not so easy if it's carpeted), which can work well as it's often where children like to draw their pictures, but you can just as easily do it at a table or desk.

2. Close your eyes and take a minute or so to centre yourself by breathing slowly and deeply into your belly. If your shoulders rise as you breathe in you need to drop them and imagine the breath going into your lungs, pushing your diaphragm down and out. As you breathe, affirm to yourself that you are preparing to do some important work, that you are allowed to spend this time on yourself, and that whatever happens you will accept and value it.

3. Now imagine a beautiful place where you and your Inner Child can meet. As long as it feels safe and comfortable it can be anywhere you like. Stay there for a couple of minutes imagining your Inner Child there with you.

4. Choose a crayon and, with your non-dominant hand, draw a picture of your Inner Child. Try not to plan how it will look, just let it unfold in its own way and time. This might feel a bit awkward and slow, but that's ok.

5. When you're finished, stop and reflect on your picture of your Inner Child. Ask yourself how it felt doing it. Did you judge how it looked? Did you criticize yourself (Inner Child) for not being very good at drawing? Or did you allow the drawing to unfold without censure or judgement?

6. In your journal or on a separate piece of paper, write what you feel about the process and about your Inner Child as s/he appears on the paper. By now, you may feel you need to take some time to absorb this new and, hopefully, enlightening experience. However, if you're ready, by all means go on to the next exercise where you will talk to your Inner Child. You will need your paper and crayons and, if you are coming back to this at a later time, your drawing of your Inner Child.

COMMUNICATING

1.   Starting with your dominant hand this time, you're going to get to know your Inner Child. You might want to start by asking, 'Who are you?', or 'What is your name?' Swap hands (and use a different colour crayon if you like) and, using your non-dominant hand, let your Inner Child respond. You might be surprised to learn that it has a different name to yours!

2.   Now you're going to have a conversation with your Inner Child. You might want to let it know that you want to take better care of it and hear all about how it feels about things. You could ask if it's ok for you both to talk to each other. If the answer is no, then honour that, thank your Inner Child (again by writing with your dominant hand) and let it know that it's ok not to talk right now. Ask if it's ok for you to come back again sometime to visit with it.

You might also want to ask if it would like to do another drawing instead of chatting. It might take some time for your Inner Child to feel it can trust you enough to be able to talk to you. If you ever experienced in your life a time when an adult told you that you had to do something that you really didn't want to do (like give a relative a kiss), then you know how powerless it feels to be forced into something against your will. By not pushing your Inner Child, you show it that you can be trusted to honour their needs and wishes.

3. If your Inner Child is happy to talk, then thank it and ask away! It might be interesting to find out how old it is. (This might give you some insight into a time of your life when Core Beliefs were set up.) You could ask how it feels, what they like or don't like, and what it wants from you.

4. When it feels right, ask your Inner Child if they'd like to draw a picture of what it is they might want or need right now.

5. Finish by thanking your Inner child for coming out to play and by letting it know that you're going to do this more often so that you can get to know it better.

As you'll be swapping crayons and hands with which to write, this could take some time, so be prepared to let it unfold slowly. Try not to rush things, and definitely try not to think about the responses your Inner Child *might* give to your questions. Just let it happen and enjoy the experience of discovering an amazing part of who you are.

I can't stress enough how important it is that you honour whatever comes from doing this work. This is a vulnerable, fragile part of you that needs acknowledgment and nurturing. In doing this, you will provide yourself with the means to begin to release some of your Core Beliefs and so enable you to lead a more fulfilling and harmonious life.

Staying Connected

Once you have made contact with your Inner Child, do your best not to neglect it by forgetting it's there waiting to be acknowledged and heard. You don't need to write out conversations or draw pictures in order to connect with your child within. At times when you feel low and unhappy -

particularly when it's a general feeling as opposed to being a reaction to something unpleasant that may have happened - take the time to sit quietly and communicate with your Vulnerable Child. As weird or silly as it may seem, talking to yourself in this way can be very therapeutic and healing.

If it makes it easier, imagine that you have a small child sitting beside you who is unhappy and feeling lonely and scared. Talk to them in a calm and caring way. Let them know that you are aware of how they are feeling and that you are there to help. Tell them that you love them and will always take care of them. Tell them how special they are. By giving yourself the time and space to reflect on how your child within might be feeling, and connecting with it in a meaningful and loving way, you will find yourself appreciating yourself more and berating yourself less.

I find working in this way with my clients helps them to create a deeper understanding of why they may do the things they do. We may only do one session where we focus on connecting with their Inner Child, but the following sessions are always enriched by their having this awareness of their Inner Child. From then on, whenever, for instance they find themselves wanting more cake or another packet of crisps, they can stop and ask themselves, 'Who wants this and why?' This then reminds them that their need isn't for food, but for love and affection. Once they realise that it's their Inner Child speaking to them through their craving, they are then able to choose not to eat and to reassure their Inner Child, instead.

In the following chapter I will go into other ways of accessing the subconscious: ways that can often lead to profound healing and self-awareness.

Chapter 12

DEEPER TRAVELS WITHIN

Your visions will become clear only when you can look into your own heart. Who looks outside, dreams; who looks inside, awakes.

C.G. Jung

Look within. Within is the fountain of good, and it will ever bubble up, if thou wilt ever dig.

Marcus Aurelius

As we have already seen, it is within the realms of the subconscious that our limiting beliefs were created and so it is there that they will be discovered and eventually released, altered, or eradicated. The subconscious mind is tuned into universal intelligence and has been tracking our lives since birth (and before), and so it knows exactly what might be causing us physical or emotional pain. In communicating directly with this wise part of us, we are opening the way for healing and growth in a powerful, lasting way.

When working with your Inner Child or, more specifically, your dreams, you are accessing the source of all your beliefs about who you are, the world around you and how you operate within it. You may by now have discovered your own limiting beliefs that continue to disrupt or wreak havoc in your life. If this is the case, then you are already well on the way to letting them go or; at the very least, transforming them. However, as they were created at such a deep, unconscious level, you will need to go there in order to achieve lasting changes - there is no point in just talking about what you have discovered and hoping that that understanding and awareness will be all you need to experience the necessary shifts in behaviour. If you had a virus in your computer, knowing it is there and knowing what it is capable of doing will not be enough to disable or remove it from your hard drive – you would need to locate it first and then do something tangible in order to delete it. I'm not suggesting that discovering and talking about Core Beliefs and how they affect you wouldn't be beneficial, it would, but only to a certain extent.

For instance, you learn that your inability to hold on to money stems from your family and how they approached finances and possibly even wealth. You discuss and explore this inherited attitude in more detail with a trusted friend or therapist and vow to make an effort to save money or at least not blow your wages within the first few days of being paid. However, there will remain within you at a deep level an almost felt need not to keep money: you may even feel compelled to purchase things you don't really need. You will be able to argue your case convincingly and, eventually, successfully. You make the frivolous purchase, feel good about it, enjoy it for a short time once it arrives or you get it home, and then start looking for the next fix. It's this habituated behaviour that you need to over-ride, and it is this deep-seated drive that is extremely difficult to shift and let go of.

This is where the following therapeutic approaches can be of lasting benefit. Once you have discovered your Achilles heel, or weak spot, you can use one or a combination of these methods to get to the root of the problem, and hopefully eliminate it from your subconscious.

HYPNOTHERAPY

One the best ways of accessing and dialoguing with your subconscious (or hard drive), is through hypnotherapy. Hypnosis is a state of focused concentration that allows you to enter an altered or deeply relaxed state similar to the stages of sleep experienced just as you drift off (Hypnogogic state) and just as you begin to awaken (Hypnopompic state). At these times, you are in an altered state of consciousness and can more readily access the subconscious realm of your mind. Repeating affirmations and doing visualisations during these periods of altered consciousness greatly improves the chances of them being more strongly imprinted on the subconscious mind, and therefore, more effective. It is also in this deeply relaxed state that we can access the memories and experiences stored in the subconscious where they have been since childhood. In this way, you are more likely to get to the root cause and origins of your limiting beliefs.

Have you ever been driving your car along a very familiar route such as the journey home from work? As you arrive at your destination you become aware that you paid no attention whatsoever to large parts of the journey. In these experiences, your subconscious mind, where you have stored this very familiar route and the habitual actions of driving a car, has taken over whilst your conscious mind was somewhere else, planning what to have for dinner or re-running a conversation with a colleague, for instance. During hypnosis, it is this by-passing of the conscious mind that provides us with the powerful means of communicating with the subconscious.

In truth, we experience many similar, ordinary situations that may inadvertently induce a light trance state. Whenever you find yourself in an environment filled with a methodical rhythm - windshield wipers swishing slowly on a rainy day can create a sense of timelessness; for some, the gentle ticking of a clock can provide the backdrop for self-hypnosis. Similarly, meditation and prayer can also be forms of self-hypnosis. In fact, any repetitive activity can provide the same sense of calm that allows us to transcend time and space in the way that hypnosis can.

During light states of altered awareness or focus, the brain shifts from the Beta waves (38-15 Hz) of normal waking consciousness, of logical, conscious and analytical thinking, into an Alpha state (14-8 Hz). Alpha brain waves are present in deep relaxation and while day-dreaming. The relaxed, detached awareness achieved during light meditation is characteristic of Alpha and is optimal for programming your mind for success. Alpha heightens your imagination, visualisation, memory, learning and concentration and is the gateway to your subconscious mind.

As I've mentioned before, the subconscious is our memory bank. Every experience, conversation, idea, or dream we've ever had is stored there. It is not bound by time or space and is a font of wisdom and creativity. Many famous people attribute their success to being able to access this place within them, either through their dreams or by day-dreaming. Even Einstein considered the imagination to be more important than knowledge when trying to find the solution to a problem.

There are many myths around hypnosis and what it actually is and what it does. Freud, the father of psychoanalysis, created a fear of the subconscious when he maintained that it was a dark and scary place filled with supressed desires and incestuous fantasies. People were worried that in uncovering the workings of their inner self, they may also uncover things that they'd rather not know or admit.

It is true that the conscious mind acts as a censor. It filters out thoughts, feelings and experiences that we find unacceptable or overwhelming, and relegates them to the subconscious. Through hypnosis, we can uncover those aspects of our behaviours that we have pushed deep down within us or that are out of our awareness, as in Core Beliefs.

A useful aspect of hypnotherapy, particularly for the purpose of uncovering hidden limiting beliefs, is regression.

REGRESSION

During regression the therapist helps you to recall events from the past, either to uncover forgotten or repressed experiences and/or emotions, or to help you go back to a time when something may have happened that is still causing you problems now in the present – either physical or emotional. By accessing a difficult event from the past during hypnosis, you will have the opportunity to view it as an observer and see it from a different perspective – one that is dissociated from the emotions experienced at the time of the event. Instead of being overwhelmed, you are able to be more objective – almost as though you are a witness to the event instead of being part of it.

When using regression to help remove limiting Core Beliefs with my clients, I often take them to a time or event that has already been identified as being pivotal to the creation of one or more of their Core Beliefs. The client will then meet and converse with that version of themselves and, amongst other things, inform them of their current age, situation and resources now available to them as an adult – very much as we might do during Inner Child work. The difference here is that we are going deeper into the subconscious. This allows us greater freedom to explore the limiting beliefs of the Inner Child and for the client to over-ride and replace them with present-time, adult beliefs/attitudes that will work in their favour.

PAST LIFE THERAPY

This isn't the place for me to go into too much detail about 'past lives' as it's a very complex area as well as still being controversial. However, having experienced the healing capacity of such an approach first hand, and having used it successfully in my own therapy practice, I feel it's within keeping to describe, briefly, how it can be of benefit in Core Belief work. It's not something I would consider using with every client, and I would need to be satisfied that they'd explored every other 'here and now' option before suggesting past lives as an alternative reason for a problem or problems.

Past life therapy or regression is a powerful tool for identifying, exploring and releasing past experiences that continue to affect a person's physical, emotional, mental or spiritual wellbeing in the here and now. This 'stuckness' may manifest as a chronic health condition, phobia, addiction, relationship issues, inexplicable repulsion or attraction to another, intense fear, or nightmares. You may even have a strong interest in another time in history or culture.

Countless people's lives have been changed for the better after using past life regression to explore current issues or disturbances. When working with clients, I emphasise that belief in past lives is not necessary in order to achieve relief or change. For me, it's more important that my clients allow the story of a past life to emerge in their imagination. For some, it helps to think of the images and feelings that come up as a metaphor for a current situation. As with Inner Child therapy, we are working with a part of consciousness that has split off from the whole and become 'stuck' in another time and place. By accessing this 'version' of ourselves, we are then able to release the trapped energy or emotion.

By identifying the emotion-laden event from the past, you will be able to change the triggering mechanisms that continue to cause so much pain and anguish in the here and now. Past life regression can help people to understand the cause of many current problems such as health or relationship issues which have origins, not in this life time, but in an experience that may be from another time and place. Through deep relaxation, you can locate the time of trauma or sadness; and, with the guidance of the therapist, begin to work through that experience and thus release any repressed or blocked emotions. These emotions may manifest as anger, jealousy or hostility held towards another. This cycle of punishment, guilt, shame, anger etc., can finally be broken now and for all time (past, present and future).

This isn't necessarily a quick-fix solution to present day issues. However, there are occasions when, having re-experienced a past life trauma, some people are able to release abnormal fear, anxiety or a physical condition almost immediately. For others, it may take several sessions in order to achieve lasting improvement.

Regardless of the initial reason for seeking past life therapy, what most people come away with following a successful recall and re-experience of a past life or lives, is a dramatic change in attitude towards being physical, relationships within this life, the meaning of death, and the experience of dying. Being made aware that we exist as an eternal being of energy - an energy that does not die but simply experiences a transformation once the physical body has been released - brings about a calm acceptance of death and a more spiritual approach to relationships and life experiences.

Those stubborn, evasive, inexplicable Core Beliefs that seem to have been created out of nothing, may finally make sense in light of uncovering past life trauma, pain, loss, or fear. This approach is worth considering if you can find no present-life emotional or psychological explanation for a physical condition, irrational fear, or unfathomable behaviour or attitude. On witnessing or safely re-experiencing this other life event, you would then be able to release it from your energy and return to full consciousness feeling real and lasting relief. I have listed some very informative and comprehensive books on past life therapy in the bibliography, within the pages of which, you can read example after example of how people have reached profound and lasting relief from all manner of physical and emotional issues.

BACH FLOWER REMEDIES

Another way to access and work through deeply held issues is through the use of flower remedies. I have already mentioned Flower Remedies in Chapter Two, but now I will go into their use in more detail.

The original flower essences were developed by Edward Bach, an English physician, homeopath, and bacteriologist. Through personal research and observations, he found that the basis for illness and disease lay in the disharmony between the spiritual and mental aspects of his patients. His research also led him to recognise that there were various personality types that related to various patterns of ill-health, irrespective of the symptoms shown by the patient.

As a homeopath, he began collecting plants and in particular flowers - the most highly-developed part of a plant - in the hope of replacing the nosodes (homeopathic preparations made from bodily tissues and fluids) with a series of gentler remedies. Over many years of trial and error, which involved preparing and testing thousands of plants, he found the remedies he wanted. Each one was directed at dealing with a particular mental state or emotion. He found that when he treated the personalities and feelings of his patients, the healing potential in their bodies was unblocked and allowed to work, which naturally alleviated their unhappiness and physical distress. Bach espoused a holistic approach to physical and emotional issues, believing that we are more than the outward physical body. He suggested that illness is a message from our inner being calling attention to something within our lives that needed to change.

In his book, *The Twelve Healers & Other Remedies*, Bach outlines the healing personality of thirty eight plants and the corresponding negative state of the person they can best be of use to. The essences are prepared using only the flowers as they grow above ground where they are bathed in sunlight and air, and because, 'they contain in their hearts the embryo seed, the continued life of the plant.' They are the plant's unique expression and work best if the flowers are collected from unpolluted areas, at certain times of day.

Nowadays it is possible to buy essences from flowers found in the Australian Bush, Findhorn, Guernsey, and even Alaska! Each wild plant has mastered the ability to grow and thrive in a particular environment. As someone born in Britain, I believe those plants native to the UK are best suited to my needs, as my body is acclimatized to operate successfully within this part of the world. For this reason, I personally prefer to use

Bach Flower Remedies, but I'm sure the essence of any plant would work well (remember, it's all about belief!).

I have used flower remedies for many years and find them to be a useful adjunct to any emotional or physical work I might be doing. Each remedy, usually made up of 3 – 4 essences, will contain a few drops of our life or 'signature' essence. In Chapter Two I described how I discovered that my signature essence is Scleranthus, and how this applies to many aspects of my being. Other essences I have used have included: Gorse for hopelessness; Oak (recommended for long-term illness) to help rebuild strength; Impatiens for impatience; and Pine for feelings of guilt and not being good enough. From these you can see how using flower essences may be of use when working with and trying to release or alter Core Beliefs.

Flower essences are safe to use and can be taken alongside prescribed medication. The only cautionary advice I would give is to be prepared for old pain or issues coming to the surface. The essences can be powerfully cathartic, like peeling back the layers of years of sadness, regret, fear, anxiety or any other emotions that we may not have fully dealt with.

There are many books on Flower Essences that explain how to create and use them for yourself; however, as with most remedies, they are often more effective if administered by a practicing therapist. As a trained practitioner, they will be able to 'prescribe' the best remedy for you and help you prepare for and work through whatever those remedies bring to the surface. As I discovered when I first started using flower remedies, it can be difficult to focus in on just two or three essences when several might seem to be appropriate.

Who's the Boss of You?

In the following chapter I will explore the kinds of more creative things you can do to access the home of your Core Beliefs and how you can use your visits there to begin or continue the journey of re-programming and/or releasing them.

Chaprter 13

CREATIVE APPROACHES TO HEALING

We need creativity in order to break free from the temporary
structures that have been set up by a particular sequence of
experience.

Edward de Bono

The past exists in multitudinous ways. You only experience
one probable past. By changing this past in your mind now, in
your present, you can change not only its nature, but also its
effect, and not only upon yourself but upon others, too.

Seth

If you've ever watched a child being creative whether it's through art, play, fantasy or dancing, then you will know that there is a place we can go within ourselves that transcends reality (or the world around us). As I mentioned in Chapter 11, *The Child Within*, for children, this is a place of complete focus and attention, pleasure, freedom and expression that, as adults, we can never reach again in quite the same way. It's not that that special place no longer exists within us, it's that we have grown so far removed from it that we no longer recognise or acknowledge its existence. Or perhaps, we sense its presence but believe we can no longer visit that place. These are the adults (and, sadly, young people), who struggle to let their hair down, to act daft, or get messy. They try their best to control their environment out of fear, as in the words of King Lear, 'Oh, that way madness lies; let me shun that; no more of that.'

What does art (meaning any form of creativity) have to do with Core Beliefs? Well, when I was in primary school, about age 8, I clearly remember having a picture returned to me by my teacher who refused to put it on the wall with the other pictures. The reason I didn't make the grade? I'd coloured outside the lines. Another time, a year or so later, a different teacher told me to stop making a mess during an art class – I was excitedly flicking the paint from my brush onto my paper to make patterns. I'd never seen this done before, but I loved the unpredictability of the paint splatters. I didn't have a natural ability to draw and so this was, to me, a joyful way of expressing myself with paint. I was careful not to splash paint anywhere except on the paper, so I had used a certain amount of control.

Those two teachers probably had no idea that in the years to come, I would internalise their instructions (for that's how I perceived their words) to keep everything neat and tidy and ordered, and that this would manifest as not being able to fully embrace even the tiniest bit of chaos. Thankfully, it was a message that wasn't repeated often enough for it to develop into something like OCD, but it has affected how I do certain things. I try to keep everything ordered. I'd love to just throw my hair up any old way and let it look haphazard, but I always feel compelled to tuck away the stray wisps so that it looks more tidy. Not a big deal, granted, but my desire to stay within the lines and not make a mess means I'm not able to really let go and flow.

As a young adult, I went to college and studied for an art 'O' Level. I wanted to be just like my very artistic friend and create paintings that were abstract or just had soft edges, smudges, layers of blended colour making up beautiful landscapes or even portraits. Unfortunately, all my paintings consisted of blocks of colour, no perspective, and very little imagination, as I tried desperately to recreate exactly what I was seeing instead of interpreting what I was seeing through my own filters of creativity and emotion. Never one to give up easily, I tried again not so long ago and realised I still can't let go enough to allow myself the freedom of being creative in this way.

Enjoying your creativity, in whatever form you choose, is crucial to being able to release the limiting beliefs about your world and your place in it. This is partly why I love doing Inner Child work so much: I get to draw with my non-dominant hand, which gives me permission to let go of the need to draw something that resembles a perfect, almost photographic, reproduction.

Julia's Story

Julia self-harmed. She was struggling to feel positive about her life and feared many things. I asked her to draw a picture of how she saw herself and her situation. She drew a cage-like prison. Within the cage she drew a bleeding heart which was in shadow. In the top right-hand corner, she drew a key. When we talked about her drawing, she told me she felt she was a prisoner of her feelings. In talking about the key, she told me she felt she had the ability to free herself but didn't yet know how. This helped us plan our sessions together so that we addressed the issues that the drawing had identified.

DRAWING OR PAINTING

Having already discovered some of your own hidden limiting beliefs, you can do something similar for yourself. Just as with the Inner Child work, you will need paper – any size or colour (sugar paper is good or even lining paper used by decorators) - and something to make marks with: Julia used coloured pencils, but you could use pens, crayons, markers, chalk, pastels, or even charcoal. At a time when you know you won't be disturbed, take a few moments to sit quietly. Try to get in touch with an attitude, behaviour or belief that troubles you. As you bring it to mind, try to feel an emotion that might go with it. This may not be something you can easily label - like 'sadness', 'anger', or 'frustration' – but hopefully, something should stir within you. Now, using your chosen medium, begin to make marks on the paper. You might have an actual image in mind, or you might just get a sense of colour or shape. If you know a piece of music – or even part of a piece of music – that stirs strong feelings within you, then play this as you do the exercise.

I once took part in a creative expression workshop and one of the facilitators played music whilst we used pastels and A3 sugar paper to express how the music made us feel. The lyrics of the song she played were in French. I don't speak French so it helped enormously that I didn't understand what the singer was singing about: I could only tap into the emotion of her voice and the music. This was a great method of drawing that allowed me to let go of my need to make neat and tidy pictures. What I created was a series of over-lapping ellipses and circles – all soft curves which I then smudged with my fingers and coloured in, only this time my colouring filled the whole page and not just within the lines! Heaven!

COLLAGE

Another way of accessing the creative within you is by making collages. There are so many ways of doing this that listing them would take up a lot of space. Typing 'emotion collage' into a search engine set on 'image' can bring up some excellent examples of how to make and use collage as a way to express your feelings. A good place to start, however, is by cutting out images, words and phrases from magazines and sticking them onto card or paper. You could even add your own words or drawings. Try not to get caught up in reading the articles or it could take you a very long time to complete!

This is the same method used to create a vision or dream board. For this version, you consider all the wonderful things you would like to experience, own, or be, then find pictures or phrases to match and then stick them all onto a board, paper or card. I like to do these at New Year to help give me focus over the coming months.

WRITING

Writing is another form of creativity that can allow you to access your inner self and world. This could be in the form of Journaling, where you allow yourself the opportunity to explore how you feel and think about the world around you. A good exercise and a way of gaining a new perspective of your life, is to write it as if it were a fairy tale or story. As well as being cathartic, this can often be the basis of something you go on to weave into a work of fiction. A friend of mine, who is an actress with her own shadow and puppet theatre company, weaves elements of her childhood into her shows. Her intention when doing this isn't necessarily to expel her demons, but it would be impossible for her not to experience an emotional release when writing her material and most definitely when she's performing it. One of her shows, *Sleeping Beauty*, tells the story of a modern day princess who loses her way and finds herself in a tower block instead of a fairy tale castle, where she is pricked, not by a sewing needle, but by a syringe. The characters that populate her stories are adapted from real life, and her experiences with them are the starting point from which she then embellishes and exaggerates in order to create a fantasy world.

There's no reason why you couldn't begin with the reality of your past and use this as the basis for weaving a story that also combines fact with fiction. You could even create a whole new version of your past, one where you experience positive things or are able to express yourself freely and are empowered to follow your bliss. Again, many famous and successful writers litter their stories with experiences or people from their own lives that they then develop into adventures and fantasy.

Why not write your future as it will be once you have successfully freed yourself from your King Kong and limiting beliefs and you know who the real, authentic you, truly is? What dreams and aspirations would you have for yourself if you were free to choose from a place of self-belief and self-trust? What kind of character would you be in the new story of your life? By writing it you give yourself more chance of living it.

Go confidently in the direction of your dreams. Live the life you've dreamed.

Henry David Thoreau

Many poets and songwriters put their life experiences into their lyrics or poems. In fact, I would bet that the majority of them fill their work with feelings about their life, loves, fears, and joys. I can remember as a teenager doing the same thing. I never had any desire to be a songwriter or poet, but like most angst ridden teens, I felt compelled to use poetry as a means of self-expression. Who knows, perhaps this activity, as a form of escape from very difficult feelings and situations, helped me avoid the need to self-harm. If I felt unbearable pain and confusion, I just wrote about it. I never intended for anyone to see my writing and would cringe to show them to anyone now (they are very clumsy and filled with self-pity and hopelessness), but they certainly helped me to express myself in a safe and pleasurable way.

These are just a few ideas of how to use creativity to explore, connect or make friends with, or even eradicate your limiting beliefs. Part of their power comes from the sense of freedom and, in some cases, relaxation, that doing them can give you. Anything that allows you to access the deeper parts of you or even your Greater Self, is going to be beneficial in dealing with stuck emotions or attitudes. If they can help you gain insight into what's behind the beliefs and behaviours that are holding you back and possibly causing you discomfort and unhappiness, then it's well worth experimenting to see what works best for you.

Now that you're really getting the swing of identifying your Core Beliefs, and you, hopefully, have a better understanding of how to deal with them, the following chapter will go into more depth about something we touched on in Part 1: the role that being part of a family has on the creation of your Core Beliefs. Here, you will find exercises that have been designed to help you uncover the crucial aspects of family life that have gone into creating the adult you are today. Armed with this knowledge, you will be able to work out which aspects of your personality are yours, and which ones you inherited from your family.

Chapter 14

FINDING YOUR OWN KING KONG

Education commences at the mother's knee, and every word
spoken within hearsay of little children tends toward the
formation of character.

Hosea Ballou

Psychiatry enables us to correct our faults by confessing our
parents' shortcomings.

Dr. Laurence J Peter

When faced with the prospect of identifying and re-programming our Core Beliefs, it can feel like an overwhelming endeavour. Where to begin? Although this chapter may not necessarily be the first in how we work with Core Beliefs, their creation and understanding of how they operate and why, it's certainly the most important. When looking for clues as to how your Core Beliefs came into being, some may be so glaringly obvious that it doesn't take much detective work to uncover the place of origin, and thus be able to begin the healing work that might be necessary.

Unfortunately, some triggers may be disguised or hidden from view. Have you ever looked at a star-filled sky and saw, just on the periphery of your vision, a cluster of stars? Wanting to see this wondrous sight more clearly, you look directly at them, or where they seemed to be, only to find that they're just a shimmering haze. You look slightly off to the side of where they were and they appear again, on the edge of your vision, twinkling enticingly. So it is with the source of your Core Beliefs. You catch glimpses of them hovering on the edge of awareness, but when you try to look at them more closely, they seem to fade into the background. In order to see that cluster of stars you need to know where to look and use a telescope. In order to see the origin of your Core Beliefs you not only need to know where to look, but you also need to use all your awareness to bring them into focus.

When I designed my Core Beliefs workshop, I knew that family work would be key; after all, family is at the heart of where it all begins. You may know the details of who was born when, maybe even how your parents responded to the birth of each child, how you felt about the birth of each sibling that followed you (if this is the case), and of course, your family situation – struggling or thriving financially, educational opportunities and expectations, emotional responses to illness, grief, anger, etc. All of this is of utmost importance when examining Core Beliefs and their consequences. It would be easy perhaps to shrug off certain incidents and experiences as just the way it was (or how families are), or something that you just have to deal and/or put up with. As children, regardless of background, we learned to amass a certain amount of resilience. How else were we to survive if we didn't learn how to navigate the challenging waters of family life and social interactions?

I wanted participants on my workshops to be able to quickly access the clues to the origins of their Core Beliefs, and to be able to examine the evidence of what could be the reasons for their creation. I felt that one of the best ways to do this would be to use family photographs. These literal snapshots in time provide us with the clues that we need in order to gain insight into the nature of our childhood and the subsequent creation of

Core Beliefs. Group photographs of this kind open the door to buried, forgotten, disregarded, or unnoticed early family dynamics. Even if the various members were told to sit together in a certain position in readiness for the photograph, something of the nature of the inter-relationships between each person will seep through into their body language and so show up on the final image.

I appreciate that not everyone has the experience of growing up within a family. You may have spent most of your young life (if not all) in the care of children's services or even being moved from one foster family to another. You will have created a very complex set of Core Beliefs as a result of this lack of stability or sense of belonging. However you were treated within your formative years will naturally still have bearing on who you are now. For you, being passed from home to home, or having to struggle with the inconsistency of paid staff acting as your primary carers, will no doubt have instilled a feeling of being adrift, of not having an anchor. You're confidence in yourself and trust in others will be extremely low and fragile. Not having experienced anything like that, I can only imagine what it must have been like not to have roots, or to be able to share family memories with those you created them with. If you had foster carers, it may still be likely that you would have been included in group photographs, although I realise that this may not always be the case. For you, the following exercises will have to be greatly adapted in order for the questions to come even close enough to work.

FAMILY PHOTOGRAPHS EXERCISE

This exercise will give you vital information about your place within your family as a small child. You may choose to do this as a written exercise -

going through each of the questions below and writing your observations as you go through them - or you could record yourself speaking your observations and answers. This method might prove the most fruitful as you will not have to consider anything other than the thoughts and ideas as they come. Later, if you wish, you can always transcribe your recording.

If you have access to early family photographs, go through them and choose two - you can always go through the questions with other photos if you choose, but for now, just stick with two - you'll be surprised how much can be gleaned just from these. The first photograph should be the earliest one you can find of your family together. Ideally, this would be your immediate family – i.e. parents and siblings. It would be preferable to choose one in which you all posed for the camera: even better if there was a seating arrangement, however formal, as opposed to one where people were caught off guard, but it's not essential. It is, however, essential that you are in the photograph. The second photograph should be one of you and your family when you were a young teenager (12 - 14yrs). Again, a posed family photo is best, but not essential.

Some of these questions won't fit with your photograph or family situation, but answer as many as are applicable to the best of your knowledge. It's possible that you may not know the answer to some of the questions. Once you've completed as much of the exercise as you can, you can always ask other family members what they remember and fill in the gaps that way.

It's important that you give yourself time and space in which to do the exercise. When I have done this exercise as part of a workshop, participants have been amazed by the emotion that was brought up for them. Some realised that what they'd always felt about certain aspects of their childhood, but may have dismissed as faulty recollection or childhood exaggeration, was actually a true representation.

Questions to Ask Yourself

1. How old are you in the photograph?
2. Who else is in the photograph and what's the order according to age?
3. Who's missing and where would they fit in (again, according to age)?
4. Who took the photograph and why was it taken?
5. What's the story behind it?
6. What is the relevance of positioning?
7. What does it say about your place / experience within the family?
8. What feelings / memories does it bring up?
9. Who were you closest to (relationship), and why?
10. Who were you the most distant from and why?
11. What was your relationship with your mum, your dad, and your siblings like at that time?
12. What might your family have been experiencing at that time?
13. What other elements of the photograph are there that might be important, e.g. clothes, objects, décor, pets etc.
14. Any other information.

When I do this in my workshops, I get people to work in pairs. Each takes a turn in explaining who everyone is in the photograph. Something as simple as this can be quite revealing. You might find yourself using descriptions of family members that provide you with insight into how you felt or feel about them. If you are able to do this with a partner, be sure it's not a family member – you want to get a clear idea of *your* place in the family and doing it with a parent or sibling will only muddy the waters. If you're doing the exercise alone, you could record what you say rather than taking notes, that way your observations and feelings flow better and are more spontaneous. This method of examining family dynamics can be so productive that after doing this exercise in my workshop, people often continue to work at home with a friend on other family photographs.

FAMILY VALUES (RULES) EXERCISE

1. What was your family background? (Economic, religious, education, environment etc.)
2. What kind of things were you told about life? Yourself? The world?
3. What was your family creed? Moral code? Belief system (not necessarily religious)?
4. What did you learn about relationships? Money? Health? Faith? Education? Food? Loyalty? Trust? The future?
5. What was your health like as a child?
6. What significant incidents do you remember? How did you/others react?

Again, this can be a very enlightening exercise to do with or without a partner. For some, they realise that a lot of their values are not actually their own, created from their own experience, but are those of their parents or care givers. They may have adopted those beliefs and values as they grew up, never questioning if it's what they themselves hold true and whether or not those values serve them now as adults.

I can remember times when someone would 'rock the boat' or question the wisdom of those in authority and I would feel uncomfortable and want to make things right. It's only now that I realise that my discomfort came from an unchallenged belief that anyone with a 'posh' accent was automatically better than me and so commanded instant respect and compliance. This attitude to class wasn't of my own making, but came from my parents. They had grown up in a generation where only those with money were well educated. This in itself became an indication that they were more superior - they had more knowledge and so must obviously be more intelligent. As a result, I found myself kowtowing to anyone who didn't have a working-class accent. Not only that, but I truly believed that I would not achieve very much if I spoke with an accent that wasn't at least neutral.

These are not strictly Core Beliefs in the sense of those that I have been exploring up to now, but they are supporting, entrenched beliefs that have a profound effect on how I conduct my life and on how far I can allow myself to succeed in that life. My mother never once said (not that I can remember anyway), 'you are not as good as others who are better off than you', but I picked up that message loud and clear from countless, subtle messages - many of which were non-verbal. It's entirely possible that these unspoken commands went into the creation of what is known as 'imposter syndrome', and the fear of being discovered as a fake.

Feeling Like a Fraud

Have you ever felt like an imposter? You get a job, or start to get clients or make sales, and you wonder if anyone is going to suss you out for the pretender you are. You live in fear that someone will point a finger and ask you what you think you're doing acting like you belong in this environment, charging for your service, writing a book about Core

Beliefs!, or whatever area you find yourself trying to become established and successful in.

A couple of years after qualifying as therapists, my partner and I opened a therapy centre. We'd only been open a week or two when an acquaintance of mine - who had been in the local bistro having a bit of a liquid lunch with a friend - came in to say hello and have a look around. I was very proud of our new centre and was happy to show it off. As we talked about how things were going and about the therapies we offered, her friend asked me about my qualifications. I became a bit self-conscious having only recently completed my training as a therapist. I tried to justify why I believed I was adequately qualified to do this work with vulnerable people. This didn't satisfy this person, who continued to harangue me about my suitability (or lack of it) for the work I was charging money for, 'what gives *you* the right to think you can do that?'

My acquaintance, understandably very embarrassed at this unwarranted attack on my credentials and integrity, ushered her slightly inebriated and bitter friend out of the door. Seething with justifiable indignation and humiliation, I sat crying as I tore sheets of paper to shreds in outrage. *How dare she come into my therapy centre, uninvited, and tear into me about my credibility as a therapist when she didn't know the first thing about me?* Once I'd got my initial fury and righteous anger out of my system, I sat down and thought about what that distressing experience was trying to tell me.

I realised that I felt like an imposter, charging people when I hadn't been qualified for very long. I had struggled with putting a price on my therapeutic services ever since we'd opened our doors and advertised our centre. I almost felt like apologising to people for taking their money. Of course, a lot of therapists experience this dilemma when embarking on their career in the helping profession. Some struggle with the belief that in working with vulnerable people (particularly with counselling), and charging them for their time, they are in some way being mercenary. Unfortunately, that's an attitude held by a number of lay people too: thinking that counsellors are fleecing people in need and making money out of their misery. However, they would never apply this belief to say, a psychiatrist or osteopath. At the time of this incident, I was struggling with this commonly held attitude, too. And my friend's companion had provided me with the perfect opportunity to face this faulty, limiting belief. Something that stems in part from my Core Belief that I am not good enough, or worthy: that I should ask for permission to breathe and take up space...or to open a therapy centre and make a living from helping people.

This stranger that came and shook up my belief in myself also gave me a gift. I hadn't realised just how much guilt and doubt I had about my right to be what I wanted to be. If she hadn't come in and challenged me the way she did, I would have known I felt uncomfortable about charging people, but I wouldn't have known just how much it was connected to my sense of unworthiness. I would have continued squirming when prospective clients enquired about fees, fighting the urge to apologise for charging and wanting to explain how much it was costing us just to keep the centre open, and how we never made enough to pay the bills let alone ourselves. I would have continued to feel embarrassed as they wrote out a cheque, wishing someone else could take care of that side of things so that I wouldn't have to deal with the discomfort and misplaced shame.

With this woman's visit, I was forced to deal with my beliefs around my integrity and my right to earn a living from this kind of service without feeling guilty. This was an important step towards valuing not only what I do, but also myself. I had to acknowledge that just because I'd only recently qualified, didn't mean I wasn't a good therapist. I had a genuine interest in helping people deal with their pain and confusion - something I had years of life experience doing for myself (and many others) in an informal way. Everyone has to start somewhere. It isn't possible to be a great anything without experience - and that takes time.

When dealing with this kind of situation, it might help to imagine that if it were a dream, what would it be trying to tell you? If this woman had appeared in a dream, I would have instantly known that I had doubts about my skills and worthiness. I would have seen it as a message that I need to take myself and my abilities seriously: that I need to value myself and what I have to offer others. If it had been a dream, this woman would have represented the part of me that believed I was not worthy. She would have been drawing to my attention the fact that I believed I was an imposter, a charlatan out to con people into believing that I was good enough to be able to help them. On waking I wouldn't feel anger towards this woman. Why would I? I would recognise her as part of me, as an aspect of myself that was trying to help me understand something about myself that was holding me back, preventing me from becoming all that I could be. All that I have a right to be.

In the next Chapter, *Heal-thy Mind, Heal-thy Body*, we will look at the deeper meaning behind illness and what it might be trying to teach us. This isn't a 'how you can heal' kind of approach, but focuses instead on where and when the need for that particular set of symptoms arose.

Chapter 15

HEAL-THY MIND,

HEAL-THY BODY

You may dislike your illness, but it is a course you have decided upon. While you are convinced that the course is necessary, you will keep the symptoms.

Seth

The best day of your life is the one on which you decide your life is your own. No apologies or excuses. No-one to lean on, rely on, or blame. The gift is yours - it is an amazing journey - and you alone are responsible for the quality of it. This is the day your life really begins.

Bob Moawad

As we clear out the old, limiting beliefs passed to us by our parents, we can begin to take back control of our bodies. Our thoughts about health and wellness stem, in most part, from what we learned in childhood about disease, sickness, and the aging process. As I've already said, children learn very quickly how being ill gets them the attention they crave. In this chapter, we will also go into more detail about how emotions and negative attitudes are manifested in the body as illness and dis-ease as a way of bringing our attention to areas of our lives in need of greater examination and change.

In Chapter 8, *Out of the Shadows*, I looked at the possible pay-offs for being ill and how we need to recognise when our ill-health is also a means for us keeping ourselves small or to gain the attention we crave. I'll go into this in some more detail later in this chapter, but first I want to look at the role our family members play in causing us to develop or prolong ill-health, for it is within the family that we learn what it means to be well and ill.

Hopefully, when you were ill as a child, you would have received the tender loving care (TLC) you needed until you were well again. Someone would tuck you up in bed or on the sofa with something special to eat or drink: In my family, we were given 'chucky egg' – boiled egg roughly chopped and mixed with butter (or in our case, margarine). This, along with the kind and soft words and the gentle stroke of a cool hand on a hot brow, became the placebo that encouraged healing.

No wonder then, that when we are adults in need of some TLC, our inner child comes to the fore with an illness that puts us in bed or on the sofa under a duvet for a couple of days. Later in this chapter, you'll see how far my Inner Child was prepared to go to get some of that TLC. Unfortunately, other than giving me a much needed break from adult responsibility, the person I most needed that TLC from was no longer living. My Inner Child doesn't know this, of course, and so she will continue to resort to ill-health in some form or other in order to recapture the safety, love and solicitous attitude that would have been administered by my mother.

Do you know someone who is forever complaining about or listing their aches, pains and imagined diseases? This is an example of the Inner

Child desperate to recreate the atmosphere of their childhood home, longing for the comfort of a caring parent. Or perhaps they didn't receive the necessary care and compassion no matter how ill they became as a child and this is their attempt to get it now, as an adult. For many people suffering from hypochondriasis, there is a fear of illness, a fear that they will succumb to a terrible disease that could, and most probably will (in their mind), lead to a drawn-out, painful death if not treated promptly and correctly. These unfortunate people have a mistrust of life and their bodies. They will no doubt have grown up with one or more members of their family anxiously bemoaning their ill-health. They believe the world is not a safe place and that germs and diseases are rife and just waiting to pounce with impunity.

A famous example of this is Charles Darwin. His father was a strict, opinionated doctor who would lecture all-and-sundry on life, death, disease, and his patients. Although well, he wore a shawl to protect him from draughts - a practice taken up, not only by Darwin, but also by his children. Darwin was convinced he was in constant poor health, but his friends could see no visible sign of ill-health and put his endless complaining of sleepless nights down to hypochondria, prompting him to write in his diary: 'Everyone tells me that I look quite blooming and most think that I am shamming.' When ill, his children would beg not to be put in the sick room as their father's anxious hand-wringing over their demise was harder to bear than the illness itself.

It's interesting to note that in the medical journal, *Perspectives in Biology and Medicine*, Dr Jay Tepperman, commented that, '...Darwin used illness to insure himself the kind of privacy he needed in order to concentrate on his great [species] problem...' With the excuse of ill-health, Darwin was free to hide himself away in seclusion with his family, eschewing social events or even discussions with other scientists about his findings and theories. His largely imagined ill-health was the perfect pretext for avoiding participation in the world, thus providing him with the safety and security of the family home he experienced as a child.

I have already stated that I believe the *Ulcerative Colitis* was created within my body partly as a way of keeping me safe - if I'm too ill to go out, then I'm not visible, if I'm not visible, I can't be harmed - but why this particular means of keeping me invisible? There are any number of illnesses and physical or even psychological conditions that would serve that purpose equally well, if not better, than something that often flares up every 9 - 12 months. How come I didn't develop any one of those?

As I have previously explained, the part of the body that exhibits the illness or condition is a clue to this. In fact, it's not only a clue, it's a signpost on the emotional map of the body. If you remember, the language we use to describe a physical problem isn't just a figure of speech. For instance, someone can be a right *pain in the neck*, or something can make us *sick to our stomach*, or we can be *gutted* when something happens that we're disappointed about. We can even find something *hard to swallow* or it can be hard to *shoulder* responsibility.

All of these expressions are meant to indicate how we feel about a situation or person, but they are actually pointing us towards where in our body we manifest these difficulties or experiences. Unfortunately, we seldom pay much attention to these clues; and so, when we really do get a pain in the neck, or a sick stomach, we look to the medical - body as machine - model to try to fix it. Something has gone wrong or invaded our bodies and so a doctor (or other medical practitioner) must be consulted to figure out what it is and how best to get rid of it - pronto. Very rarely do people - especially doctors - consider asking, not just '*what's*' the matter with you, but *'who's'* the matter with you? Who is it that is giving you a pain in the neck? Who is it that is making you sick to your stomach? What situation is causing you to have pains in your shoulder?

Imagine how much our health system would change if that was the first thing we thought of when we developed a pain or an illness? We could still get help from orthodox medicine in serious or life-threatening situations, but we may prevent something from developing and really getting a grip if we were to consider what it was our body was trying to draw our attention to. Thankfully, there are several books that more than adequately cover this kind of 'mind-body' healing or 'meta-medicine'.

Unfortunately, I knew very little if anything about the body-mind connection when I developed *Ulcerative Colitis*. I'm not sure that even if I had understood what my body was trying to tell me I would have been able to staunch its progress. Something as pervasive as bowel disease does not come overnight or even over a few days or weeks: this kind of thing can be years in the making. As such, it can be years in the healing (or, very rarely, it can happen in an instant).

In the years since I began my search for a mind-body connection to the *Colitis*, I have discovered many things about myself that I didn't know before: things I might never have come to know about had I not had this illness. In, *Why People Don't Heal and How They Can*, Caroline Myss talks about illness emerging to 'physically guide us onto a path of insight and learning upon which we would never have set foot.' In learning about the possible causes of my developing *Ulcerative Colitis*, I learned about how I operate in the world and relationships. I learned how I would use illness as a means to getting attention (firstly from my mother), how it brought the reward of sympathy from others, how it got me out of doing things I didn't want to do: all the things I spoke of in Chapter 8, '*Out of the Shadows*'.

Part of the path to healing for me has involved learning to let go of illness as a dishonest means of getting the attention or easy time free of responsibility that I often crave. I can remember actually being excited at the prospect of going into hospital as it meant I would be able to relinquish responsibility for pretty much everything - being a mother, a wife, a wage earner, even a strong, capable woman. I was tired of carrying so much responsibility, and being in hospital meant I didn't have to make any decisions about life or even my treatment - it was all taken care of.

As I had medical insurance that paid out for each day I was in hospital, it was even more of a bonus! As soon as I realised what a draw hospitalisation was for me, I set about ensuring I had those needs met in other ways. I learned to say I needed a break or to be looked after by my husband. I'm not saying I solved it all in one fell swoop, but I've never spent another day in hospital since.

Energy in Motion

It's hard to believe that a small child can feel deep anger at their treatment by others. So often they withdraw or act out in ways that don't seem connected to the inner rage they may be feeling towards another person. They grow up to become difficult teenagers, always getting into trouble, never able to behave appropriately, seemingly angry at everyone in authority. It was the anger I felt as a four year old child that was never acknowledged or expressed that eventually contributed to the development of *Ulcerative Colitis*. It was the anger I continued to supress growing up as a teenager that caused it to be so severe, and made it difficult for me to heal.

When we experience anger that we deny or disallow it has to go somewhere. Emotion is, after all, e-motion - energy in motion - and that energy needs to be healthily felt and expressed in order for it to complete its circuit and not get stuck somewhere in the body (anger is usually stored in the gut).

Dawn's Story

Dawn is struggling to overcome Bulimia. As I have already alluded, eating disorders are, in part, connected to control. Controlling unexpressed anger can also be a contributing factor. For Dawn, who had recently separated from her fiancé, it was hard for her to express anger at the way she had been treated by her ex. Whenever we broached the subject and I asked how she felt about certain aspects of that painful experience, she would quietly say that she felt, 'a bit peeved'. This hardly seemed appropriate considering the way in which her ex had handled the separation. It took a lot of deep breaths and stammering before Dawn could admit, even to herself, that she felt anger towards her ex. Like me (and lots of women, I suspect), Dawn was too busy understanding and appreciating her ex's motives to be able to get even close to the anger she really felt towards him and her situation. (It seems Dawn couldn't remember seeing her mum angry, and realised that 'peeved' was the word she would use to describe anger.)

What I discovered about my own way of handling unpleasant emotions - particularly anger - is not to acknowledge it in the moment, or sometimes not at all. This means that it could be days after an upsetting incident before I realised that I was actually annoyed about what was said or done. At the time, I would acquiesce and even help the other person to feel better or that it's ok to do or say the things that I later realised were not really acceptable.

What I (and people like Dawn), was effectively doing in these situations - like when being told something unpleasant or difficult - was bypassing my heart. My head would nod and agree with the reasons and excuses, and I would concur that it's a sensible, reasonable thing to do and that it's ok to do it. In these kinds of situations I wasn't even aware at the time that I should be angry or indignant: I was far too busy wanting to look after the person, making sure they were ok, to even consider that it might have been upsetting for me. There would be a delay in my emotions and my body making a connection. Everything would take place in my head, reasoned out, weighed up and measured in an, oh so reasonable and easy-going manner.

Thanks to my Core Belief work, this is now something I am able to recognise and acknowledge more readily. Nowadays, when I am on the receiving end of something unpleasant, I'm more and more able to *feel* it in the moment (or very soon after) and react appropriately. In this way, I avoid the physical repercussions of not being congruent about how I feel in upsetting situations and issues.

In the past, that righteous anger went straight to my gut, where I stored it up with all the other unexpressed anger and resentment. Consequently, I developed a very inflamed and irritated colon which struggled to deal with all the negative emotion I was holding on to. Understanding the body-mind connection, I endeavoured to pinpoint the times of my life when I have felt anger that wasn't acknowledged or expressed at the time: beginning with the rape I experienced when I was four.

As a spiritual person who believes that we all serve a purpose in each other's lives, I at first tried to feel gratitude and then compassion for the man who raped me. He was, after all, possibly struggling with learning difficulties (although I only have my mother's interpretation of his behaviour), which may have affected his ability to distinguish between the right and wrong way to express love for another person, particularly a child. As a spiritual being, he was working through his own learning and in some way that was connected with mine (perhaps we had a 'soul contract' to be the provider of this experience in our lives?). But there is always free will, his actions weren't pre-determined and he didn't *have* to carry out his urges in that way - something he will have to face and deal with when he reviews this physical life once he has passed.

I, in some ways foolishly, tried to do 'the right thing' spiritually by forgiving this man for what he did to me. Forgiveness is an incredibly important aspect of living a healthy, happy life and it's something we would do well to cultivate in our lives. And yet, it needs to come *after* acknowledgement of our pain, disappointment, anger, resentment or whatever other emotion we may feel towards another for the part they played in something that deeply affected us. If we try to jump straight to forgiveness because we believe that's the spiritual or healthy thing to do, we're denying our true feelings and pushing them deep within where they will fester and cause us physical problems in the long run. Better to do all the shouting, crying, lamenting and even hating first, that way you're then free to feel your way to forgiveness and letting the pain go.

I still believe that ultimately the man that raped me played a part in my learning as I did in his, but what was foolish was the fact that I bypassed, once again, the righteous anger and rage I should have felt at being abused in such a way before I went on to finding forgiveness. He had no right to violate my young and fragile body. He had no right to force me into what belongs in the adult world of sex, for his own pleasure. I had a right to be angry with him for hurting me and betraying the trust I had in him. But at four, there wasn't any precedent for such anger and rage. No-one told me that what I might have been feeling *was* anger, or anything else, for that matter. If I did do or say anything at that time that alluded to my true feelings, I'm sure, being unable to handle their own pain, my family would have hushed me up or quickly changed the subject.

In being too quick to forgive others their weaknesses and shortcomings, we disallow our own totally acceptable feelings of hurt and confusion. For me, this was the most difficult part of accessing the anger within: allowing myself to feel the anger towards my parents - my father in particular - for not protecting me. Reason and logic dictates that there was absolutely nothing he could have done to prevent what happened. As far as he and my mother were concerned, I was playing happily with a group of friends on the green right outside our home. But logic and/or reason will not have even been on my four year old radar. All that I would have known is that my daddy (or mummy) didn't come to save me.

I didn't face or acknowledge my anger towards my dad until I came to do more inner work on anger towards the man who raped me. I was punching the stuffing out of a large cushion, calling him for everything for doing what he did to me. Suddenly, in the midst of this, I heard myself shouting at my dad for not protecting me. For a brief moment I hesitated: surely I couldn't reasonably blame my father for not doing something to stop him? But then I went with it and gave the cushion a few more punches for my dad's involvement. When I was exhausted from all the shouting, punching and crying, I lay on the floor and hugged my (four year old) self and told her she was safe and that I would protect her. I then fell asleep and woke an hour or so later feeling lighter and more at ease than I had been when I started.

Are You Your Illness?

As well as a means to gain attention and affection, ill-health can also be a way for us to avoid those things that cause us anxiety or upset. As we have seen in earlier chapters, even something like an addiction can be a way for us to keep ourselves small and taken care of. Just as we might use our health as a way of getting what we need, we may even use events from our past for the same purpose.

I have met people who will play on a traumatic or difficult past experience whenever they find themselves in a situation where they are likely to be taken to task or expected to do something they would rather not do. This, '*woundology*', (as Caroline Myss refers it), is reflected in the need to be with others who speak the same language (about illness or abuse, for instance), and share the same mind-set and behaviours. These are people who define themselves by their emotional and/or health wounds. They have invested so much of themselves in their health condition or past trauma that they find it very difficult to let it go for fear of finding themselves alone and without the means to evoke a sympathetic response from others.

It is important that you make yourself familiar with just how far you define yourself around your condition or history. You have to uncover the pay-offs and benefits of being stuck in your illness or traumatic experience and then decide if you are ready to let it go and move on into a new way of being. So much illness reappears and spreads to other parts of the body because we have not taken the time or the trouble to truly get to know the reason for its existence and how we will operate once we are free of it. As you peel back the layers of old, out-dated beliefs about yourself and the world, you will find yourself moving forward into a new way of being, a way of health and vitality. It is possible - it just might take a lot of time and trouble, but it's worth the effort. You are worth the effort. If you don't believe that then you might as well add extra years to your sentence of misery.

Imagine you are your own bank. Instead of depositing money into your self-bank, you deposit self-love in the form of self-esteem, self-worth and self-value. It is this currency that adds to your wealth of health, happiness and success. Others can also add to your abundance account in the form of interest, by giving you positive praise and support and by recognising your worth. But you must first have something to add interest to. You must begin the process of self-love in order to grow your abundance account - and by abundance I mean in all things, not just money. You do not need others' approval or acceptance in order to be well and happy. By letting go of the need to have sympathy, attention or an excuse to say no, you let go of illness and staying small, and welcome in the ability to be a whole human being.

You now have the means and the awareness at your disposal to be able to seek out your own Core Beliefs and to begin the process of eliminating those that do not serve you from your life. In Part 3, I use examples from the film world to give yet another possible means of developing your skills at recognising the creation of Core Beliefs and how they operate. This may be a more whimsical approach to Core Beliefs, but you will still learn a lot from this section of the book and from the films discussed. On top of that, it's good practice!

PART THREE

CELLULAR TO CELLULOID

Chapter 16

ALL THE WORLD'S A STAGE

Life's like a play: it's not the length, but the excellence of the
acting that matters.

Lucius Annaeus Seneca

One good thing about acting in film is that it's good therapy.

Denzel Washington

Building on the story of King Kong as a way of demonstrating how and why Core Beliefs exist, this part of the book continues to illustrate the creation and influence of Core Beliefs and the parts that carry out those beliefs, by examining them in action in various films. I have chosen movies from a variety of eras and genres; and, in choosing them, have tried to present a cross-section of society, background, philosophy and education both fictional and biographical. To this end, you will encounter characters rich and poor, old and young, well educated and not so well educated. The only thing they might have in common is that they were part of a family – even if that family comprised only one parent. In other words, their development as children was shaped, in most part, by the influence of those closest to them – an experience every single one of us shares.

In searching for appropriate films, I tried to find those that adequately demonstrate the roots of the main characters' Core Beliefs. So for the majority of them, we will be able to get an insight into their childhood – even if only through flashbacks or dialogue, as in *Prince of Tides*. I also didn't want to only use films in which key characters portrayed glaringly obvious Core Belief traits that were created out of equally obvious traumatic experiences.

For obvious reasons, I wanted to use films in which we see the journey of Core Beliefs from their creation right through to manifestation or revelation. In choosing these particular movies, I felt I would be able to illustrate more comprehensively just how Core Beliefs can and do affect the lives of the main characters as adults. This will hopefully give you a better understanding of how your limiting Core Beliefs might be affecting you in your life, and so provide you with a starting point for dealing with them.

And so, within each of the following chapters, I will explore various films, the main character's journey to adulthood, and the issues they face as a result of the Core Beliefs set up in childhood. I will give a basic story outline and then move on to identifying the Core Beliefs in operation and linking them to the experience, repeated messages, family values etc., that created them. We will then explore their adult behaviour in light of this new awareness and see for ourselves how those Core Beliefs are influencing them almost on a daily basis – certainly at times of great stress, pressure or expectation.

Not all of the movies I've used are fictional. In order to make this concept as accessible as possible, I have also included examples from real life, as in the case of Howard Hughes (*The Aviator*) and Margaret Thatcher (*Margaret* and *The Iron Lady*). Some of the examples are more obvious than others, but I have tried to avoid those that scream 'Here comes a Core Belief!' mainly because, for most people, they are not always easy to spot: some will hit you over the head and some will sneak in round the back, but they will be there. Once you've had practice, you will be able to see Core Beliefs in operation from a mile off. You might not be able to determine why it was set up in the first place, but you will know it's there and what its M.O. is (*modus operandi* – Latin, meaning method, a way of doing something).

What would really help is if you didn't just read about these films, but actually took the time to watch them. That way you can see the progression for yourself. The understanding might even be more powerful this way for you; especially if, like me, you are a visual person. You might want to even watch the films before reading about them to see how many Core Beliefs you can identify and how they are linked to what created them, i.e. the relevant experience. Whichever way you decide to go about it, even if that means not watching the films (or only some of them), you can gain just as much insight about Core Beliefs by reading about the films as by watching them. It makes no difference.

With the exception of the first film to be discussed, *The Aviator*, and the last, *The Kid*, I've no particular reason for choosing the order of the films. I've chosen the biopic on Howard Hughes as an opening simply because it ties in with Jean and her development of and struggle with OCD. These two people couldn't be any further apart in almost every aspect of their lives, and yet, they were and are both victims of their beliefs – beliefs that were given to them by a parent or parents. As we shall see, they share a common thread – it is the fearful child within that dictated (and for Jean, still does dictate) the adult they became. I chose *The Kid* (not to be confused with the Charlie Chaplin film of the same name), because it's light-hearted and fun to watch – and I prefer to end the book on a smile!

Chapter 17

FEAR OF BEING VULNERABLE

As human beings, our greatness lies not so much in being able
to remake the world - that is the myth of the atomic age - as in
being able to remake ourselves.

Mahatma Gandhi

Life isn't about finding yourself. Life is about creating
yourself.

George Bernard Shaw

THE AVIATOR (2004)
Director: Martin Scorsese
Writer: John Logan

The Aviator is based on the mid-section of Howard Hughes' life: the period
covering his early 20's to his late 40's. As with all films, which usually last
anywhere between 90 – 120 minutes, episodes in people's lives are chosen
for their capacity to show significant developments in the story, depth of
emotion, integral relationships, and important decisions and their
repercussions. This is another reason why I've chosen to use films as a
medium for the exploration of Core Beliefs. Like a laser beam, films focus
the light of awareness on noteworthy moments from the story they are

depicting, and highlight those salient - often crucial - events that might otherwise be missed among the myriad of life experiences. When writing a biography, the author must choose pertinent moments from their subject's life, and condense what might span decades into something that is concise, readable, and that keeps the readers' interest. If they were to include every conversation, every trip, every nuance of every relationship, etc. the book or film would not only take a lifetime to write, but another to read or watch: within it we would lose the thread of the subject's journey.

And so, in *The Aviator*, we see a snapshot of Howard Hughes' life, loves, successes and failures. More importantly for us, we see the creation of Core Beliefs, and watch as they destroy one of the richest men to have lived.

The film centres on Hughes' life from the late 1920s to 1947, during which time he became a successful film producer and an aviation magnate while simultaneously growing more unstable due to severe Obsessive Compulsive Disorder. The opening scene is of Howard Hughes at the age of about 8yrs old, standing in a bath in front of a roaring fire in a sumptuously decorated and furnished room. Kneeling before him is his doting mother, Allene. She slowly washes her son's body; and, as she does so, she gets him to spell the word 'quarantine', over and over.

I've not read any of the many biographies written about the world's most famous recluse, so I don't know for certain if he ever spoke of his mother bathing him in such a way. What I do know from the research I have done, is that she was consumed with an intense fear for his health and safety, and so most likely lavished far too much attention on him – as many parents of an only child are wont to do. I am an avid film-watcher, and have an MA in Screenwriting, so I also know that writers and film makers will exaggerate an incident to make a point. They need the viewer to understand something as quickly and as clearly as possible. This image of Hughes' mother bathing her naked son as he repeats the word 'quarantine', lets us know that this is where his troubles began. In our terms, this is the kind of experience that created his Core Beliefs, and the filmmakers really bring this point home when his mother asks, 'Do you know what the world will do to you? You're not safe.'

This is why films are so good at illustrating the creation of Core Beliefs. They reduce what probably took several years of warnings – both verbal and non-verbal – to one, short scene. Allene was terrified of her son's exposure to germs, and the possibility that he would catch Typhus or Cholera (diseases that were prevalent at that time).

The Film – The Story

When making the First World War film, *Hell's Angels*, Hughes' excessive attention to detail and his determination to make it as realistic as possible, meant that it took him over three years to complete. Constantly striving for perfection and unhappy with the tiniest of details not being to his liking, Hughes made and re-made what was (until 1939 and the making of *Gone with the Wind*), the most expensive film ever made. As with the planes in his infamous aerial acrobatics, the budget climbed higher and higher as he assembled the largest private air force in history - close to 150 planes - shooting and reshooting dogfights and bombing sequences. Three pilots died; and so, understandably, some pilots refused to re-do the scenes for fear of their lives, leaving Hughes with no option but to do some of the flying himself. Sound was invented towards the end of shooting, causing Hughes to re-make it with Jean Harlow replacing the lead actress, who was Norwegian and whose accent was now at odds with her character.

In *The Aviator*, we see Hughes develop a relationship with Katherine Hepburn who later dumps him for Spencer Tracy. He then takes up with a fifteen year old girl, who is later supplanted by Ava Gardner. This is apparently only a taste of his romantic liaisons, which allegedly included affairs with both men and women. In what we are shown of his relationships in the film, he is controlling, paranoid and obsessive, going so far as to bug Ava Gardners' bedroom and telephones.

Hughes had major dealings with the Army Air Forces during the Second World War, and was contracted to build an XF-11 reconnaissance aircraft and the enormous troop transporter, "Spruce Goose" flying boat. Over these years, Hughes' OCD worsens, characterised by his repetition of phrases and words, his increasing fear of germs, and his repulsion of anything tarnished, or in some way, imperfect. (Unhappy with how fabric apparently bunched up along the seam of one of Jane Russell's blouses, he wrote a detailed memorandum to the film crew explaining how it should be fixed.) During a test flight of the XF-11, he pushes it beyond its limits and one of the engines malfunctions, causing the aircraft to crash; he is severely injured and takes months to recover.

Through his inability to produce the Spruce Goose on time, he is accused of war profiteering and his house is searched by the FBI for incriminating evidence. Watching investigators handling his possessions and tracking dirt everywhere, Hughes experiences a major psychological trauma and he sinks into a deep depression, shuts himself away in his screening room and grows detached from reality.

Having eventually come through this particular self-imposed 'quarantine', Hughes successfully test flies the flying boat – something so huge, no-one believes it could possibly fly. This achievement seems to have freed him from his inner demons, but he quickly relapses after seeing strange men, who may not be real, wearing germ-resistant suits. He begins repeating the phrase "the way of the future" over and over in an effort to restore calm to his anxious thoughts. Hughes has a flashback to scenes from his boyhood: being washed by his mother, resolving to fly the fastest aircraft ever built, to make the biggest movies ever, and become the richest man in the world.

There were other aspects of his life portrayed in the film – his owning the majority interest in Transcontinental & Western Air (TWA), the predecessor to Trans World Airlines; his rivalry with Juan Trippe, chairman of the board of Pan American World Airways (Pan Am), and his determination not to let Hughes challenge his company's success; Trippe getting his friend, Senator Owen Brewster, to introduce the Commercial Airline Bill, which would give Pan Am a monopoly on international air travel; and Hughes appearing before Brewster at the Senate Committee to answer allegations of war profiteering – but these are unnecessary details in a book about Core Beliefs and their creation.

Despite all of the obvious negative outcomes of Hughes' Core Beliefs, there are positive aspects to them, too. Hughes was a successful businessman, entrepreneur, industrialist, film maker and aviator. He certainly had vision and the confidence (arrogance?) and determination to realise his dreams. But who is to say that coming from such a wealthy family in America, where freedom includes the opportunity for prosperity and success and an upward social mobility achieved through hard work, he wouldn't have achieved such success anyway? However, if our parents create within us a set of ideals that produce the adult we become then it's easy to see how positive and negative influences can be intertwined.

Childhood – The Setting

Allene Hughes was so consumed by fear for her son's health that she went to extraordinary lengths to protect him from coming into contact with anyone who might be contaminated. To this end, she would check him every day for diseases, and was overly cautious about what he ate. This concern extended to her paying excessive attention to his teeth and his bowels. These fears and her ever watchful 'house arrest', caused Hughes to become an introvert from an early age: neighbours recalled often seeing the solitary boy riding his bike in circles around the driveway of the family home. He was discouraged from making friends for fear they were germ carriers, thus giving him the excuse to avoid social contact and subsequently to avoid pressure likely to be created by that contact. Unable to gain assurance that their son would not contract polio at summer camp, Hughes was kept home. He attended camp the next year, but the following year he avoided attendance by complaining of headaches and bad dreams: possibly an example of *Avoidant Personality Disorder* - a means of escaping social pressures by using the excuse of illness.

As an adolescent, Hughes was paralysed for several months and unable to walk, the cause of which was never diagnosed and so had no physical basis. The paralysis gradually disappeared and was undoubtedly an early manifestation of what became a lifelong pattern of withdrawing in times of stress. Shortly after this episode, when Hughes was 16 years old, his beloved mother passed away, followed by his father's sudden death less than two years later. His parents had been his world; and Hughes, understandably, went into a deep depression. At the age of only 18 years, the young adult Hughes inherited 75% of his father's million-dollar estate.

The Core Beliefs – The Creation

With his mother's constant attention to and concern for his health and wellbeing, it's not surprising that Howard Hughes went on to develop such crippling OCD. As we know, a young child's brain is like a sponge, soaking up everything around it. If it sees or hears something often enough, or if there is strong enough emotion attached to an event, it is likely to create an imprint on the brain. This imprint will remain in place unless, over time, the words and actions that created it are sufficiently diminished in frequency and intensity so as to render the experience almost non-existent. Or, in later years, more positive, life-affirming messages are communicated, demonstrated and validated on a regular basis.

Hughes' limiting and negative beliefs were reinforced over and over, both verbally (which includes not only the vocabulary used, but the intonation and emotional intensity), and non-verbally (frowns, face screwed up in disgust or repulsion, etc.). What his mother succeeded in doing was creating in Hughes' mind a world beyond the safety of their home that was filled with danger and disease; and that ultimately, we have no effective defence against germs.

As with Jean in our earlier example, Hughes may have been able to keep his OCD under relative control as long as his mother (primarily) and father (who was often absent from the family home and so would not have had much influence or input into the rearing of his son) were around to keep him safe and protected. Once his precious mother died, what to him was his first line of defence also disappeared. Who would watch out for him now and protect him from those unseen forces that have the capability of wiping out, not only individuals, but entire communities? How would he safely navigate his way through life without his mother's relentless vigilance? Unable to contain his fears or have them alleviated by his mother, Hughes went on to develop the OCD that would eventually contribute to his death.

Adulthood – The Consequences

By the time Hughes was 25 years old, he was already displaying obvious signs of mental illness. Close friends described how he was obsessed with the size of peas and would use a special fork to sort them and arrange them by size on his plate. As well as the memo about fixing Jane Russell's costume, he once wrote a staff manual on how to open a tin of peaches – including directions for removing the label, scrubbing the can down to the bare metal, washing it again and pouring the contents into a bowl without touching the bowl.

He would spend months at a time never leaving his darkened screening room. His diet at those times would consist of chocolate, chicken and milk. He would urinate into empty bottles and containers, which he kept in the room with him. He was surrounded by boxes of tissues which he would continuously stack and re-arrange. Throughout those periods, he would sit naked in his chair – often with tissues or a pink napkin over his genitals – watching hours and hours of films.

Ironically, for someone with an extreme fear of germs such as Hughes displayed, in the final years of his life he neglected his hygiene to the point where he never washed, brushed his teeth or cut his hair or nails. This was possibly due to the fact that he had developed another psychological condition, Allodynia – extreme pain on being touched. Even his staff was required to wash their hands multiple times and cover them with tissues when serving his food. According to Raymond D. Fowler, the man assigned to conduct a psychological autopsy on Hughes, 'he didn't believe germs could come from him, just from the outside.'

The influences in Hughes' childhood affected his adult life in profound ways – of that there is no doubt. As a result of what his ex-wife described as 'smother love', Hughes seemed to have developed – amongst other things - Avoidant Personality Disorder. Those who suffer from this disorder often consider themselves to be socially inept and avoid social interaction for fear of being ridiculed, humiliated, rejected or disliked. His overly-close relationship with his mother may also have led to his obvious misogynistic attitude toward women.

When Howard Hughes died in 1976, his body was in such a deteriorated state of health, the FBI had to resort to identifying him by his fingerprints. He was severely malnourished, and his hair, beard, finger and toe nails had grown grossly long. Due to several serious air crashes, he was in constant pain and had been addicted to codeine for most of his adult life. He would administer pain killers intravenously; and, after his death, X-rays revealed broken-off hypodermic needles in his arms.

Hughes' Core Beliefs were incredibly powerful and deeply entrenched in his psyche. However, as with all Core Beliefs, his fears of contamination by germs were not his own, but those imposed by the dissemination of, and exposure to, his mother's Core Beliefs, many of which she would have inherited from her family. By inherited, I do not mean a genetic inheritance, but one that is acquired. Despite the commonly held doctrine that many mental health professionals ascribe to, as far as I know, no-one has discovered the gene for OCD; and, in my opinion, they never will. I believe these habits and behaviours are learned on the laps and in the constant company of similarly afflicted parents and care-givers.

I also believe that if you can learn something, then you can un-learn it. Of course, it will take longer to re-programme and/or remove the limiting beliefs and habits that constitute something as insidious as OCD; but, with the right approach, it can be done.

Chapter 18

FEAR OF LOVE AND ADULTHOOD

*For a long time I was scared I'd find out I was like my
mother.*

Marilyn Monroe

*Nothing has a stronger influence psychologically on their
environment, and especially on their children, than the
unlived lives of the parents.*

Carl Jung

A TASTE OF HONEY (1961)
Director: Tony Richardson
Writer: Shelagh Delaney

Written in ten days by working-class teenager Shelagh Delaney, '*A Taste
of Honey*', epitomises the mother/daughter relationship in all its
complexities and diverse nuances. Delaney, dissatisfied with contemporary
theatre - which at that time gave only a middle-class perspective on life -
felt that she could write something that resonated with people from her
own background with more realistic dialogue than could be found in such
plays as *Variations on a Theme* by Terence Rattigan, which was currently
being staged. She also felt that Rattigan's work showed, 'insensitivity...to

198

homosexuals'. '*A Taste of Honey*' was a huge hit, winning several awards as a play and as a film and became one of the defining plays of 1950s working-class and feminist cultural movements.

Delaney was born in 1939 in Salford, England. She attended five different schools from the age of 5 to 9yrs. She failed the 11+ - an exam taken by some students in their last year of primary education, governing admission to various types of secondary school – and was subsequently sent to a Secondary Modern. At the age of fifteen, she was transferred to a Grammar school, where she learned (to her surprise) that she knew more than most of the other pupils.

In the short documentary, '*Shelagh Delaney's Salford*' (a *Monitor* film for the BBC by Ken Russell) she says that, 'No matter where I am, no matter what I do, I shall always be a restless person.' She goes on to talk about travelling abroad and how she would get so homesick for England and Salford, that she would have to fight the urge to return. However, once home in Salford, she would soon become restless and want to be on the move again. Are these hints at her Core Beliefs in action?

The Story

The story centres around Jo, a fifteen year old girl from Salford. She lives with her mother, Helen and they move around a lot, often doing 'moonlight flits' to avoid paying back-rent. It's clear from the start that Jo and her mother have a difficult relationship; which is reflected in the many squabbles and arguments they have, and in the fact that Helen acts as if she doesn't want Jo in her life. Straight away we can see that Jo is clearly resentful of her mother. The opening scene has them on the move to a new flat: a flat that Jo has never seen until they move in. When she tells her mother that she doesn't like it, Helen responds with, 'When I find us somewhere to live I have to consider something far more important than your feelings...the rent. It's all I can afford.' It's clear from this statement that Helen doesn't consider Jo's feelings or opinions to be important enough to be taken into account. The flat has a sitting room-cum-kitchen and one tiny bedroom; which means Jo has to share the bed with her mother.

Jo and Helen act more like peers than mother and daughter, with Jo calling her mother by her name. At times it's hard to tell who is the adult and who is the child. Jo is quite serious and mostly dresses older than her years, often reprimanding her mother for her immature behaviour and attitude to life. Helen dresses like someone 20 years younger and often behaves impulsively, and like a petulant teenager who can't get her own way - very '*Ab Fab*' and Jennifer Saunders, but without the humour. Helen even goes so far as to tell Jo, 'It's your life, run it your own way. I've got enough to do looking after myself.'

We are soon introduced to Peter, Helen's love interest and Jo's rival for her mother's affection and attention. He is sexually demanding of Helen - who is eight years older than he is – but she seems disinterested in him until he proposes to her, promising to move her into a new house with him: Jo is not included in this future arrangement.

Jo soon meets Jimmy, a black sailor whose ship is on a stop-over at the local shipyard. Her brief relationship with him epitomises all that she wants from her mother – tenderness, affection and attention. They have fun together, laughing and joking, not taking life too seriously. He proposes to her, and actually gives her a ring. As he pulls the box out of his pocket, he also pulls out a toy car. Jo likes the ring but is more interested in the car, playing with it as a child might. She insists that her mother would not disapprove of her having a relationship with a black man. But later in the play, when Jo eventually tells her mother of her relationship with Jimmy, Helen is more scandalised by his colour - perhaps highlighting the discrepancy in what Jo believes of her mother and what is actually true - than by the fact that he is a sailor and so will be more than likely using Jo for what he can get. Their affair is short, possibly only spanning a few weeks, and when Jimmy tells her that he is going off on a six-month tour of duty, Jo is pragmatic about his leaving. She knows he won't come back even though he is genuinely sincere when he says he will.

Jo leaves school, where she was the class joker, and gets a part-time job in a shoe shop. She has aspirations to be an artist: something that her mother, surprisingly, supports and encourages. It's at the shop that Jo meets Geoff. They become close friends and spend a lot of time together. With her mother living with Peter, whom she married (Jo was not invited to the wedding), Jo moves into her own flat. Before long, Geoff moves in with her and begins to look after Jo in a way she's never been looked after by her mother. He is caring and attentive towards her and even decorates the flat. Early on in this arrangement it becomes clear that Geoff is gay. When Jo announces she is pregnant (to Jimmy), he begins making baby clothes. He is so caught up in his fantasy of a home and family that he proposes to Jo. She rejects him telling him that there isn't a 'marrying love between us, thank God!'

In her relationship with Geoff, Jo is able to derive a sense of security from the fact that he is gay and so is not sexually attracted to her. He is safe to be with, almost mothering her in his care and attention. Unfortunately, it's his sensitivity and gentle nature that prevents him from standing up to Helen when she returns on the scene and begins to bully him out of the flat. Peter has thrown Helen over for another woman and she now needs somewhere to live. She is threatened by Jo's relationship with Geoff and makes it clear that he is not needed by Jo, or wanted by her. Geoff allows himself to be ousted from the flat when Helen moves in: there isn't room for two mothers in Jo's life, even if one is a gay man and the other a flibbertigibbet of a woman with loose morals and without a trace of maternal instinct.

Childhood – The Setting

We don't see anything of Jo's early years in the play. However, there's no doubt from her interactions with the other characters (particularly her mother), and the lifestyle they have, that she didn't have any secure or nurturing attachments. With her mother's constant need to escape and hide from irate landlords, Jo will never have experienced a stable, consistent home life. This rootlessness will have also been mirrored in the comings and goings of the men in her life. She learns that her mother's husband was not actually her father, and that her father – who was 'retarded' - divorced Helen when she became pregnant with Jo.

Given the comments made by Helen about motherhood, such as: 'Bearing a child doesn't put you under any obligation to it', it's entirely probable that she coached Jo to call her Helen and not Mum – a title that would have constantly reminded her of her responsibility and lack of freedom. When speaking to Peter about his desire to marry Helen, Jo refers to her as 'my old woman', indicating that they never had a conventional mother/daughter relationship. It's as if to Helen, Jo only really exists in a physical way, an inconvenient encumbrance that has to be worked around, controlled and endured in her life rather than included, considered or involved in any meaningful way.

Jo shares a bed with her mother/rival/peer, and with a teddy. This implies that there is an aspect of her development that has been frozen in time. The teddy and playing with the toy car, indicate the child within that has never been able to experience that stage in her life. Jo has not been able to grow through and out of childhood and into the next developmental stage – adolescence. She is a young adult, but emotionally she is still a little girl starved of her mother's affection. When out on a trip with her mother and Peter (Helen, in a rare display of concern fuelled by guilt, invites Jo along despite Peter's displeasure), Jo is openly hostile towards Peter. When he comments that she doesn't like her mother very much, Jo responds with, 'Well, she doesn't much care for me.' Peter responds by calling her a 'jealous little cat', to which Helen retorts quite without conscious awareness of the implications, 'She's always like this when I'm affectionate with anybody.'

Like many children, Jo is afraid of the dark. However, as a young adult, she makes the distinction that the darkness she fears is that which is found 'inside houses'. This is an oppressive, confining darkness that threatens to engulf her. It's a darkness she would have been left alone in as a child, the darkness of isolation and abandonment. Helen was determined to live her life on her own terms despite the fact that she had a child to look after.

Jo comes closest to sharing this feeling of rejection when she tells Geoff that she used to try to hold her mother's hand, only to have her mother pull away from her. She has grown up knowing that her mother's affections would never be directed toward her or that her own attempts at closeness would not be reciprocated. Demonstrating her deep awareness of her lack of a place in her mother's heart, Jo states, 'she always had so much love for everyone else, but none for me.' Helen seems almost ignorant of the fact that as a mother she should nurture and comfort her child, protecting her from harm and disappointment. Her insensitivity doesn't seem borne out of a desire to hurt or punish Jo, it's as if she has no awareness of the damage her words might do. When she tells Jo, 'I never thought about you! It's a funny thing. I never have done when I was happy', it's almost as if she is just thinking out loud, with no thought for the impact it might have on her daughter.

Core Beliefs – The Creation

Jo's low self-worth and insecurity will have been profoundly compromised by her mother's inconsistency and her rejection of Jo and her role as a mother. She undoubtedly would have made it implicit that Jo - whose birth apparently revealed her infidelity to her husband - was to blame for her subsequent divorce. This in itself would have led Jo to believe quite rightly, that she was a mistake, an unwanted hindrance to her mother's freedom and happiness.

Like all children with insecure attachment issues, Jo had a deep-seated love/hate relationship with her mother. As a child she will no doubt have screamed and cried inconsolably for her mother whenever they were separated, only to ignore and reject her when reunited. These children feel abandoned every time their mother (and it is most often the mother) leaves them, but are unable to trust their dependability when they return. Because of this yo-yoing of love and rejection, they will often be unable to form healthy attachments. They will go to the first person that shows them even the tiniest bit of affection, only to treat them so badly that they succeed in pushing their love away. They treat the object of their love and attachment so poorly because they don't believe they will stay and so try to protect themselves from the pain of rejection by doing it to them first. They will then miss that person and long to be reunited with them, only to start the whole process again if they return.

For Jo, this instilled a set of Core Beliefs that revolve around not being able to trust her feelings or the feelings of others. Nothing is permanent in a life where even your home can be taken away from you at a moment's notice. She has learned that she is the only person she can rely on. Despite Geoff's sincere desire to be present in her and the baby's life, Jo cannot accept this declaration of dependence, and tells Geoff that, 'You're nothing to me. I'm everything to myself.' To Jo, love and commitment are impermanent and unattainable.

It's important to note that Helen is not a cruel or malicious woman. She is capable of moments of tenderness, or at least concern, for her daughter, as when she laments, 'Oh Jo, you're only a kid. Why don't you learn from my mistakes? It takes you half your life to learn from your own.' This is one of the few instances where Helen actually behaves like a parent instead of Jo's peer. She seldom speaks to Jo of the things that mothers usually discuss with their daughters. Her view of life, love and marriage are skewed, most likely from her own experiences of being a daughter.

Adulthood – The Consequences

We never see Jo needing to compete for her mother's affection with a female friend. If Helen had had any close relationships with women, that might have provided Jo with a positive role model for womanhood, and perhaps even a small bit of mother-love. There doesn't appear to be a grandmother or aunty to fulfil this role for Jo, to give her another perspective on what it means to be a woman. Jo and Helen are women adrift in a sea of men who, for one reason or another, cannot provide either of them with enduring love. Unfortunately for Jo, these transitory men are also her only masculine role models. She has no more idea what to expect from a father than she does from a husband.

As a young woman, Jo declares that she hates love and hates motherhood. How could she feel otherwise? Her only experience of both has been given her by a woman who cannot think beyond her own needs. She has seen that in order to have happiness and to feel good about yourself (albeit gained at the expense of others), you need a man, not a child.

Jo doesn't pursue her aspiration to train as an artist, something that she is naturally gifted at – something that was even endorsed by her mother. To Jo, this is merely a dream, a fantasy, but it also represents a potential means of escape from her dreary life. It would be understandable if Jo had this as her primary reason for not wanting a baby; after all, her mother didn't want Jo because she would tie her down. But Jo doesn't want a baby because she doesn't want to be, or end up like, her mother. Even so, there is a certain ambivalence in this. Her mother is an attractive woman as demonstrated by Peter's sexual demands, and Jo wants to almost rival her mother in that respect. She asks if she is like Helen and, when told no, claims to be relieved saying, 'I'm glad no-one can see the resemblance between us.' Later, when Geoff warns, 'If you don't watch it you'll turn out exactly like her…in some ways you are already, you know', she is annoyed and pushes him away from her. She might want to be attractive like her mum, but she doesn't want to *be* like her.

Throughout the film, Jo desperately tries to free herself from her dependence on her mother. She strives to establish herself as an individual:

which may account for why she has a black boyfriend and a gay friend – these are as strong a statement of independence from her mother as she can get. In denying motherhood, womanhood, and love, she is trying to detach herself from Helen's dominating personality; and yet throughout most of the film, she exists in relation to Helen – seeing everything through the filter of Helen's attitudes and behaviours. These are the actions of the insecurely attached child within her. Continually caught in the cycle of push-me, pull-me that epitomises love/hate relationships: she needs her mother, but doesn't want her.

Helen is an exuberant, powerful woman for all her insecurities. She loves life - as long as it's on her terms – and anyone in her company will be sure of a good time filled with bonhomie and raucous laughter. Unfortunately, this is a side of Helen that Jo is never allowed to witness or enjoy. There is no doubt that Helen is a flawed woman and an unsatisfactory mother: it's no surprise that Jo wants to reject the role of mother for herself. She dislikes milk, which could also symbolise her rejection of Helen and motherhood. She mocks Geoff for being more maternal than she is. While he is busy preparing the flat for the baby's arrival, Jo is actively avoiding consideration of how she will cope. When she does allow herself to contemplate it she exclaims, 'I'll bash its brains out! I'll kill it! I don't want this baby, Geoff. I don't want to be a mother. I don't want to be a woman.'

To Helen, Jo is the reason she's unable to partake in a life of hedonism and self-indulgence, living only in the moment. Jo shares this trait with her mother, unable to plan ahead and unwilling to consider the possible consequences of her actions. Their lives not only revolve around a cycle of depravation, but also around familial and relational dysfunction. Without other powerful forces for good in her life, Jo is doomed to perpetuate Helen's experience of being a woman and a mother. She too will look at her baby and see the future she'll never have, the nurturing she never received, and the confirmation that love never endures and always leaves you miserable and alone.

Chapter 19

FEAR OF BEING WEAK

If we could read the secret history of our enemies, we should find in each man's life sorrow and suffering enough to disarm all hostility.

Henry Wadsworth Longfellow

The only reason I always try to meet and know the parents better is because it helps me to forgive their children.

Louis Johannot

THE IRON LADY (2011)   **MARGARET** (2009)

Director: Phylida Lloyd   **Director:** James Kent

Writer: Abi Morgan   **Writer:** Richard Cottan

This chapter is unusual in that I will be referencing two films rather than one. *Margaret*, was a made for TV film that focused primarily on Margaret Thatcher's spectacular rise and fall. It took only eleven days for the most powerful woman in the world to be seen as a tearful figure in the back of a car being driven away from Downing Street and her place as a major player in world politics. Almost Shakespearean in its execution and finale, this major tragedy sees Margaret Thatcher lose what seems to be the one thing she really cares about - power - changing from celebrated leader to deposed victim before our eyes.

In *The Iron Lady*, we are given glimpses of Thatcher's life prior to her Premiership in a series of flashbacks. We see her as a young aspiring politician, a new and struggling mother, and a wife. But the central theme of the film is one of grief and loss. Through her interactions with her deceased husband, Denis, we are party to the loss, not only of respect and reputation, but also of her sense of self as she declines into dementia. This once powerful woman, who caused tremors of civil unrest throughout Britain, is reduced to an ordinary woman shopping for milk at the corner shop: apt, when you consider her background.

Margaret Hilda Roberts, the daughter of a grocer, was born on 13th October 1925 in Grantham, Lincolnshire. She went to Oxford University and then became a research chemist, retraining to become a barrister in 1954. In 1951, she married Denis Thatcher, a wealthy businessman, with whom she had two children. In 2002, after a series of minor strokes, Baroness Thatcher retired from public speaking. She died from a stroke on April 8, 2013, at the age of eighty-seven.

Of the two real life stories to be included in this book, Margaret Thatcher's is possibly the most provocative of all. In part because she has only recently died, but also because she was renowned the world over for being Britain's first female prime minister and for introducing domestic policies that divided the country and which resulted in her being held equally with utter contempt and deep admiration, with very little in between. She was one of the dominant political figures of 20th century Britain, and the ripples of Thatcherism continue to have a huge influence.

My reason for choosing her as a subject for this book was based mainly on the fact that it was her father's influence, as opposed to her mother's, that shaped the woman and politician she would become. Generally, it is often mothers who hold the most sway over the upbringing and shaping of their children; however, this isn't always the case, and I would not like to present an unbalanced view one way or the other.

The Films – The Story

Although both films give a perspective of Margaret Thatcher that mainly focuses on her years as a politician, it is in *Margaret* that we get more of an insight into her relationship with her father. Her rise to fame, first as a politician then later as prime minister, is well documented. Unlike Howard Hughes, there are many interviews with, or profiles on, Margaret Thatcher. As early as 1970, when she was the new Education Minister, she was the subject of a BBC Panorama special, right up to her being interviewed for *Married to Maggie*, a Channel 4 documentary about Denis Thatcher, which was filmed a couple of months before his death in 2003. Because of the proliferation of material and documentation on her career and certain aspects of her earlier life beyond politics, it's unnecessary to describe the story of each film as it unfolds.

Margaret gives what seems to be an honest and balanced view of her life, albeit from the Left-wing perspective. It depicts her steely determination and power in the past, contrasting it with her mental confusion and frailty in later years. This is as much a study of the last days when parliament looked and sounded like a boys' public school, her ministers portrayed as male weaklings, fighting a constant battle with their strident female leader. In fact, Baroness Shirley Williams, in a documentary about Thatcher's rise to power, put her dominance over her male ministers down to their profound awe of women borne out of their childhood experiences:

> '...*brought up by a nanny, his mother is a slightly distant, authoritarian figure... He goes to an all-male school where matron is a figure of real awe, or fear... she will be a key figure of authority. So you have a nanny, a rather distant mother, a very stern matron [...] they didn't know how to confront a woman, how to disagree with her, or how to take a different line.*'

The scene in which Geoffrey Howe (played by Anthony Head) is on the receiving end of a cringe-worthy dressing-down in cabinet, reinforces the strength of the control she had over her male colleagues. In a speech she gave in 1949, she actually refers to the then Labour government as being, 'a bunch of little boys fascinated by machinery they can't help fiddling with.'

There are moments of tenderness, particularly between herself and her husband, Denis. Her son, Mark Thatcher, appears to have been her favourite for whom she couldn't do enough, to the extent that we even see her cleaning mud from his shoes. Her relationship with her daughter, Carol, was doomed to emulate that of hers with her mother, Beatrice Roberts, who didn't even get mentioned in her autobiography. Elsewhere, she briefly mentioned her mother claiming that she 'loved her mother dearly, but at 15 we had nothing more to say to each other.'

The Iron Lady gives much the same portrayal of the former prime minister – a personal as well as political account of her life. As I said earlier, in this film, her political career is shown primarily through flashbacks, with the main story centring on her years when she was developing dementia and seemingly had no awareness of her husband's death several years earlier. This is a stark contrast to that of the formidable intellect of a career woman intent on taking power and reigning over the country as prime minister. What we see is a weak, old woman struggling to find her place in a world that has discarded her - a world where she had ultimate authority - and that has now left her behind.

This is also a study in grief and regret. Thatcher sacrificed her family for her career. Even Denis spends most of his time on the periphery as she forges her course through the male dominated world of British politics. Carol is seen constantly trying to win her mother's attention and affection, and failing. When trying to tend to her when she is confused and tired, she is told, 'The last thing I wanted to do when I was your age was fuss around my mother.' There is never any mention of Mark in this film, who at that time was living in South Africa. Instead we see Thatcher speaking to him on the phone when he once again makes excuses as to why he's cancelling yet another a visit.

Both films include flashbacks to her early years in power, revealing her drive to succeed – the drive that ultimately led to her downfall. They document the events that occurred just prior to and during her time as prime minister, focusing on her winning the leadership over Ted Heath, being elected as prime minister in 1979, and the contentious policies and decisions that divided a country and threw it into a state of conflict, sedition and perpetual dispute. Hers was a government that saw riots, strikes, pit closures, bombings and war. We see her making the decision to sink the General Belgrano during the Falklands war, despite the fact that she had been informed that it had turned and was sailing away from the conflict. The war, the start of which had further polarized opinion of her policies, now saw her as Britain's heroine. It turned her fortunes around – from being the most despised woman/politician to being the nation's beloved saviour.

However, it was around this time that support for her amongst her own ministers began to waiver. The Poll Tax - another controversial levy that threatened to create a bigger divide between the haves and the have not's of Britain - caused more riots and violent protests all over the country. Despite advice from her ministers to consider the impact her stringent - and in some ways Draconian - policies were having on the country as a whole, she would not budge. She only listened to those who agreed with her decisions and even considered putting someone else in place as prime minister while she continued to run the country her way from the wings.

Her scathing attack on Geoffrey Howe during a cabinet meeting, in which she criticised his ability to do his job and even went as far as to correct the wording, grammar and punctuation of his report, resulted in his total dissatisfaction with her leadership and her - by now tyrannical - behaviour, and ultimately led to his resignation. On November 13th, 1990, eleven years after coming into office, Geoffrey Howe made the lethal resignation speech that stunned the country and sealed Thatcher's fate. Within ten days, Thatcher was ousted by her once loyal all-male ministers. Unable to gain enough votes to retain leadership, she was deposed and had no choice but to resign.

In *The Iron Lady*, we see what happened to Thatcher as she continued her life out of the public eye - placidly going about her days in a growing fog of dementia until finally letting go of Denis and coming to terms to life without him. *Margaret,* on the other hand, ends as she leaves Downing Street for the last time. Having run the gauntlet of staff, many of whom are clearly indifferent or relieved to see her go, she pauses at the closed door. As Crawfie, her faithful dresser, dabs tears from her mistress' eye, Thatcher takes a breath, throws back her shoulders and nods her readiness to have the door opened, releasing her to the awaiting multitudes of press. In stark contrast, the Hollywood version with Meryl Streep, portrays the deposed Thatcher gliding elegantly and stoically towards the door along a path bedecked with huge bunches of red roses. As she steps on petals, she pauses at the door, visibly shaken at the prospect of leaving and of facing the public in her humiliation. Denis, forever at her side, lays a gentle hand on her shoulder as he nods to the doorkeeper to open the door.

Both films depict a dramatic, historical event that tells a story as old as politics itself: the powerful leader who becomes so detached from reality that it destroys them. What isn't shown in either film is something that most people had never before witnessed in one of the most formidable leaders of the country - a show of genuine emotion. Filmed by news cameras on the day of her resignation, we see her visibly tearful as she climbs into her car ready to be driven away from Number 10.

Childhood – The Setting

Both films cited in this chapter make it abundantly clear that the childhood influence of Thatcher's father created the woman and politician she became. Having two daughters and no son, Alf Roberts instilled in his youngest daughter, Margaret, a sense of ambition, drive and self-reliance that forged the mind-set that enabled her to fight her way to the top of politics in Britain, and become a force to be reckoned with on a global scale. Her father was not only a successful grocer owning two shops, but also a Methodist lay preacher and an Alderman within Grantham county council (a titular term denoting a high-ranking councillor chosen by elected members of the council as opposed to voters), eventually going on to become Mayor.

As a child, Alf allegedly kept Margaret separate from the other children, making her walk the long way round to school so she could avoid the poorer houses. In school she was known as 'Snobby Roberts', more evidence that she behaved differently to the other children. She spent her formative years accompanying her father to Chapel; and, from about the age of thirteen, she would also accompany him to the Rotary Club and council meetings. Members of the family have commented that although she was four years younger than her sister Muriel, she inherited her father's temperament and love of debate. With Alf being so involved with the town council, politics was a frequently discussed subject in their home above one of the shops.

Her mother features very little, not only in the films discussed here, but also, as previously stated, in Thatcher's autobiography, and didn't even get a mention in her daughter's Who's Who entry. Apparently, she kept the house scrupulously clean and even made the girls' clothes by hand. Thatcher once said that her mother 'was always weighed down by the home. Always being in the home.' She admired and possibly adored her father. She saw him hold sway at council meetings, spouting his own brand of Methodist politics: believing that people should stand on their own two feet, advocating self-advancement, and unyielding loyalty to personal truth. 'Service Above Self', the young Margaret Roberts believed, were the words engraved on the heart of the man who gave her integrity.

Within the Roberts' household, there was only room for one person to take up space in her father's affections. It's clear that he bestowed on his youngest daughter all of the dreams and aspirations a father would normally inculcate in a son and heir. A neighbour of the Roberts' family when Margaret was a young girl observed that Mr Roberts, 'saw himself in Margaret from the start, nurtured that.' This focused attention on her daughter would have left Beatrice side-lined in all important matters. Consequently, she transferred all her affection to her eldest daughter, Muriel; who, by all accounts, favoured her mothers' traits.

Core Beliefs – The Creation

With her father's positive approval being dependent on her showing him her ability to be self-reliant, loyal and unwaveringly pragmatic it was inevitable that she would grow to become a woman with high ideals and expectation, not only of herself, but of those around her. It's been said of her childhood that it, 'forged in her the strength and the character to impose the values of the corner shop on the entire nation.' Unfortunately for her – and arguably for a large percentage of the British population – the rigidity of her childhood was something that made it almost impossible for her to comprehend or accept viewpoints that in any way differed from her own.

Those who bought their groceries from her father's shop have accused Alf Roberts of being 'a mean old bugger', who allegedly economically and sexually exploited his female employees. One customer remembers him as:

> *'[...] the domineering force. He was very, very scary to me as a little girl. He would pick who he chose to serve in the shop. He'd stand there in his brown overalls looking you up and down. I'd really hate going in there. He would look over his glasses at you, frighten you to death, very stern.*

"What do you want, child?" Most of the shops would give families a bit of credit until the end of the week, but never Mr. Roberts.'

From roughly the age of 13 years old, Thatcher would attend council meetings at the town hall with her father, who was then Mayor. At these meetings she would see 'grown-up men in their smart suits with their pipes and their chains dangling in their pockets.' Even at such a young age she exhibited the drive to be seen as equal amongst these (locally) powerful men who made decisions that affected the lives of the residents of Grantham. 'One always felt so small. One had to fight to be heard, you see. Fight again and again and again, against your smallness, against him, but not like a girl. That's why they laugh at me now, isn't it? Me as a man.'

It's not clear at what age she became aware of the knowledge that, following the birth of her sister, her parents had hoped for a boy. We can only imagine what might have been said or intimated at in the privacy of their home that had instilled in her such a strong sense of being the usurper, the cuckoo in the nest. Something that would have certainly caused her to feel, deep down at her core, the desperate need to prove her worth, to be approved of and allowed to stay. She also realised early on in life that the person she needed to convince and influence the most in her favour, was her father. She referred to herself as, 'Daddy's, but not Daddy's girl, d'you see? He took me everywhere. Chapel, Rotary Club, council chambers.' It's clear that Alf Roberts inculcated within the young Margaret the mindfulness that she had to be the boy he never had, to meet the standards and values he would have forced upon his son and heir.

Retired Labour minister, Leo Abse (who interestingly enough, has an interest in psychoanalysis) observed Thatcher in action at the Commons on a regular basis. He asserted that Thatcher's 'stentorian behaviour' was the result of her being rejected by her mother and having an overwhelming attraction to her father. He goes on to posit that her extraordinary insistence on self-reliance was an expression of her unconscious desire to destroy her guilty sexual feelings for her father! All very Freudian. In my opinion, her striving to achieve success and respect within a male dominated arena had less to do with an Electra complex than it was with wanting to be accepted by the father that made it clear she was the wrong sex and would therefore have to prove her worth amongst her male peers and betters.

It's possible that although her father was, in her opinion, 'university, college material', his lack of money meant that he would not be able to reach that pinnacle of academic achievement. Instead, he had to satisfy his need for power and superiority by saving to buy a corner shop: a place where he ruled supreme over employees, customers and, no doubt, family alike. It was his frustrated ego and the cultivating of his daughter in the ways of power-hungry men, that prompted him to pay for her to have Latin lessons from a local grammar school teacher so as to enable her to apply to Oxford.

Baroness Williams commented that in observing female politicians, she has come to believe that, 'the relationship between father and daughter is absolutely crucial – whether Mrs. Ghandi, Benazir Bhutto, Margaret Thatcher herself, me, Barbara Castle – the same thing is true over and over again. It's the father's influence in believing his daughter can achieve almost anything, which is all important.' The then Chief Press Secretary, Bernard Ingham said that '…her moral courage was the mark her father left upon her. I think her entire being reflected her upbringing.'

Despite all of this, she can be seen to have been a resilient child (what child isn't in the face of an overly strict and authoritarian father – or mother, for that matter?), who was inspired by the words of Churchill (she has been considered the most dominant prime minister since Churchill), and Kipling. In *Margaret*, we see her learning the Kipling poem, *The Law for Wolves*, by heart:

> *'Now is the law of the jungle, as old and as true as the sky.*
> *And the wolf that shall keep it may prosper, and the wolf*
> *that shall break it must die.*
> *And the creeper that girdles the tree trunk, the law runneth*
> *forward and back;*
> *For the strength of the pack is the wolf, and the strength of*
> *the wolf is the pack.'*

Adulthood – The Consequences

With her father's all too obvious disdain of women and those in a lesser financial position or status than himself, it's obvious to see how Margaret Thatcher developed a similar disdain for all things feminine. And it was this inclination towards a masculine, left-brain disposition that created within her an aversion towards domesticity and a nurturing, maternal nature. She grew up to believe that a woman's place was most definitely in the home – unless of course, you were of a certain disposition and background. In her book, *Backlash: the Undeclared War Against American Women*, feminist author, Susan Faludi wrote that, with the exception of Baroness Young, 'Britain's first female prime minister failed to put another woman into her cabinet of 20 or so males.' As for supporting working mothers, she seemed to actively discourage other women from following her example. Thatcher's biographer, John Campbell, even went as far as to say that, 'She was keen on education but she didn't believe in [childcare] places that primarily allowed women to go out to work. She believed that was an abdication of the mother's role.'

It seems to me that Thatcher had done such a good job of subjugating her femininity in order to win the approval of her father (in her early years) and male politicians (also in her early years in the political arena), that she may have indeed thought of herself more man than woman; and, therefore, entitled to the same treatment and opportunities as her male peers: something which did not include staying at home with the children. In *The Iron Lady*, she can be heard declaring to her strongest ally, Denis Thatcher, 'One's life must matter, Denis. Beyond all the cooking and the cleaning and the children, one's life must mean more than that.' Is this merely fanciful, poetic licence claimed by a screenwriter trying to imbue a sense of severance from any maternal, nurturing instincts? Or true sentiments as reported by those closest to her? If the latter is true, then to Thatcher, fame and fortune were more important than family.

The ultimate price Thatcher paid for this calculated divorce from her true, feminine nature (and by this and what follows, I do not imply that women should not aspire to success or great standing in industry or academia), was the distance it created between herself and her children. It's no secret that Lady Thatcher was closer to her son, Mark, than she was to her daughter, Carol. This is no surprise given her admiration of all things male, left-brain and masculine. Carol's femaleness would have been too close for comfort for a women intent on eradicating most of her own right-brain emotionality.

As ever in this kind of family dynamic, Mark could do no wrong – even when he needed bailing out of financial difficulty or being bought out of house arrest in South Africa (to the tune of £265,000): whereas Carol would have found it difficult to find a way into her mother's affections.

Apparently, there was never any show of tactile affection within a family where, 'hugs, cuddles and kisses never seemed to be on their agenda'. An observation from a boyfriend of Carol's was that there was 'more chill than warmth', between mother and daughter and that although Carol admired Margaret from a distance, she 'did not enjoy being close to her.'

The Thatcher family is a good example, plain for all to see, of how the childhood environment influences not only the children of that time, but the children to come and, as we have seen, the children beyond that. This is the vicious cycle that comes to dominate family members for generations. These family dynamics are created by the Core Beliefs operating within each member: behaviours, values and attitudes that will go on being replicated throughout time unless awareness of the source – the Core Beliefs - is reached and a healing of childhood wounds takes place.

Chapter 20

SIBLING RIVALRY

I don't believe an accident of birth makes people sisters or brothers. It makes them siblings, gives them mutuality of parentage. Sisterhood and brotherhood is a condition people have to work at.

Maya Angelou

A sister is a gift to the heart, a friend to the spirit, a golden thread to the meaning of life.

Isadora James

IN HER SHOES (2005)
Director: Curtis Hanson
Writers: Jennifer Weiner (novel); Suzanna Grant (Screenplay)

Rose and Maggie Feller have nothing much in common (apart from being sisters), other than the size of their feet. Rose is an attorney at a top law firm in Philadelphia, who works long hours, and struggles with her low self-esteem and physical appearance. She collects designer shoes (which she never wears), because regardless of her size, they always fit. Maggie, on the other hand (or foot!), is a party animal, who only just graduated from high school, changes jobs as often as she changes her designer clothes, is self-centred and is the epitome of the 'blonde bombshell'.

The Story

The opening scenes show how the sisters are polar opposites, with Rose going to work and lamenting that she is not like 'thinner women who wear [...] things designed to excite men'. At the same time, we see Maggie having casual sex in the toilet at a bar. When Rose comes to collect her, she is passed out on a sofa. Rose drives her to their emotionally unavailable father's house where Maggie has been living, only to be told by their cold step-mother that she is no longer welcome and will have to move in with Rose.

From Rose's reaction, it's clear that this isn't the first time she's had to take parental responsibility for her younger sister. She resents having to once again provide her with a place to sleep and insists that it is only a temporary measure, and that Maggie has to find a job and move out as soon as possible. This is old ground for the both of them and Rose has had enough.

The next day, before leaving for work, she hands Maggie a newspaper in which she has circled jobs she feels are appropriate for her. These are the type of jobs - in offices - that she herself would seek out and are effectively way beyond Maggie's skills or experience. What Rose has missed when telling Maggie, 'You have so much potential. Find something you're good at', is that Maggie is actually very good with fashion and make-up. These are the things that inspire her and make her feel good, but Rose doesn't consider them to be of any real value and so doesn't consider that area of work as a possibility. Left alone with implicit instructions to get interviews with prospective employers, Maggie spots an advert for a presenter on MTV. Borrowing a pair of Rose's precious designer shoes, she travels to New York for the audition.

Despite the fact that Maggie's bubbly personality and sexy, trendy appearance gets her noticed, she is unable to read the autocue as she is dyslexic. From Rose's attitude toward her sister's intelligence, 'She's pretty, but real stupid', it's obvious that this debilitating condition has never been diagnosed – not even by Maggie herself, who also believes she is stupid. Needless to say, she doesn't get the job and ends up working at a dog grooming parlour.

Coming home from work one evening, she meets two strangers (both attractive, young men) in the street. They flirt and she agrees to go and have drinks with them. Later, when going home, one of them wants payment in kind for the money he spent on Maggie. When she makes it clear that she's not interested, he becomes aggressive and his more likable friend has to intervene to save her from what could have turned into a serious sexual assault.

Maggie is deeply disturbed by this event: it's possibly the first time she has not been in control of an interaction of this nature with a man. She reverts to 'frightened child' mode and goes to her work place to 'borrow' a dog that is being boarded there. She takes the dog back to Rose's apartment and cuddles up with it on her bed recalling a time from her childhood when they had a dog for a day, '…the best day.' When Rose returns home from work to find the flat in a mess with Maggie snivelling on her bed with a dog, she loses her patience. Rose is so accustomed to Maggie's promiscuity and recklessness, that she doesn't realise how much the incident has affected her, and so doesn't recognise Maggie's need for comfort and reassurance. She shouts at Maggie and tells her she has to leave. She then goes back out, leaving Maggie to cry alone.

Maggie reverts to type and decides that if Rose is going to throw her out then she is going to wreck the only thing she holds dear, her shoes.

Systematically, she goes through the shoes breaking the heels and putting them back on the shelves in such a way as to be unnoticeable. As she is preparing to leave, cavorting around the apartment in a shirt and knickers, Rose's new boyfriend from work calls. Unabashed by her semi-clothed state, Maggie invites him in. Before long the inevitable happens and Rose returns to find them both in bed together. This is more than she can bear and she tells Maggie she never wants to see her again.

Shocked out of her work-centred focus by Maggie's actions, Rose takes an unprecedented leave of absence from work and 'accidently' becomes a dog-walker – something that she ends up enjoying as a way to get herself fit.

This was also a turning point for Maggie, who seeks out the grandmother they thought was dead. Whilst looking for money at her father, Michael's house, she discovers a pile of birthday cards intended for her that he had withheld. The second half of the film focuses mainly on Maggie reconnecting with her grandmother, Ella, in Florida where she lives on a retirement complex. She turns up on Ella's doorstep wanting to know the truth about her mother. Ella takes her in and before long, Maggie has settled down to her comfortable role as a selfish, manipulative teenager, who just pleases herself, 'loafing around like a princess'. She settles in for an easy time of sunbathing, swimming in the complex pool, drinking to excess, and inevitably, trying to steal from her grandmother.

Ella catches and challenges Maggie who makes up an excuse for why she was rifling through her chest of drawers. Ella knows what she's up to and tells her the money's in her sock drawer. Maggie explains that she's trying to save up to go to Los Angeles to be an actor. Ella suggests she try to get work at the complex medical centre and offers to match whatever she earns. Maggie begins to work as an auxiliary nurse, and soon finds that she's not able to get away with looking after No.1.

Even though she starts off in her usual casual manner – just doing the bare minimum in order to save up her money - something has changed within her and she begins to enjoy the work. This is in part due to the fact that Maggie is befriended by an elderly, blind resident/patient who asks her to read to him. Realising she is dyslexic, he helps her to overcome her lack of confidence by getting her to read out loud to him. This, and her grandmother's genuine interest in her, helps Maggie to overcome her self-centredness and to become aware of the needs of others around her. As other people start to believe in her, she tries harder to be part of Ella's life, develops more respect for herself, and even cuts down on her drinking. Ella and her friends soon discover Maggie's natural flare for fashion and accessories, and very quickly she is in demand as a personal shopper for most of the female residents at the complex.

Inevitably, Ella wants to know what life was like for them growing up with their mother - her daughter. Maggie responds petulantly about Ella's lack of involvement in their lives and is told to 'grow up'. Maggie then says of her mum, 'She was special, different from other mums. She used to surprise us.' It later transpires that such surprises often consisted of such things as finding a tiara in her lunch box, but no food.

Back in New York, Rose is unable to open up to her new boyfriend, Simon. She finds it hard to tell him about her life and how she feels. They get engaged, but he refuses to marry her until she can talk to him about her feelings, fears and concerns. As she grapples with this ultimatum, she receives a letter and plane ticket from Ella. Rose turns up at the complex and is surprised to find Maggie there, as she had no idea where she'd gone after she'd kicked her out.

Whilst reminiscing with Ella, Rose and Maggie describe a special day they shared with their mother just before she died. Although they recall much the same events, certain aspects of the story don't quite match. For instance, Maggie didn't realise that the 'great day' happened two days before their mother's death. They both tell Ella about how their mum woke them up really early – each contributing bits of the story as they go along, demonstrating how their interpretation and perspective of the same event differs. Maggie's tone is wistful and dreamy, as though she is telling a fantastic fairy tale. Rose is more down to earth and matter-of-fact. It is during this exchange that Maggie learns that her mum's death wasn't an accident as she'd been told.

Maggie: Mum woke us real early. It was a school day and it was dark out.

Rose: It was winter.

Maggie: She put us in our best party frocks and dragged us down to the kitchen which was…

Rose: … a mess…

Maggie: …covered - every counter - in fudge. She'd been up all night making it. She drove us right past school up to a shop in New York.

Rose: Which was closed because it was only eight in the morning.

Maggie: That's right. And we hung out in the car.

Rose: Eating fudge for breakfast.

(Their mum thought she would make a fortune selling her fudge to the shop.)

Maggie: We went in and she was so beautiful. She was wearing this long velvety gown...

Ella: At eight in the morning?

Their mum spilled the fudge all over the jewellery counter and they had to leave. Maggie tells Ella that their mum told them that they could each have a present. Rose was given a Nancy Drew book and Maggie got a puppy, which they called Honey Bun and only had for one day. Maggie believed that they only had it for one day because their dad thought she was too young to have a puppy. Rose explains to her that he was mad about the whole day - he'd had no idea where they were, and the school had called asking what was going on. Maggie didn't remember that their parents had had a huge fight, and Rose explains that that was because she was in her room playing music. Rose had taken her there and had put music on so she wouldn't hear them, especially as their dad was saying that their mother was unfit and that he was going to put her away.

Now the truth is finally out. Ella tells them that her estrangement from the family grew out differences of opinion she and her son-in-law had over treatment for her daughter – should she do as Ella wanted and stay on medication that she didn't like taking, or should she stop taking them and risk hurting herself? According to Ella, Michael hadn't tried hard enough to get her to take her medication, and so each blamed the other for her subsequent suicide. It was this that broke the family apart.

With the truth out in the open, the sister's relationship with each other and their estranged grandmother was able to finally heal. Soon after this, there is a surprise visit from Simon (Maggie had written and told him Rose was pregnant as a ruse to get him to come), and Rose returns with him to the city where they marry. Maggie buys Rose a wedding dress paid for out of her earnings as a very popular and much in demand senior citizen fashion consultant and personal shopper. The film ends with Rose finally able to appreciate and wear her designer shoes, and Maggie better able to consider the effect her behaviour has on feelings of others.

Core Beliefs – The Creation

Rose

Rose's lack of spontaneity comes in part from her childhood experiences and in part from the fact that she is the eldest. As such, she is responsible, hard-working, has taken on the parental role, and is self-sufficient (remember, this isn't hard and fast, just common traits). However, the fact that she witnessed her mother's erratic behaviour from the view point of being the older sibling, means she took a more serious approach to Maggie's care – almost assuming the informal role of *in loco parentis*.

In entering the imagined world of her character via what we know about families and the setting up of Core Beliefs, we can surmise that her mother's behaviour taught Rose that it isn't safe to be spontaneous: people don't react kindly and even throw you out of shops if your behaviour isn't what's deemed socially acceptable. As an adult, her attitude to Maggie's spontaneity, difficulty in relationships, inability to express herself emotionally, workaholic nature, and hoarding beautiful shoes she never wears, shows us just how uncomfortable she is with expressing herself creatively, impulsively or intimately. To her, this kind of behaviour leads to anguish, embarrassment and even death in the form of suicide. Her Inner Child will equate impulsivity with being out of control and with a lack of concern for the needs of others. Which is why she struggles so much with Maggie's self-centredness: she sees this as her being on the same path her mother was on, and consequently does not want to witness the self-destruction of someone else she loves.

For Rose, it isn't safe to act out or be creative in any way. But she is her mother's daughter and her need for creative expression leaks out in her almost compulsive shoe buying and hoarding. She likes to own them and look at them, but she could never contemplate taking them off the shelf and wearing them. To do so would be to walk in her mother's footsteps – an apt metaphor for her shoe obsession. Each time she looks at them she will be reminded on a deep level of what potentially lies in store for her should she ever lose control and take a risk.

In order to protect herself further from developing her mother's mental health issues, Rose buries herself in her work: always the first in and always the last to leave. From her reaction to the stress of her job, it's clear this isn't because she loved it, but because she would worry about what would happen to her without all the people to please, all those tasks to get done, 'Maybe they were the things that were holding me together and without them, I'd fall apart'. She had to keep a grip on her mental health at all costs and so used work as a way of avoiding the descent into madness she feared was waiting for her should she relax for even a minute.

Her relationship with Maggie is fraught with peaks and troughs – mostly troughs – because on some repressed level she is envious of Maggie's ability to act spontaneously, to have casual relationships and to flit from job to job seemingly without a care in the world. She would also resent being the responsible one – believing that if she didn't keep Maggie in check, she, too, could lose her grip on reality and may also end up being sectioned, on medication, or committing suicide. In reaching the end of her tether with Maggie, she showed she had also reached a place where she was ready to relinquish her hold on their relationship. The two of them would have gone round in circles with one being in charge and in control and the other being irresponsible and always getting into trouble. Neither one would be able to break free of this dynamic in their relationship until pushed to the edge: as Rose was when Maggie did the unforgivable and slept with her boyfriend.

Although this resulted in her cutting all ties with Maggie, deep in her heart, Rose grieved for the loss of her sister. However, they could never have successfully re-connected if neither of them had changed in some way. Rose learned that a degree of spontaneity is good for the soul and brings unexpected benefits: in the form of a new outlook on life and an enjoyable way to get fit – something that boosted her confidence and self-esteem. For Maggie, it was having people (particularly her grandmother and the patient in the hospital), take the time and trouble to see her potential that enabled her to let go of old habits and finally get to like and accept herself.

Maggie

As the second and younger child, Maggie is irresponsible, self-centred, failed at school, has addictions (alcohol), is promiscuous and feels like the outcast of the family. Also in true birth order style, she was protected from the truth: Rose shut her in her bedroom and played loud music so she couldn't hear their parents fighting – especially as their father was threatening to have their mother sectioned. She was also protected from the truth about her mother's death, being led to believe she died in a car accident (she did die in a car crash but it was a deliberate act, not an accident).

It's interesting that the youngest child in a family treated in this way, does not ask to be protected from the truth or the harsh realities of life, and yet they often pay the price in the form of resentment from older siblings for being excluded and sheltered from having to deal with the pain of family problems. They often then grow up with a distorted view of the family dynamics and history, believing it to have been one of idyllic days of fun and group activity – a little like *The Waltons* where everyone gets on perfectly and the (very) occasional family disagreement is fixed and forgotten quickly and with very little hassle.

Maggie's view of the world is almost a magical one of being in a continued state of grace where no harm can come to her. Her journey to maturity is hastened by the incident with the man who wants payment for the drinks he bought her. Suddenly, she is not as charmed as she perhaps believed herself to be. In fact she realises – possibly for the first time – that she can be naïve when it comes to the motives of others. As a child, her pretty face and guileless behaviour would have meant she didn't get into trouble with her parents. Being the youngest child combined with her bubbly, playful nature possibly meant they wouldn't have had high expectations of her academically – something that may have accounted for her undiagnosed dyslexia.

Not being a witness to the down side of her mother's illness and behaviour, she would have seen it as fun and exciting. Being protected in the way she was, she would never have seen the darker side of her mother's illness. To her, her mother was a playful, free spirit who dressed in ball gowns in the day time, and put tiaras in her lunch box instead of food. Stifling her impulsivity would have been akin to denying or betraying her mother. Maggie would have felt close to her mother, who probably encouraged her flighty and impulsive nature. Whilst Rose's controlled and careful manner no doubt drew stern looks of disapproval from their mother – something Maggie would not have been able to cope with.

Adulthood – The Consequences

To Maggie, growing up and maturing, meant growing further away from her mother: whereas Rose learned to quell her spontaneity for fear of it leading to death. To her, their mother was a fairy princess. To Rose their mother was a mentally unstable, unpredictable woman who blew hot and cold. Staying in her head – logical, rational, ordered – and away from her heart, was Rose's way of staying safe.

When her world didn't crash around her feet after leaving her job and taking up dog walking instead, she learned it was safe to do things that weren't planned or measured first. Maggie learned that having a certain amount of order and predictability in your life doesn't necessarily spell death by boredom.

By the end of the film, both characters had discovered how to be more of who they wanted to be and less of who they'd become due to their mother's irrational behaviour. They were able to rid themselves of some of their Core Beliefs and create a new set based on choice, bringing with it a more balanced view of the world.

Chapter 21

THE SOUTHERN WAY –
Denial, Repression, Humour

You will find peace not by trying to escape your problems, but by confronting them courageously. You will find peace not in denial, but in victory.

J. Donald Walters

Confront the dark parts of yourself, and work to banish them with illumination and forgiveness. Your willingness to wrestle with your demons will cause your angels to sing. Use the pain as fuel, as a reminder of your strength.

August Wilson

PRINCE OF TIDES (1991)
Director: Barbara Streisand
Writer: Pat Conroy (Novel and Screenplay) and Becky Johnston (Screenplay)

This is probably the most 'on the nose' film explored as part of this book and the creation and consequences of Core Beliefs. By 'on the nose', I mean the most obvious in terms of how childhood experiences relate to and affect adult behaviour, attitudes and values. It may not be apparent until nearer the end of the film just how much his family history shaped the experiences of the main character, Tom Wingo, but the clues are there from the beginning. Now you know what to look for, you will clearly see - in Tom's approach to dealing with pain, uncomfortable emotions, and how he relates to his wife and children - Core Beliefs in full-on action, even if you don't know the whole picture of how they were created.

This film uses flashbacks to show us the history of Tom and his siblings. As each one unfolds, we are given deeper insight into Tom's personality and the reasons for his biting sarcasm and his avoidant behaviour. At first it seems that perhaps his parents were the cause of most of the children's unhappiness as adults. Their behaviour towards each other and the children is undoubtedly crucial in the forming of their adult selves. However, a single traumatic event which happened when Tom was thirteen, created a set of behaviours and beliefs that would haunt them all for years to come – an event that perhaps contributed to the death of Tom's brother, Luke, and the repeated attempts at suicide by his twin sister, Savannah.

The Story

The film opens with what appears to be a scene of an idyllic lifestyle in an even more idyllic setting. Three happy children play together with their dog, whilst their mother affectionately watches them as she shells beans. The voice-over from Tom Wingo, the adult, describes himself as being 'the son of a beautiful woman and also a shrimper's son'. The first hint we get that things aren't as perfect as they appear is when Tom says that his father would have made a good dad, 'if he hadn't been so violent'.

We see the children running together towards and along a jetty. Together they jump into the lake as Tom's narration tells us that this is what they did when things got scary or unpleasant. Holding hands, they would stay submerged under the water, 'and when our lungs betrayed us, we would rise towards the light'. (This is almost a foreshadowing of how they would deal with their painful memories from the past – submerging them until it became impossible to bear and their lungs – their emotions – would betray them.) This was a ritual that kept them safe, for this was a 'silent, soothing world where there was no pain: one without fathers and mothers'. Through the narration, Tom goes on to inform us that this was a long time ago before he made the decision not to have a memory.

In the present, Tom, a football coach, lives with his doctor wife, Sally, and three daughters in a beautiful beach house in South Carolina. It's interesting to note that Tom has married a doctor, and later has an affair with a psychiatrist. It's a commonly held belief within therapy that people with a history of trauma often unconsciously seek out partners with whom they hope to have a healing relationship. Unfortunately, his marriage is far from healing, as he unable to allow himself the intimacy that is necessary in a healthy relationship.

Tom learns from Sally that his mother, Lila, is on her way. He's openly hostile towards his mother and states that not only does he hate her, but that he actually enjoys hating her. When she arrives a little later, the first words out of her mouth are an admonishment for not watering the shrubs by the door. She tells Tom that Savannah has attempted suicide – again – and that her psychiatrist has requested that someone must go to New York to be with her. Tom is distraught to hear of his sister's attempt to take her life again, but his distress turns to fury when Lila tells him that she can't go as she needs to be around for her husband's birthday party. This is the first glimpse we get of Lila's self-interest and subjugation of her children's needs for those of her own. Besides, Lila moans, Savannah would only blame her, 'you children always blame me for everything'. Tom asks if he detects a note of guilt and from then on, mother and son verbally lunge and parry at each other in an all too familiar battle of snipes and gripes and accusations.

Tom reluctantly goes to New York to be with his sister: reluctant because he hates the big city. At the hospital where Savannah is being treated, he meets her therapist, Dr. Susan Lowenstein. She explains that she needs him to help her put together the missing pieces of Savannah's story so that she can better treat her. She asks why his father didn't reply to her telegram and Tom tells her it's because he only likes good news; and, as 'the shrimp are running good', this takes priority over his children's needs. When things get too painful, he goes on to explain, the Southern way is to either avoid the situation or laugh. Dr. Lowenstein wants to know when they cry, to which Tom replies, 'We don't'. Although unhappy at having to share private thoughts and memories with the psychiatrist, Tom is equally desperate to help his sister, and so he grudgingly agrees to meet with her to fill in the gaps of Savannah's life.

It's through these meetings that we learn about Tom's (and thus, Savannah's) childhood. Unable to truly enter into an honest review of their childhood, Tom at first pulls out the usual, glossed over recollections of incidents and memories that tell the story of an unremarkable family, describing his mother as 'a perfect woman who had a love of language and an appreciation of nature'. This is the last desperate attempt of a man to hold his family system together at all costs. Ever revealing flashbacks and recollections slowly unravel a history of violence, abandonment, secrets and denial, which also portray the binding love and commitment of siblings as they struggle to cope with the legacy of those lies and denials.

One of the most poignant flashbacks comes as Tom prepares food in Savannah's kitchen. It is of a time when his mother had made a meal using wine to flavour an otherwise dull meal of chicken and rice. His father, Henry, spits out the food in disgust. Lila describes it as 'elegant food', and the young and innocent Tom, trying to defend his mother, says that he thinks it's good. Henry pushes him aggressively and Tom gets upset, causing Henry to make fun of him by asking if he's going to cry. 'What've I told you about crying? There'll be no crying in this house! Put your hands on your lap! Sit up straight! Savannah, go get this little girl one of your dresses.' Luke tries to stop his dad and tells him to pick on someone his own size. Lila, ever the placator, offers to make Henry another meal and calls Tom into the kitchen with her where she tells him and Savannah that, 'if you marry into nothing, you get nothing'. This statement sums up Lila's view of her world and expectations of life.

She then proceeds to make a meal for Henry with dog food, onions and rice. Tom watches in awe and admiration at his mother's defiance and audacity. Usually powerless to effectively stop her husband from abusing her children – particularly Tom - she uses food to express and vent her anger and frustration. This is a safe way for her to retaliate against his violence and aggression towards herself and her children. Understandably, cooking becomes Tom's means of salving his own pain and discomfort when he feels powerless: the kitchen is his place of safety, his sanctuary.

Tom later shares this memory with Savannah's psychiatrist (whom he calls by her second name, Lowenstein). He goes on to tell her that his mother burned all of Savannah's childhood journals because she wasn't happy with Savannah's disloyalty to the family. Savannah responded by writing poetry that her mother wouldn't understand. In effect, Lila was trying to destroy Savannah's memories of her past – something she succeeded in doing only too well. This may have been why Tom became her memory. If, as it seems, the siblings embodied denied aspects of each other, and Tom was Savannah's memory, then she was his emotional expression and Luke was his courage and fortitude. As someone with Dissociative Identity Disorder will fragment themselves into parts in order to cope with trauma, Tom portioned out parts of himself to his siblings for safekeeping: even his mother was given pieces of his psyche in the form of his hate and anger. He describes himself to Dr. Lowenstein as a, 'Courteous, Southern boy. Did what I was told. Responsible. Normal. Dull'.

He visits Savannah in hospital, but she is still unable to communicate. Instead she lies inert in his arms as he reads her a poem by E.E. Cummings, [anyone lived in a pretty how town]:

> *'Women and men (both little and small)*
> *cared for anyone not at all*
> *they sowed their isn't they reaped their same*
> *sun moon stars rain*
> *children guessed (but only a few)*
> *and down they forgot as up they grew'*

In another session with Dr. Lowenstein, he recalls that when he and Savannah were about seven or eight, his mother gave birth to a still-born baby. She told them it had died because they were bad. Henry wrapped the baby in a towel and put it in the freezer. Later that night, Tom came down stairs and saw Savannah sitting in the rocking chair with the baby. She was telling it that it was the lucky one as its death meant it wouldn't have to live with them. When Tom asked her about it the next day, she didn't remember doing 'such a crazy thing'.

Sally calls Tom and asks him not to come home at the weekend. He guesses that she is seeing another man. Later, he writes her a letter telling her that he wishes the words 'I love you' weren't so difficult for him to say.

In another flashback, we see Lila calling Tom into her bedroom where she is reclining on the bed. She cuddles him as she tells him she loves him more than the other two children, and that he is her favourite. She gets him to promise to keep it a secret: something he does for twenty years. When he does finally tell Luke and Savannah, he is shocked to learn that she had said the same thing to them. This is when he tells Lowenstein that 'Women are more devious than men. They're great at keeping secrets. You smile when you lie. Expect a man to be a tower of strength then, when it turns out he has a few weaknesses, insecurities, what do you do? Run around and betray him!

Tom has been invited to a party at a neighbour's apartment. As a friend of the neighbour, Lowenstein has also been invited. After doing a slow dance together, they leave and Tom takes her home. It is at this time that they become more intimate and she invites him up to her apartment to meet her son, Bernard. A teenager, Bernard is sullen and rude to Tom and his mother. Embarrassed at his behaviour, she sends him to his room and apologises to Tom, who reassures her that he's not offended by Bernard's typical teenage behaviour. She tells him he wants to play football but isn't very good, and that his father, Herbert, who is a world renowned violinist, doesn't approve. Tom agrees to coach Bernard whilst he is in New York.

In a bookshop looking for a birthday present for his daughter, Tom discovers a book written by his sister entitled, *The Southern Way*, and published under a pseudonym. (He'd seen a collection of poems under the same name in her apartment but hadn't realised it was his sister until then.)

He is furious at Lowenstein for keeping this from him. She accuses him of acting like a petulant child and goes on to explain that it wasn't for her to disclose. She tells him that when Savannah first sought her out for therapy, she used the pseudonym and had fabricated a life as the daughter of Jewish survivors of the holocaust. Lowenstein was intrigued by this and wondered what it was Savannah was trying to survive. Tom and Lowenstein have a row and she invites him to dinner by way of an apology.

During dinner, Lowenstein tells Tom that Savannah's book idea had come from a dream she'd had, and which had images that terrorised her, including three stray dogs. She wants to explore this with Tom but he changes the subject and begins to flirt with her.

Over the weekend he spends at home celebrating his daughter's birthday, Sally tells him that her lover wants to marry her. Instead of erupting and having a fight as he would usually have done, Tom understands – even sympathizes about his wife's dilemma. The next day, as he watches Sally decorate the cake with her daughters, he remembers a birthday when his mum and dad had a huge row. Henry had been watching football on the television and refused to join in the celebrations. Lila had switched off the TV and they began to argue. Luke blasted the TV with a shotgun and told his shocked father, 'Now you can watch your kids blow out their candles'.

The next day (in present time) Tom is on his father's boat with his daughters. He tells his dad that they love him. True to form, Henry ignores the comment and starts talking about a football game. At first, Tom frowns, then he smiles indulgently at his father and lets the matter ride. This is another significant moment in Tom's healing journey. Instead of arguing with his dad about his inability or refusal to accept the love of his grandchildren, Tom perhaps recognizes how Henry is covering his own inadequacies around intimacy: something that, until recently, Tom was apt to do, himself.

Lila is now married to a rich and influential man who once hit Tom when she had taken him to apologize for hitting his son in self-defence. She now has the life-style she always believed she deserved and was born to achieve. Tom visits his mum in her luxury home and tells her that he's going to talk to Dr. Lowenstein about Callanwolde. At first she feigns ignorance, and then reminds him it's a secret. She admonishes him for always living in the past, and reminds him that she never looks back on the past, choosing instead to 'close the door' on it. Tom is angry about this and asks whether she has closed the door on Luke and his death. She is hurt by his remark and asks him who taught him to be so cruel. 'You did', he says, 'You also taught me that even if someone nearly tears you apart, you can still feel love for them.'

Back in New York, Tom is at last ready to divulge the real reason why Savannah is tormented so much that she wants to end her life. When he and Savannah were thirteen, they were in the house with their mother having fun dancing together. Suddenly, there is a pounding on the door. Tom answers it only to find three men who have escaped from a nearby prison, Callanwolde, standing on the porch. They push past him into the house and embark on a frenzied sexual attack on Lila and Savannah. As he describes this traumatic event, he omits his experience at the hands of these vicious criminals. When Lowenstein asks him what he was doing while this was happening he just shrugs feebly. She presses him on why he didn't go for help, and he mumbles, 'Coz'. Lowenstein tells him that that was a child's answer. It's clear from Tom's body language and facial expression that he has now regressed to a frightened, confused, thirteen year old boy.

Lowenstein, unwilling to let him off the hook, presses him about the third man: what was he doing? It's then that Tom admits that he was being raped, too. He expresses his guilt that he didn't do anything to stop any of the men, and Lowenstein reminds him that he was only a child. His shame was further intensified when he saw Luke watching through a window. He looked up to his big brother and couldn't endure him being a witness to his having something so unspeakable done to him. This is further compounded when Luke bursts in and shoots two of the men with the shotgun, whilst his mother killed the third one by stabbing him in the back with a large pair of scissors.

Instead of comforting her violated children, she insists that they clean the place up, telling them, 'It's over. Get these carcasses out of here, clear up the mess'. The children then set to work helping their mother remove every sign that the men had even been in the house. They bury the bodies and carry on like nothing had happened. Lila ensured their secrecy by threatening that, 'The minute you tell anyone is the minute I stop being your mamma.' It seems that Lila's desire to be seen as acceptable by the social league she longed to be part of, over-rode what should have been a natural, maternal response to ensure her children were comforted and allowed the space and time to come to terms with what had happened to them. Three days later, Savannah made her first suicide attempt.

When Lowenstein asks Tom how he is feeling after disclosing the truth about his past, he smiles and says he's relieved. He then reverts to his usual defence mechanism by making light of what happened and what's just taken place, saying in a jokey way, 'The laundry's clean. The ghosts are out of the closet'. Once again, Lowenstein refuses to accept this response as congruent and so gently challenges him by stating that he's done a really good job at covering his pain. The real catalyst comes when she says, 'That thirteen year old boy is still in a lot of pain.' At this point, Tom begins to lose his resolve and begs Lowenstein not to do this to him, i.e. don't make him go there, into the pain.

Lowenstein speaks softly to him, reassuring him that it's ok, and he begins to cry, then to sob as she continues to soothe and comfort him in hushed, whispered tones. Soon he is crumpled up, head in her lap as she strokes his hair and encourages him to let go. This is what his mother should have done all those years ago – comforted her traumatised children (and herself – she didn't even give herself the permission and time to acknowledge her own pain).

Tom is invited to dinner by Lowenstein's husband, Herbert. He uses the occasion to belittle Tom's Southern ways and heritage, talking to him as though he's an unintelligent hick. Tom takes it in his stride, but is angered into action when Herbert turns his acerbic put-downs onto Susan. Tom retaliates by taking Herbert's million dollar violin and threatening to drop it from the balcony of their penthouse apartment unless Herbert apologises. He does, but only grudgingly and Tom insists he also apologise to his wife. Again, he does, but there's no real sincerity in his words – he's just afraid for his violin. Tom leaves and Lowenstein follows him, asking him to take her with him back to his apartment. This marks a turn in their relationship, and they go from being professionally linked by Savannah's need for healing and treatment, to being emotionally linked by both of their needs for intimacy.

Soon after this night of lovemaking, Lowenstein takes Tom to her lakeside cabin for the weekend. They spend an idyllic, romantic, passionate couple of days together and contemplate the possibility that they could be together as a couple. Tom is even able to tell Lowenstein that he loves her;

however, she forewarns Tom (and us) that this is probably not likely to happen as she believes Sally will want him back.

Back in New York, Savannah is finally home, and Tom tells her that his marriage is on the rocks and that he might stay with her longer. She reminds him that he couldn't possibly leave the South as he loves it too much. She tells him she's writing a new book called, *The Prince of Tides*. Tom assumes the title refers to Luke, and tells her he would be very proud. Savannah corrects him: the book will be dedicated to Tom – her memory.

As predicted by Lowenstein, Sally calls and asks Tom to come home. Tom and Lowenstein spend a last evening together knowing they can never be together as Tom is the kind of man who would always do the honourable thing and stay with his wife.

For the first time, Tom, who earlier in the film had said that he always seems to disappoint anyone who tried to find the good in him, now feels that he has something of value to offer the women in his life. With this newly acquired ability to acknowledge and express his feelings, he returns home to the South; where he is not only a football coach, but also a teacher and 'a much loved man'. The final words from Tom, the narrator, reflect his journey with Lowenstein: 'I'd learned to love my father and mother in all their outrageous, flawed humanity. In families, no crimes are beyond forgiveness.'

Core Beliefs – The Creation

I'm sure that by now you are very familiar with the process of creation when it comes to Core Beliefs. Again, I refer back to my description of *The Prince of Tides* as being an 'on the nose' kind of film when exploring Core Beliefs. As you read through the previous section on the story behind the film, you will have seen obvious clues as to why Tom Wingo was the way he was. However, I'll re-iterate certain points in the story that contributed to establishing his set of behaviours, values and attitudes that dominated his adulthood and wreaked havoc on his marriage, career and self-approval.

So what did Tom learn from his parents (and siblings) about family values and rules? Secrecy seems to be the biggest, most enduring rubric for the entire family. No-one is allowed to air the family's shortcomings and social inadequacies for fear that they (or at least, their mother) will be considered low-bred. This comes from Lila's narcissistic need to be seen as an 'amazing woman', who has been cheated by birth and marriage out of her rightful place in cultured, refined society. Her struggle to live in a world that doesn't recognise her innate sophistication creates an ever-widening chasm between her and Henry, and ultimately the children. It's Lila's aspiration to be a member of the elite social league that drives her on and forces her to deny her children any chance of healing after their traumatic experience. Indeed, so strong is this desire to fit in and be seen as worthy of high society's prized regard, to be seen as someone above the usual detritus of life, that she will go to any length to cover even the slightest trace of anything that might threaten her fragile façade.

This, then, is the powerful message driven home almost on a daily basis – you must hide your true self, your true self is something to be ashamed of, something that you must strive to deny or change at any cost lest you be discovered as an ordinary, mundane person, unworthy of respect or approval. Add to this the equally as powerful message – thou shalt not tell the truth or be disloyal to your family or the Southern Way – and the future is one filled with self-deception, pretence and denial.

Of course, Lila ensured her children's compliance with her instruction to say nothing to anyone about the rape by threatening to remove herself as their mother if they breathe a word about it – even to each other, seems to be the unspoken but implied directive. The children, then, knew that acknowledging their trauma in any way could result in the removal of their mother's love, approval and protection. Which, as we are now aware, equated to – keep quiet or die.

As a result of Lila being unable to provide the safe environment the children should have expected of her, and of her inability to perform as the 'good enough' mother, Tom's (and no doubt, Savannah's) sense of trust and security in the world was shattered. The internalisation of the traumatic experience sets up within Tom a struggle that would play out for his whole life: until, that is, he met Dr Lowenstein.

As she cleaned the blood from the walls, Lila's repeated mantra, 'This never happened, this never happened', is an attempt to eradicate the event from existence – whether in reality or memory. This then served to instil within the children a deep-seated conflict between the reality of their experience and the need to protect the family system of not speaking of those things considered unpleasant or vulgar.

Another contributing factor to Tom's lack of self-esteem and self-worth came from the cruel taunts and treatment at the hands of his father. The scene around the dinner table when Henry spits out the food he considers to be garbage, is filled with a whole host of commands, instructions, values, behaviours – enough to create a King Kong of monstrous proportions!

Henry thinks the food has been ruined with the addition of wine – something Lila will have done in an attempt to rise above the mundaneness of their usual simple fayre. This gives the children two opposing instructions – never be satisfied with the ordinary and simple; and, don't try to improve yourself or try anything new. Then Tom, in an attempt to defend his mother and thus demonstrate his loyalty to her, ends up on the receiving end of Henry's disdain for sensitivity - evidenced by the sneering and mocking words and tones he uses when Tom gets upset. The messages here are: only girls are allowed to cry; crying is for sissies; the kitchen is for females; and, it's not safe to be loyal or defend the ones you love. However, Tom will have also learned: how to retaliate without violence; how to use your intelligence to outsmart others; and that cooking can be a form of escapism. It was Lila's response to her husband's bullying (putting dog food in his meal) that prompted Dr Lowenstein to ask Tom if he got his sense of humour from his mother: more evidence that not all Core Beliefs are negative and to be routed out and removed at all costs.

Adulthood – The Consequences

As an adult, (and pre-Lowenstein) Tom was unable to reach his full potential – as a parent, husband, teacher, or football coach. For him, intimacy was equated with betrayal, mistrust, deception and loss of self. He could relate to his children in ways in which his parents could never do; however, in so doing, he would be likely to indulge them a little too much, letting them do whatever they wanted with few boundaries. Sally, on the other hand, would have to tread carefully in expressing her need for love and attention from Tom, lest he perceive those needs as akin to his mother's craving for his abiding loyalty at any cost. Saying, 'I love you', came at a price – denial of your true self and your own needs. Tom stated to Lowenstein, 'you can't trust people (*women? his mother?*), especially around love'.

Tom's projection of his mother's traits onto Sally (and later, onto Lowenstein), became so dominant in their relationship that he was unable to see her as a woman in her own right. What he'd said earlier about women expecting men to be a tower of strength, but then abandoning them (*him*) when they show any signs of weakness or insecurity, was aimed consciously at his wife for having an affair whilst he wrestled with his demons, but unconsciously at his mother for all of her betrayals.

The sense of humour that Tom uses to such good affect whenever he, or anyone else, gets too close to sensitive or potentially painful circumstances is clearly something that he would be loath to lose altogether in his quest for self-realisation. Humour can act as a healing force, but it can be used equally well as a means of preventing deep, inner reflection. 'Gallows' humour – the kind favoured by Tom – is used to cover discomfort and unease when faced with illness, adversity, or death, and is a form of distancing yourself from your true feelings and the power of those feelings to bring you to your knees.

However, through his relationship with Lowenstein (who plays the part of the 'good enough' mother), Tom is able to face his demons, which allows him to then move through the pain and into true healing. As long as he continued to deny his justifiable pain, he ran the risk of sending it somewhere into his body where it would likely fester and cause all manner of health problems. Savannah had already embodied her demons to such an extent that she needed to use extreme measures to exorcise them. Killing herself seemed to her to be the only way to free herself of the torment and despair caused by repressing such horrific memories. Although she didn't fully develop Dissociative Identity Disorder, she did create an alter ego that was allowed to acknowledge her pain and the fact that she had survived something horrific.

As Savannah split herself in order to cope with her pain and suppress memories from her childhood, so too has Tom separated himself out between his siblings: Luke was his courage and defiance, Savannah his emotions and sensitivity. In expressing his pain and bringing the past into the light without covering it with a blanket of humour or sarcasm, Tom showed great courage and thus integrated that aspect of himself once held by his brother. However, whilst he was engaged in supressing the righteous pain of his Inner Child, it was left to his sister to carry the burden of sensitivity for him. She took on all of his pain and made it her own. Forced to face and challenge the blind loyalty of the Southern way, and to step out of victim role with his wife, Tom is finally able to fully integrate and connect with his feelings at a deep level: something that allows him to take on the role of caregiver to his wife and children. In so doing, he not only saves himself, but also Savannah, who can now bring her pain out of her body and into the open, where she can then let it go and begin the journey to true healing and recovery.

Once Tom took the risk to engage in his close relationships in a meaningful and truly intimate way, he was able to begin his journey towards discovering his true self: a self that had all the resources he never believed he was capable of having. This meant he was able to enjoy the pleasure he gets from football coaching instead of being oppressed by his mother's view of it as being something beneath him: clearly a belief created by her need to be seen as an amazing woman, adored and accepted by what she considered to be the higher social group. As for teaching – something his mother did approve of – he was able to continue with that and derive pleasure from it on his own terms. It may have been a career encouraged by his mother's need for status, but Tom was able to separate that out from his own enjoyment of teaching by bringing the choice to continue with it into conscious awareness.

This consciously choosing life paths, values and behaviours, can only come about once their origin has been identified and examined: is it mine, if not whose is it? Tom's journey to self-realisation took place in the form of informal therapy with Dr Lowenstein, reading his sister's poetry, helping Bernard to experience and feel good about wanting to do something that gave him pleasure despite his father's disapproval (something that mirrored Tom's journey of separating out his desires from that of his mother's), and from having an intimate relationship with Lowenstein.

In the following film analysis, we get to see a more playful, lighter view of the consequences of suppressing your Inner Child and their needs.

Chapter 22

BACK TO THE FUTURE

The child is the father of the man.

William Wordsworth

Men do not quit playing because they grow old; they grow old because they quit playing.

Oliver Wendell Holmes Jr.

THE KID (2000)
Director: Jon Turteltaub
Writer: Audrey Wells

This is a more whimsical perspective of how Core Beliefs are created in childhood and how they play out in adulthood. As I said previously, I chose this one as it has a more comedic approach to a potentially serious subject; and, after the previous film, I don't want to end the book on a downer!

In *The Kid*, the main character, Russ Duritz, has spent most of his adulthood life supressing and denying who and what he was as a child. As a successful image consultant with wealthy clients, the dissatisfaction and displeasure he felt towards his childhood physical appearance and personality, lies at the heart of his motivation. Every time he does an image make-over for a client, he effectively removes another part of himself. This is aptly summed up in the insightful words of '*The Kid*', aka, Rusty (Russ' younger self and Inner Child), Russ 'helps people to lie about who they really are so that they can pretend to be someone else'.

Again, there are spoilers ahead, so please be warned: if knowing how the film ends will ruin it for you, then make sure to watch it first! It's a Disney film made for children - and the child within - which means it's an easy ride that should leave you smiling.

The Story

The Kid starts with a red bi-plane noisily coasting through a blue sky. This seemingly random appearance of the plane continues to inter-cut the opening scenes in which we see Russ with a client who is upset about something that's been written about her. He is impatient, rude, and has no empathy towards, or sympathy for the woman, believing that emotion is unnecessary and pathetic. As she cries, he mimics and belittles her for being so self-pitying.

Later, on the flight home, a woman sitting next to him chats excitedly about her new job as a news anchor. She asks what he does for a living and, when he tells her, she gets even more excited - she believes it wasn't an accident that they are sitting together - and asks him for advice about the way she presents herself. In true cynical-style, Russ (who also doesn't do excitement), responds with, 'The cosmic purpose of our sitting together is so I can give you free advice? What do I get out of it?' She agrees to shut up once he's done, and so he gives her a blunt appraisal of her image.

Sitting in his sports car on the freeway, the red bi-plane swooshes dangerously low over his head, causing him to instinctively duck. He tries to share his outrage at the pilot's reckless behaviour with other drivers on the road; but, by the blank or quizzical looks he gets, it seems no-one else saw it.

He arrives at his the office to find his dad - with whom he has a strained relationship - waiting for him. He's not happy to have him there and tells Janet, his office assistant, to interrupt in 60 seconds so he can get rid of him. His dad is moving and had asked Russ for help, to which Russ reminds him he sent him a cheque, which will have to do as 'time is money and my time's worth more than a mover's.' Undeterred, his dad asks him to dinner – his sister and her children are going to be there and Russ hasn't seen them in a long time. Russ isn't interested and his dad reminds him that there are things in the attic he may want: childhood memorabilia. Russ asks his dad when the last time was that he asked for anything from him in the last 20 years, thus making it clear that nothing has changed in that respect.

Russ meets with another assistant, Amy, at a baseball stadium. She tries to engage him in normal chit-chat by asking how he is. When he rebuffs her, she tells him to just have a go, but he's unable to give his words any warmth or sincerity. Besides, he doesn't have time for social niceties. They go into their meeting with the stadium manager Bob Riley, who had promised to set aside 5% of ticket sales to fund a baseball camp for disadvantaged children, but actually kept the money. In danger of going to jail at worst and irrevocably ruining his reputation at best, Russ has him make a video of some children throwing pies at him as punishment in a bid to get him off the hook. Amy is upset about this and feels that the video is unethical. Trying to prove to Amy that he has morals, Russ throws the tape away: something that thrills Amy and restores her belief in Russ's honour. Outside, Amy gets excited at seeing the full moon and tries to get Russ to share her enthusiasm; but again, he's not interested and makes fun of her. She's disappointed – she had wanted to see the kid in him.

Russ returns home and sees a small child running around his gated property. Furious with the laxity of the security firm, he calls Janet and demands that she get them to increase the security system – he wants Rottweilers, electric fences, a moat with lava. Later, he hears a noise and goes to investigate armed with a baseball bat. Outside, he finds a red toy plane on his front step. It has the name, 'Rusty', painted on it, and he contemptuously assumes it has been left there by his father. Back in bed he is awoken by the noise of a boy playing with the plane in his front room. Russ chases him outside, but the boy escapes by riding off on a Chopper bike. Jumping in his car to give chase, they eventually end up at a small plane airfield. He sees the boy entering the Skyway Diner, which sits incongruously in the middle of the airfield. He follows him inside, but there's no sign of the kid and none of the customers has seen him. A policeman leaves the diner and Russ calls after him for assistance. Once outside, the officer has disappeared, as has the diner, leaving Russ to believe he is having hallucinations.

The next day, Russ goes to see a psychotherapist for some strong medication to stop him hallucinating. Entering her office he tells her he wants to get straight to the point as he has an appointment in ten minutes. Unfazed by his brusque, business-like manner, the therapist calmly tells him he's entitled to a 'fifty minute hour', to which he replies he only needs a five minute hour. Pacing the floor, he tells her he doesn't want or need therapy as he's 'not like the other nut balls' she sees in her office. He only has one issue and that's that he's seeing things: first there was a man in a plane and now there's a kid. The therapist asks if the child is someone he knew from his childhood. His eye starts to twitch and he claims it's dry eyes. He's adamant that his problem doesn't have anything to do with his childhood as he's forgotten it, and that it's, 'in the past, where it belongs'. The therapist challenges this belief by stating that whatever it is doesn't want to stay in the past. She gives him a prescription insisting he come back the next day – he's having hallucinations for a reason and needs to find out what it is.

After returning home, Russ finds the kid watching television and eating popcorn. He asks him who he is and what he's come for. He tells Russ his name is Rusty, and he'd come to take his toy plane, but when he saw the television and the popcorn he couldn't resist. Seeing similarities in their mannerisms, Russ and Rusty begin comparing memories and birthmarks. They eventually figure out that the only explanation is that the boy is actually him as a kid. Something that seems significant about the timing of his appearance is that in two days' time, it will be their birthday – Russ will be forty, and Rusty will be eight.

Russ takes Rusty to see Janet, and is even more perplexed that she can see him too, meaning the boy is real. Later, in Russ' car, Rusty gets upset and starts crying – he's scared and confused and he wants to go home. Unfortunately, he doesn't know where he lives, which annoys Russ even more than his crying. Rusty defends himself by reminding Russ that he should know as it was his home too, but Russ doesn't remember as they lived in 12 different homes when he was growing up. They somehow find themselves at one of their old houses, and Rusty recalls some of the more memorable things that happened to them whilst they lived there, but Russ can't remember any of it. Rusty starts crying again when he sees that another family lives there.

Back at Russ' house, Rusty runs around calling for Chester, the dog he was planning on having when he grew up and had a truck, and is devastated that he grows up to be someone who doesn't have a dog. He lists the things that Russ doesn't have, that to Rusty signify adulthood: he's old, not married, doesn't have a dog, and doesn't fly jets, and concludes that he's grown up to be a loser.

A little later, he gets excited about the moon. Russ admonishes him just as he did with Amy: the moon isn't anything to get excited about. Deflated, Rusty remarks, 'I'll never get excited about anything again – obviously'. Unable to hide his curiosity, Rusty asks Russ why the moon is sometimes orange. Russ struggles to answer: he doesn't know. Again, Rusty's treasured expectations of himself as an adult are dashed, 'I grew up to be a guy who doesn't know anything.'

When Russ gets up the next morning, Rusty has gone. Relieved, and believing his delusional episode is over, he goes to meet with a potential client at a working breakfast. Unfortunately, Rusty turns up and, nose pushed against the window of the posh restaurant, he cries that he's hungry. Russ goes outside and is trying to discreetly get rid of him, but Amy comes out and sees him. Russ tries to pass Rusty off, unsuccessfully, as his nephew. Promising to buy him breakfast – and so get rid of him - Russ takes Rusty away intending to find a cheap café. Rusty points up to the sky to where the red bi-plane is using smoke to spell out, 'Eat Here'. Also in smoke is an arrow pointing to the Skyway Diner, which has appeared on the street in front of them.

Whilst they eat, Russ tries desperately to figure out why Rusty is there. Maybe, he says cruelly, it's to put him on a diet as he's so 'chubby'. Rusty says what he would really like is to not get his 'butt kicked' so much at school. Russ excitedly jumps on that as a possibility, and decides Rusty is there so that Russ can help him learn how to defend himself.

Russ takes Rusty to meet one of his clients, a boxer who is getting married the next day and asks him to teach him a few moves. Later, Amy takes Rusty to her place for ice-cream, instructing a bewildered Russ to follow. Once he's there she challenges him about the similarities between him and Rusty, causing Russ to admit that Rusty is a close relation. This leads Amy to believe that Rusty is his secret love child. Rusty wants to tell Amy the truth, and they begin to argue. As Amy watches the two of them fighting, she sees just how similar their gestures and mannerisms are; and, shocked by the truth of the situation, she faints.

Once she recovers, she and Russ talk, whilst Rusty - watching TV - scratches and picks at his skin. Russ thinks Rusty is embarrassing – he needs a haircut and speaks funny. He's repulsed by his eight-year-old self and wonders if Amy despises him for being such a pathetic dweeb. 'No' she says, 'do you?' Russ winces and tells her that when he looks at Rusty, 'all I see are awful memories: memories I've been spending my whole life trying to forget.'

At the wedding, Rusty decides that Russ and Amy should be together. He gives Amy a rose and proposes to her; but Russ whisks Rusty off to the car park before Amy can answer. Amy follows them and tells Russ that her answer would've been that she would think about it, and so should he. Panicking, Russ goes for the car and comes back to find Rusty watching news footage of Riley being pied in the face by a group of children. Amy is disappointed and shocked that Russ crawled into the dumpster to retrieve the video tape: she thought he had changed.

In the car going home, Rusty asks Russ what happened between the ages of eight and forty, and Russ fills him in on 'their' achievements and turning points: he just about made it through high school; he's smart and so made it to UCLA; in college he began to feel better about himself; he joined the track team; saw a speech therapist; worked his butt off; and got an MA in Business. Unimpressed with these alleged accomplishments, Rusty sums him up as a 'dogless, chickless guy'.

That evening, watching TV, Russ sees the newscaster from the plane. He goes to the studio to meet her and they go for a coffee, where he tells her what's been happening to him. Unfazed by his incredible story, she tells him she thinks it makes sense that his 8 year-old self would time travel to straighten Russ out. Russ is shocked at the possibility that Rusty had turned up to help him remember something from his past. Now it's her turn to give him a blunt appraisal of his life: he's turning forty; hasn't acquired anything of any real value; he has hardly any friends; barely talks to his family; and has just lost the only woman in his life who means anything to him. This last bit about Amy shocks Russ and he denies that she is anything more than his neurotic assistant, but then the penny drops. He asks the newscaster what she would do differently if she were in his place. She would tell her younger self that everything is just fine, she says, adding, 'How many of us turn out the way we think we will when we were kids?' Demonstrating the changes that are slowly taking place for him, Russ actually thanks her for her help.

Russ goes home and calls Janet, apologising for ringing so late. He asks her to cancel all of his appointments for the next couple of days, and to find out why the moon sometimes looks orange. He and Rusty then spend some time together, during which Rusty talks about his young life in the hope of triggering a memory in Russ. They drive around the city, trying to find out why Rusty is there and what Russ needs to fix from the past so that Rusty can go home, and Rusty tells him more about the kids that keep ganging up on him.

As they drive through a tunnel, a red car with a barking Golden Retriever dog on the back seat passes them, and Russ suddenly recalls his eighth birthday when he had a fight with the bullies who were abusing a three-legged dog named Tripod. When they emerge from the tunnel, they have travelled back in time to Rusty's eighth birthday in 1968. At the school, Russ's presence and support helps Rusty win the fight and save Tripod. Rusty now has the possibility of an alternate outcome. However, nothing seems to have changed as they thought it would. Russ suddenly remembers that because of the fight, his sick mother had to come to school for him that day.

Russ follows Rusty and his mum home and they arrive just as Rusty's father pulls into the drive. After gently escorting his wife inside, he turns on Rusty and angrily shakes and scolds him for getting into trouble and causing his mother to leave the house. He tells Rusty that he's killing her; and, as Rusty cries, his father roughly rubs his tears away, telling him to stop crying and grow up.

Russ gently tells Rusty that his mother will die before his next birthday. Rusty asks if he did it and Russ reassures him that he didn't cause his mums death, explaining that his father was angry and scared because of the huge responsibility of raising him alone. As he wipes tears from his own face, he realises how he got the twitch and tells Rusty that he hasn't cried since that day.

They go to the Skyway Diner, where they talk about the fight and congratulate each other on their birthday: but they can't understand why nothing seems to have changed. Suddenly, the dog from the car in the tunnel comes in and goes directly to Rusty. They hear a man calling the dog: its name is Chester. They follow the man outside and see him standing by a plane with a group of people and the dog. The man looks across at them and comes over to where they're standing, the pair of them gobsmacked as they realise that he is an older Russ.

The people by the plane are his children and Amy is his wife. Russ realises it was this future version of him that had set everything up. The older Russ smiles enigmatically, 'I bet you've got lots of questions?' he says. 'Well, don't worry about it - you've got 30 years to figure it out'. He tells Rusty that it was especially nice seeing him again. Calling the dog, he returns to his family and they all board the plane and fly off into the night. As Russ and Rusty watch them disappear, they shout excitedly, 'We grow up to be a pilot!' Russ raises his face to the sky and triumphantly calls out, 'I am not a loser!' When he turns back to speak to Rusty, he finds himself standing alone and back in the present. He tenderly says goodbye to his younger self, and sincerely thanks his future self.

Russ returns home, makes plans to help his dad with his move, gets Janet to buy tickets to Hawaii which he then gives to her; and, with a Golden Retriever puppy in his arms, goes to see Amy.

Core Beliefs – The Creation

Once again, it's quite obvious where Russ', Core Beliefs began; and, for some of this evaluation, we will have to read between the lines. Even before that fateful day when he had the fight and then had his tears roughly wiped away with the stern instruction to 'stop crying and grow up', Russ was busy creating Core Beliefs about his world and his place in it. We never find out if his sister is older or younger than him; but, as the only boy, he would've looked to his father for guidance on how to be a male in the world.

The fact that he and his family moved around a lot – 12 times possibly before he became a teenager – would have left Rusty with a sense of displacement, instability and unpredictability: not easy for any developing child to cope with at the best of times. Add to this the fact that Rusty's mum will have been gravely ill for some time (possibly a year or so), and you can see how he would have grown up believing the world is a dangerous, capricious place.

To then have the guilt of in some way being responsible for your mother's illness and death, is a huge burden to carry on such young shoulders. At seven or eight, Rusty will have totally integrated this belief – that he caused his mother's cancer and subsequent death – and lived it as indisputable truth. This belief would have contributed to the creation of an image of himself as being someone who is dangerous to know and love – especially if you're a woman!

Adulthood – The Consequences

Rusty, the boy with an enthusiastic yearning for adventure and fun, grows up to be Russ, the man with little interest in anything beyond success and making money. The simple, innocent imaginings that had brought Rusty pleasure as he allowed himself to indulge in his dreams and fantasies, had been supplanted in his adult self with the need to always be in control of his emotions and to never let imagination or dreams get in the way of reality. Real life was a business: a business that deals with facts, figures, and cultivating the right image and persona.

263

Russ had been so untrusting of his younger self – the self that caused death and misery – that he had done all he could to eradicate all trace of him from existence. He'd done such a good job, that he then used this skill to re-imagine and re-invent others who were dissatisfied with themselves and also wanted to be someone else. It's understandable that Russ would have seen his shortcomings – speech problem, weight, even his imagination – as part of the image he had of himself as the harbinger of misery and disaster. No wonder he wanted to re-invent himself as a cool, controlled, calculating businessman. As a small boy, he hadn't been able to control anything; and, consequently, his world seemed to be a place of chaos and pain.

As an adult, he had succeeded in making it a place where he called all the shots, had people doing his bidding, had clients lining up for his services and advice, and where there was no room for sentiment or empathy. After all, his dad (his hero) had told him to 'stop crying and grow up', and if that's what it took to win his hero's respect and approval, then that's what he would do. In keeping with this powerful command, Russ never cried again, and spent his whole life being a grown up, devoid of sentimental, self-pitying emotion. Unfortunately, he'd also jettisoned enthusiasm, excitement, tenderness, and love.

Ultimately, for the purposes of this book, I chose *The Kid* because of the more whimsical approach to the creation of Core Beliefs, and the premise that it's never too late to change your ways and become a more fully rounded, happier individual; but, what I most love about this film, is that it is also about time being simultaneous (which would seem to be the only explanation for what was happening). Despite the title I've given it, it's not about time travel, but allows us a glimpse of the possibility of moving from one 'time' to another in order to facilitate positive change and growth.

I know this book leans heavily on the biological nature of development and the effects of stress and trauma on the brain, but I feel it's also important to consider the potential for tapping into our Greater (or Higher, if you prefer) Self, in order to access greater wisdom and guidance on how to make lasting changes in the brain through new experiences and awareness. In creating the opportunity for Russ *the Younger* to gain a new perspective on something that happened in childhood – something that went on to create a neural pathway in his brain that told him life is unpredictable and fraught with pain – Russ *the Elder* was able to help himself to achieve those things that Rusty had dreamed of and hoped for. It's clear he was still a savvy, successful businessman in the future, but he had also mastered being fully present in his relationships and emotional life.

I find this aspect of the film - the depiction of past and future selves impacting on the present self – fascinating. I love the idea of a future self visiting with an earlier version of itself in order to impart wisdom and guidance. I believe that we can access this *future* version of ourselves whenever we meditate or focus our attention on a problem we may be experiencing. Perhaps, when we gain insight or inspiration, it is coming from part of our expanded (past, present, and future) self working in partnership with our Greater Self to bring through the support and guidance we need.

CONCLUSION

Who's The Boss of You?, is intended to help you discover those limiting behaviours and attitudes that are running in the background of your being. I wrote it with the intention of aiding you in the process of identifying those areas where you might be sabotaging your dreamed of life of happiness, health and success and why that might be happening. To this end, it is necessary to focus on the past – particularly early childhood and teenage years. The intention is to help you recognise your limiting beliefs and to realise that not all of them will have been of your own making. Knowing that a lot of the values you hold and adhere to as an adult may not necessarily have been chosen by you, gives you the freedom to examine them and decide whether or not they are still serving you (if they ever did). Those that are limiting you in some way can be let go of and replaced with those that mean something to you. Those that serve you can be maintained or even enhanced.

The important thing to remember is that you do have choice – but only if you have awareness. Those behaviours that operate on automatic pilot can be destructive if not taken in hand and made to operate in a way that brings you a sense of wellbeing and satisfaction. Equally important to remember is that we all operate from a place of free-will: there is no destiny or fate waiting in the wings to trip you up or bring you the partner of your dreams. You do that with your thoughts and your beliefs. Wherever you're going, whatever path you're on, you can always change direction at any time. Changing your mind about something literally means *changing your mind*! Not only do you set up a new path in life, outlook and expectation, but you also create new paths in your brain that help you to stay on that path.

This is why it's so important to focus on what you *do* want and not on what you *don't* want. As I've said, in order to create the life you deserve it can help to understand past events and experiences, but without dwelling on them for too long. In the same way, knowing what you don't want helps you to discover what you do want. The trick is not to focus on negative or limiting beliefs or experiences, but to use awareness of them to highlight the positive unlimited desires that stem from them. And so, 'I don't want to have to do a, b or c', then becomes, 'What I do want is x, y and z'.

A healthy mind and attitude – whether considering it from the perspective of Law of Attraction or psychological wellbeing – looks to the future with positivity and excitement. By all means, visit the past as you try to make sense of your present, but don't set up home in the negative memories, reliving them and playing them on an endless loop in the cinema of your mind as if it were all still happening to you in glorious Technicolor. When we do this, we can't help but bring up all the past emotions too, and we once more become embroiled in the old resentment and frustration. The subconscious cannot tell the difference between what's gone, what's here, or what's to come. If you feel sadness about the past and replay how you were wronged and how that left you feeling that the world is a cruel and hurtful place to be in, then your subconscious will react as if that were the case now, in the present. Remember, to the subconscious there is only the here and now. In Law of Attraction terms, this means you will generate new experiences that mirror the old.

Once you've identified the area in your past where you became stuck in a certain way of thinking, behaving, or feeling, or discover a family value that isn't your own and isn't one you want to have as your own, then get straight on to doing something about letting it go, or changing it in some way. Then you can choose to focus on those times that brought you joy and a sense of fulfilment and satisfaction. Hold those in your thoughts and watch them grow, attracting more and more experiences with which they resonate. If only one person made you feel good about yourself, then concentrate on whatever it was they did that succeeded in creating within you a sense of value and self-appreciation. Bask in the pleasure of those memories and more and more opportunities for you to have similar experience will come to you.

As you go through the process of remembering and exploring family rules and attitudes, it's important to bear in mind that past events won't be remembered in the same way by everyone. Your version is your version, and each member of your family will have their own version. Theirs may not tally completely with yours (or anyone else's). This doesn't mean theirs is wrong, distorted, or a bare-faced lie, it's just that they experienced it through a different filter to you. They took various aspects of an event – some of which you may not even have been aware of - and they built a story around them that helped them to make sense of their world, as seen through their eyes.

There's no need for, and nothing to be gained from, insisting that everyone remember how awful a certain party was, if the majority remember it as being fun and entertaining - there may be some family members who don't even remember it at all! This in itself can provide you with a rich source of material for you to work on for yourself. Let them have their memories and version's, there's no need for it to cause you any unhappiness or frustration. You know your version of events and what it left you with, and that's all that matters.

By working through the exercises, speaking to family and friends, keeping a journal, making an effort to remember and then work with your dreams (and perhaps even watching the films), you will find yourself experiencing life in a conscious way: more aware of who you truly are with each day that passes. Taking the time to get to know and accept yourself - with all your faults and frailties - is a gift: not only for yourself, but for those you share your life with. Having figured out your triggers, you can enjoy your life more fully and know that in ways that really matter, *you* are the boss of you.

RECOMMENDED READING & REFERENCES

Bach, Edward, *The Twelve Healers & Other Remedies* (Pilgrims Publishing, 2002)

Blair, Linda. *Birth Order* (Piatkus, 2013)

Byrne, Rhonda. *The Secret* (Beyond Worlds, 2006)

Cappacchione, Lucia. *Recovery of Your Inner Child* (Simon & Schuster / Fireside, 1991)

Chopra, Deepak. *Quantum Healing: Exploring the Frontiers of Mind/Body Medicine* (Bantam, 1989)

Crisp, Tony. *Dream Dictionary: An A-Z Guide to Understanding Your Unconscious Mind* (Dell Publishing, 2002)

Cummings, E.E. *anyone lived in a pretty how town* (Liveright, 1994)

Dethlefsen, Thorwald and Dahlke, Rudiger. MD. *The Healing Power of Illness* (Element Books, 1997)

DeMarco, Frank. *Imagine Yourself Well* (Rainbow Ridge Publishing, 2015)

Douglas, Ray. *Dreams and the Inner Self* (A Blandford Book, Cassell Plc, 1999)

Dychtwald, Ken. *Bodymind* (Jeremy P Tarcher, 1977)

Faludi, Susan. *Backlash: The Undeclared War Against American Women* (Three Rivers Press, New York, 1991)

Faraday, Dr Ann. *Dream Power: Learn to Use the Vital Self-Knowledge that Lies Stored in Your Dreams* (Berkley Books, 1982)

Emoto, Masaru. *Messages From Water* (HADO Kyoikusha Co., 2001)

Hay, Louise L. *You Can Heal Your Life* (Eden Grove Editions, 1988)

Koran, Al. *Bring Out the Magic in Your Mind* (HarperCollins, 1972)

Kaptchuk TJ, Friedlander E, Kelley JM, Sanchez MN, Kokkotou E, et al., *Placebos without Deception: A Randomized Controlled Trial in Irritable Bowel Syndrome*, (2010)

Lipton, Bruce. *The Biology of Belief* (Hay House, 2008)

Missildine, Hugh W. MD. *Your Inner Child of the Past* (Simon & Schuster, 1963)

Murphy, Dr Joseph. *The Power of Your Subconscious Mind* (Prentice Hall, 1988)

Myss, Caroline, PhD. *Why People Don't Heal and How They Can* (Bantam, 1998)

Pert, Candace, B. *Molecules of Emotion* (Simon & Schuster, 1998)

Price, Allison. *Writing from the Source* (HarperCollins, 1999)

Roberts, Jane. *How to Develop Your ESP Power* (Rider & Co. Ltd, 1988)

_____*The Seth Material* (Prentice-Hall, 1970)

_____*The Way Towards Health* (Amber-Allen, 1997)

Roselle, Elly. *Changing the Mind - Healing the Body* (Ugly Duckling Editions, 2005)

Satir, Virginia. *Peoplemaking* (Souvenir Press, 1998)

Shapiro, Debbie. *Your Body Speaks Your Mind: Decoding the Emotional, Psychological, and Spiritual Messages that Underlie Illness* (Piatkus, 1996)

Siegel, Bernie, S. *Love, Medicine & Miracles: Lessons Learned about Self-Healing from a Surgeon's Experience and Exceptional Patients* (Arrow, 1988)

Scovel-Shinn, Florence. *The Writings of Florence Scovel-Shinn* (DeVorrs & Company, 1988)

Stewart, Kilton. *Pygmies and Dream Giants* (Colophon Books, 1976)

Tepperman, Jay. Dr. *Perspectives in Biology and Medicine*

Verny, Thomas, with Kelly, John. *The Secret Life of the Unborn Child* (Summit Books, 1981)

Weiss, Brian. MD. *Through Time into Healing* (Piatkus, 1995)

Williston, Glenn and Johnstone, Judith. *Discovering Your Past Lives: Spiritual Growth Through a Knowledge of Past Lifetimes* (Thorsons, 1995)

Wooder, Bernie. *Movie Therapy: How it Changes Lives* (Rideau Lakes Publishing, 2008)

Woolger, Roger. *Healing Your Past Lives: Exploring the Many Lives of the Soul* (Sounds True Inc., 2004)

_____*Other Lives, Other Selves*: A Jungian Psychotherapist Discovers Past Lives (Thorsons, 1999)

For further information about booking a therapy session, workshops, talks or training, please visit **www.kriswilliams.org**

Printed in Great Britain
by Amazon.co.uk, Ltd.,
Marston Gate.